GODS, HEROES, & KINGS

Gods, Heroes, & Kings

The Battle for Mythic Britain

Christopher R. Fee
with David A. Leeming

OXFORD

UNIVERSITY PRESS

2001

OXFORD
UNIVERSITY PRESS

Oxford   New York
Athens   Auckland   Bangkok   Bogotá   Buenos Aires   Cape Town
Chennai   Dar es Salaam   Delhi   Florence   Hong Kong   Istanbul   Karachi
Kolkata   Kuala Lumpur   Madrid   Melbourne   Mexico City   Mumbai   Nairobi
Paris   São Paulo   Shanghai   Singapore   Taipei   Tokyo   Toronto   Warsaw

and associated companies in
Berlin   Ibadan

Library of Congress Cataloging-in-Publication Data
Fee, Christopher R.
Gods, heros, and kings: the battle for mythic Britain
/ by Christopher R. Fee with David A. Leeming.
    p.   cm.
Includes bibliographical references (p.) and index.
ISBN 0-19-513479-6
1. Mythology, British.   2. Christianity and other religions—Great Britain.   3. Literature,
Medieval—History and criticism.   4. British literature—History and criticism.   I. Leeming, David Adams,
1937–   II. Title.
BL980.G7 F44   2001
820.9'15—dc21   00-068156

FOR EMMA AND MORGAN

ACKNOWLEDGMENTS

Thanks are due to the Provost's Office of Gettysburg College, which provided me with paid leave for a semester at a crucial time. Both Ian Clarke and the English Department reading group at Gettysburg offered valuable comments concerning the introduction, and Mark Drew, Cinda Gibbon, and Mindy Wilson tackled indexing chores with gusto. Finally, many thanks to the students of my medieval literature, British mythology, and Scandinavian studies courses, who were enthusiastic about this material and helpful in their criticism of our methodology.

Christopher Fee

preface

Lo! The spear of Wodan One-Eye clashes against that of Shining Lugh! Listen! The strains of Heimdalr's trumpet blast call the hosts of the dead to battle as Thunor and Sucellus—hammer-gods both—struggle for supremacy. . . . The Isles of Britain have been a battleground for gods for thousands of years, and those who know how to listen may yet hear the echoes of the thunderous conflicts of old.

IN MORE PROSAIC TERMS, the central premise of this book is that one may view medieval British literature not only as an assertion of dominant Christian traditions but often also as a complex and vibrant confluence of mythic influences: in the medieval literary traditions of Britain, the voices of the gods of the Celts, Romans, Saxons, and Vikings combine in a chorus that can seem chaotic and confused, but one that also offers us a rich and distinctly British melody.

Although we have attempted to avail ourselves of the most up-to-date scholarship concerning the literatures and mythologies we have discussed, our primary goal has been to render a readable examination of our topic aimed for a general audience. We have collated as many source materials as possible, and wherever practical we have indicated where we have had to make substantive or stylistic choices among a number of options. Furthermore, we have tried to remain true to the spirit and the flavor of the narratives and the mythic archetypes they represent, and thus in some cases we have taken the liberty of conflating material from a number of sources in order to tell the best story possible; we have attempted, however, to stay as much as possible within the parameters of the range of available records. We hope that our work will prove a useful general reference tool to nonspecialist scholars and an engaging introduction for students. Much of the present work is based on our classroom treatment of the myths, sagas, texts, and concepts at hand, and is then, we hope, more user-friendly than more academic works on the same theme. Selected, approachable sources for further reading are noted at the end of the book, and are divided into subject areas. All the works consulted in the completion of this book are included in the general bibliography.

Our treatment of the myths and sagas, as well as our choice of medieval works, is meant to be suggestive in theme rather than comprehensive (or even representative) in scope. It would be beyond the pale of a book of this length—and, indeed, beyond that of one designed for a general readership— to attempt to deal with every identifiable myth or mythic element that could be associated with medieval British literature. Moreover, mythic material enters the medieval British narrative traditions through a great many sources, many of them continental, quite a few of which are themselves medieval. That said, our goal has been to attempt to outline the general lines of a relationship between medieval British literatures and the rich mythic traditions that preceded the medieval period on these islands.

Celtic and Germanic influences abound in medieval British literature, but it is an ironic paradox that we can—in one breath—acknowledge that we have much more to say about Germanic myth than about Celtic myth, and— in the next—still allow that the Celtic Arthurian tradition is by far the best-known, most often replicated, and longest-lived mythic source for British literature. This has to do with both the origin and the nature of the Celtic material that informed the British literary tradition; this is to say that our knowledge of the pre-Christian Celts is largely limited to the archeological and classical literary records, and it is difficult to know how much of this earlier cultural system filtered down to the medieval Christian Irish, Breton, and Welsh, or indeed to the French and then the English, both of whom later co-opted the Arthurian tradition. Moreover, much of the medieval Arthurian tradition in Britain was focused through a continental lens, and it is only by examining English, Irish, Welsh, Breton, and French sources side by side that one can begin to understand the relationship of this material to older Celtic mythic systems and beliefs. It should be said, then, that this is not a book focused upon Arthuriana: we examine a handful of works containing Arthurian material, including *Sir Gawain and the Green Knight* and Chaucer's "The Wife of Bath's Tale," in the light of what we know about Celtic culture and the Irish and Welsh mythic traditions. We leave a more thorough examination of all things Arthurian, however, to the many, many books dedicated to that subject.

Much of what one can say about Germanic mythology in general comes from the Scandinavian sources, and the Germanic tradition in Britain is no exception. We attempt to sketch for the reader an outline of the relationships among older Germanic, Scandinavian, British Germanic, and medieval German mythic elements, but it is easy to confuse so many similar gods, sagas, and heroes. This ease of confusion underscores the reason for including these closely related traditions: it is our belief that the medieval Germanic materials (that is, the Scandinavian, Middle High German, and Anglo-Saxon) all reflect similar preliterate Germanic mythic traditions, and we have included as much material as practicable in order to give the reader the fullest sense of the most important elements and archetypes of these traditions that survive into medieval British literature. We also discuss a number of English folk traditions and place names, current well into the modern period, that have an ancient Germanic mythic provenance; such elements perhaps most vividly illuminate the resilience of British myth. In all cases we attempt to amplify the voices of the ancient pagan gods of Britain that speak to us yet through the words of their medieval Christian children.

CONTENTS

GODS, HEROES, & KINGS

INTRODUCTION

The islands of Britain have been a crossroads of man, myth, and god for thousands of years. Massive standing stone circles such as that at Stonehenge, ancient Stone Age villages such as Skara Brae, and imposing chambered tombs (also known as cairns or barrows) like Maes Howe all provide mute testimony to the civilizations that existed in Britain at least five thousand years ago. These monuments—some older than the pyramids in Egypt—provide tantalizing clues to the religious beliefs and rituals of the peoples who left them. Some scholars have suggested a religious system based on myths and rites of fertility and of sun worship. In fact, historical and literary records reveal little before the arrival of the Celts from mainland Europe.

The Celts, a group of related tribes who by early in the third century BCE were a significant presence in Europe from the Balkans all the way to Greece and Asia Minor, sacked Rome in 387 BCE; later, as every student of Latin knows, Celts fought Julius Caesar as Gauls in lands now called France and Germany. The Celts who invaded the British Isles during the last five centuries BCE came in waves of mutually hostile groups speaking different dialects. The descendants of the Gaels (Goidels) are still found in Ireland and Scotland. Relatives of the Gauls, the Cymri, and Brythons (Britons), including the Belgae, are the source for people in Wales and Cornwall (and Brittany in France). The word *British* comes via the Middle English *Brittish* and the Old English *Bryttisc* from the Breton *Bryttas*, a word for the Celts of the British Isles. The ancient Celts and their beliefs displaced the earlier indigenous Stonehenge peoples and their gods, although the Celts perhaps appropriated some of the earlier customs. They most certainly put old ritual sites and structures to new uses; this sort of recycling of pre-existing sites and traditions, such as the probable use of stone circles in Celtic druidic rites, happened again with each new set of invaders of Britain.

Like those who lived in Britain before them, the Celts lacked a practical writing system, and thus before their conversion to Christianity they were not a literary people, at least not in the modern sense of the word. It is only because of interaction with the Romans—and before them, with the Greeks— that accounts of the Celts were recorded. Herodotus, Hecataeus of Miletus, and, of course much later, Julius Caesar all wrote about the Celts. But among themselves, the Celts, like their Germanic neighbors to the north, passed their stories and traditions down through the generations by word of mouth. Our understanding of the Celts during their preliterate period comes, therefore, largely from the pens of their enemies.

The first challenge to the Celts in Britain was the Romans, who first crossed over what we now know as the English Channel in force under Julius Caesar in about 50 BCE. Although these new invaders consolidated their control of the southern portion of the island in less than two hundred years, they never reached Ireland, and they won only marginal footholds in Scotland and Wales. Where they did conquer, though, the impact of Roman civilization was very great indeed, as the multitude of Roman baths, villas, roads, and walls proclaims in Britain to this day. Furthermore, from a mythological point of view, the Roman influence upon the British Celts is of particular interest, as is that of the Celts on the Romans. The Romans were tolerant rulers, leaving many local customs, social structures, and religious practices in place, only putting a stop to those rituals deemed bloodthirsty, barbaric, or unseemly. Many of the religious ceremonies and military customs of the Celts were distasteful to their Roman overlords—human sacrifice and ritual headhunting being chief among these—but few of the gods of the Celts seemed alien to the Romans, and the worship of these deities was not curtailed. Indeed, the Romans made a practice of accepting foreign gods into their pantheon as new manifestations of old familiar spirits.

The golden age of Roman rule was to be short-lived, as by the middle of the fifth century CE affairs elsewhere in the empire required the removal of the Roman legions; they would never return. Germanic raiders and pirates— from modern day coastal Holland, Denmark, and Germany—who had begun to raid Roman Britain around the year 300 CE, now pressed their attacks on the nearly defenseless Celts, who appear to have won a short respite from these marauders in a great battle fought in about 450 CE. It is from this shadowy historical event that the legend of King Arthur seems to have been born. In any case, by the year 500 CE the Germanic Angles, Saxons, and Jutes had returned in earnest, and they soon drove the British Celts to the margins of the island—to Wales, Scotland, and Cornwall—and across the sea to Ireland and to Brittany.

These Germanic tribesmen brought with them such gods as Tiw, Thunor, and Frige, to whom the more familiar Tyr, Thor, and Frigg correspond in the Norse pantheon. Theirs was a dark and brooding religion, and bloodthirsty, too: contemporary continental historical records and archeology agree that human sacrifice was practiced by these northern peoples. The most demanding of these gods was Wodan—Odin to the Norse—from whom Wednesday takes its name, and in the name of whom countless animals and humans were strangled or hanged. Further, the rather dismal Germanic view of the afterlife probably hastened the conversion of the Anglo-Saxons to Christianity. At the behest of Pope Gregory the Great, the first Roman Catholic mission to the kingdom of Kent was established at Canterbury by Augustine in 597 CE, and the conversion of the English was accomplished within a century; as we shall see, however, some heathen practices and motifs remained for much longer.

Although the Anglo-Saxons suffered occasional setbacks in their drive to overrun the British Celts, the story of the two or three centuries following their initial mass invasion is primarily one of the conquest of Celtic territory tempered by a great deal of squabbling among the invaders themselves. Eventually seven main Anglo-Saxon kingdoms were established in what would become England (from the Old English *Engla Land* or Land of the Angles, one of the Germanic tribes), with an ebb and flow of power between Northumbria in the north, Mercia in the Midlands, and Wessex in the southwest. Although they mainly drove out their Celtic neighbors rather than assimilating them, these Germanic invaders were highly influenced by the peculiar religious rituals and beliefs and unique artistic forms of Celtic Christianity, which had been imported into the north of Britain from Ireland before Augustine arrived in Kent. The Roman form of Christian worship represented by Augustine eventually held sway over most of Britain, as established in a synod held at Whitby in 664 CE. Regardless of the victory for Roman Catholicism, by this time a Celtic stamp was indelibly affixed to the character of Anglo-Saxon Christianity. This character is perhaps most notably illustrated in the ornate Celtic interlace and animal figures of the manuscript illuminations of the monastery at Lindisfarne in northeast England, and in the intricately carved stone crosses such as the one at Ruthwell in southern Scotland, which combines Christian imagery with Irish artistic patterns and Germanic runes and poetic heroic sensibilities. Furthermore, stories of saints and their miracles were the most popular narrative form of this period in Christian Europe. As we shall see, the indigenous British saints' lives likewise illustrate this blending of religious, mythological, and symbolic traditions.

The Anglo-Saxon conquest of Britain was really only the first in a series of Germanic invasions of the island. In 793 CE the first Viking raid of England took place at the monastery at Lindisfarne, and this event marks the beginning of a presence in Britain that culminated with the crowning of a Danish king of England, Cnut, in 1016 CE. The Vikings were Scandinavian (primarily Norsemen from Norway and Danes) adventurer-raiders who were first cousins to the Anglo-Saxons, who were following the same migratory patterns to Britain, and who made their way, like the Celts, to Spain and Asia Minor but even farther, to North America. The etymology of the term *Viking* is uncertain; the Old English *wiking* has to do with a war band, and hence may denote a warlike pirate, while the Old Norse *vikingr* comes from a root meaning "bay" or "inlet," and thus may refer merely to those associated with those places and the crafts that plied them. These Scandinavian invaders still adhered to the old religion, and thus their appearance in Britain reinvigorated the old pre-Christian Germanic elements in the cultural melting pot.

The Anglo-Saxon period drew to a close with a final wave of Germanic invaders, the Normans, who conquered England under William in 1066. Although they came from France and used the French language, the Normans were partial products of the Germanic Frankish people who conquered Gaul in the sixth century CE, and, as their name (*Norman* = Northman) indicates, of the Germanic-Scandinavian Vikings from northern Europe. The Normans brought with them new social and governmental approaches, and it was also during the Norman period that new literary forms began to take shape in Britain, forms which would reach their greatest flower in the retelling of some of the myths, legendary histories, and narrative motifs brought by the preceding waves of invaders.

Each of the groups who came to Britain brought with it legends of heroes and myths of gods, rites of sacrifice and other religious practices, belief systems particular to each culture, place, and era of origin. With each succeeding wave of invasion, new mythic systems came into contact and conflict with the older systems already established in Britain. Indeed, these waves of invasion themselves sometimes generated new mythic traditions, to which the legends of Arthur certainly attest. New gods sometimes supplanted old gods, but often traditions merged and accommodated one another, bringing to life new, uniquely British mythic systems. This accommodation is even true of Christianity, which was, for example, transformed by Celtic culture into something quite unlike its continental counterparts. In Britain, as nowhere else in Europe, Germanic, Celtic, classical, and Christian influences came into contact, conflict, and eventually confluence; the consequent assemblage of ancient heroes, gods, and practices resulted, long after "pagan" beliefs were assumed dead and gone, in a particularly rich, fertile, and volatile medieval literary tradition, a tradition through which it is possible to gain genuine insight into the shadowy gods of ancient Britain.

Although we are most interested in examining how the various cultures and mythological systems of the British Isles tempered and transformed one another, ours is fundamentally a comparative study. This is to say that we will examine the mythic systems of the British Celts, Romano-Celts, Anglo-Saxons, and Vikings side by side according to certain more or less universal categories or archetypal motifs, the mythic manifestations of the unconscious ways in which all human societies construct their religions and understand their roles in the physical and spiritual universe. Through a comparison of Celtic, Roman, Germanic, and Christian realizations of the universal themes of creation, the hero quest, and apocalypse in Britain, for example, we will achieve a clearer view of a peculiarly "British" mythology, a British way of articulating the human condition.

Any comparative examination of British mythology must explore the tension created by two related oppositions: that between Christian and Pagan cultures and that between literate and oral cultures. In a study of the history of the development of British mythic traditions these two oppositions are inextricably mixed. Although the Romans and the Greeks—and other Mediterranean and Near Eastern peoples—were literate long before the time of Christ, literacy as we understand it came to northwestern Europe only as an aspect of Christianity. It is possible that certain Celtic and Germanic methods of inscription for messages and charms may predate Christianity, but these systems (e.g., the Celtic ogham and the Germanic runic scripts) would be ponderous for recording narratives of any length and might in fact have been based upon Roman models in the first place. It is, in any case, safe to say that storytelling in both of these cultures was fundamentally an oral art form, and that it was only with the coming of Christianity that these ancient mythologies found a form of written expression that has survived to the present day. Before moving on to the myths themselves, then, it will be beneficial to touch very briefly on the nature of oral culture and to discuss in broad terms how and why British Christianity was transformed by its contact with the Celtic and Germanic mythologies.

Oral storytellers work in ways fundamentally different from their literate counterparts. While a written story—once committed to paper—remains static through multiple readings, oral storytellers did not ply their craft through rote repetition of the same stories; instead, working from a bare outline of characters and events committed to memory, a storyteller wove a new narrative in each retelling of any particular story. The general players and conflicts remained the same, to be sure, but the storyteller also drew upon a huge hoard of stock characterizations and associations, mythic elements, poetic metaphors, and the like. The Anglo-Saxon epic *Beowulf*, to take one example, contains a host of colorful metaphors—called "kennings"—that allow the poet to mention the same thing or concept over and over without boring repetition. "Whale-road" for sea and "sea-wood" for ship are classic examples of such kennings and often seem odd to a modern reader. Further, today's reader of *Beowulf* often becomes lost in the network of vague allusions to unrecounted episodes and the series of fully recounted but seemingly unrelated asides that disrupt the main narrative of the poem. All of this material must have been clear to the original audience and would in fact have shifted from telling to telling, as the poet strove to emphasize different points. This underscores that, when we read written versions of oral traditions, it is important to look for narrative patterns, much as we look for archetypal patterns in our reading of mythology. The patterns of repetition, poetic metaphor, and stock characterization, for example, often reveal to us those elements considered most important by the culture from which the story comes.

The myths and legends of any people have much to tell us about the nature of that people, and the early British cultures are revealed to us, in some small part, as much by the types of stories they told and the way that they told them as by what any given story was about. Poets were revered in early Celtic culture, just as the *scop* (the "shaper" of words or oral poet) held a special place in Anglo-Saxon society, and the *skald* (the scop's Nordic cousin) among the Scandinavians. Such respect for storytellers is a common attitude among those who rely on oral tradition and fundamentally rests upon the storyteller's role as repository for family history, religious ritual, protective charms, medicinal knowledge, and all of the cumulative lore and wisdom of any society that has no other way to pass its traditions from one generation to the next.

This book is a comparative study of the conflict and confluence of the mythologies of ancient Britain, and such a study requires that we examine closely how Christianity—which became the dominant cultural system in Britain—helped to transform the mythological systems that predated it, and how it in its turn was transformed through contact with the earlier systems. We must begin this examination by noting that the story of the early Christian church in Britain is largely the story of the Irish church, and thus Irish narrative traditions and forms played a particularly important role in the development of British Christianity. The conversion of the Irish is traditionally attributed to Patrick, and the general consensus is that this conversion took place late in the fifth century. Just as the Romans never reached the shores of Ireland, however, the Irish church in many ways remained independent of and different from the Rome-based church throughout the early medieval period. Once again, distance and lack of contact were primarily responsible for this independence, but Irish social structures also played a role. Ireland at the time had no real urban centers, no system of well-maintained Roman roads, and no centralized political infrastructure. The model of Christianity that developed in such an environment, then, was as decentralized and autonomous as its Roman Catholic counterpart was rigidly hierarchical and dependent upon authority from Rome. Therefore, while the medieval continental church maintained an important monastic tradition, fundamentally it was structured around the parish, the diocese, the archdiocese, and their relationship to one another. The Irish model, on the other hand, was entirely monastic and idiosyncratic, and therefore drew, from monastic cluster to monastic cluster, upon different samplings of a wide variety of Celtic belief systems, literary models, artistic traditions, and interpretations of Christian scripture. This idiosyncratic nature most overtly manifested itself in the Irish art and manuscript tradition of the period, influences which were extremely important in the development of the Anglo-Saxon church in Britain. Important areas of contention with the Roman Church included such matters as the unique Irish tonsure (the method of the shaving of the head of monks), and the method of calculating the date of Easter. These conflicts came to a head in the struggle for supremacy in Anglo-Saxon Christianity, as we have already noted, but it is important to add that Celtic and Germanic heroic literary traditions gave birth to an Anglo-Saxon understanding of the nature of Christ as warrior that was equally idiosyncratic.

In sum, then, these British cultures were on the margins of Europe in every sense of the word: isolated from the center of the Christian West geographically by water and temporally by the long and difficult journey from Rome; surrounded by a cultural chasm as difficult to bridge as the physical ocean; steeped in ancient traditions that were alien to the Mediterranean cultures that spawned Roman imperial culture and Christianity, but that were at the same time resilient and adaptable. The interaction of Christianity with these older cultures was particularly noteworthy as a result of the marginal position of Britain, and the resulting cultural and mythological context was highly volatile; although Christianity undoubtedly carried the day in Britain, all of the mythologies of Britain were transformed through their contact with one another, and the literary tradition of medieval Britain is a testament to the long-term influence of early pagan narrative traditions upon later Christian Britain.

THE MYTHS

1

THE PANTHEONS

The word *pantheon* comes from the Greek *pan theon*, meaning literally "all the gods." A pantheon is an overview of a given culture's gods and goddesses and reflects not only the society's values but also its sense of itself. A pantheon directed by a thunder-bolt-wielding autocrat might suggest a patriarchy and the valuing of warrior skills. A pantheon headed by a great-mother goddess could suggest a village-based agricultural society. To confront the pantheon of the Egyptians is to confront a worldview marked by a sense of death and resurrection and the agricultural importance of the cycles of nature. The Greek pantheon is a metaphor for a pragmatic view of life that values art, beauty, and the power of the individual, and that is somewhat skeptical about human nature.

In Britain there are several pantheons to be considered under two major headings: the Germanic, which includes the Norse and the Saxon deities, and the Celtic, which includes the gods and goddesses we associate with Wales, Scotland, Cornwall, and especially Ireland. These are the lands of the so-called insular Celts, whose mythology must be seen in relation to their continental relatives—especially the Gauls described by the conquering Julius Caesar. The whole question of British-based pantheons is complicated by several factors. First, the often violent confrontations and destructions or assimilations of ethnic groups and their religions—Celtic and Roman, Romano-Celtic and Germanic, Saxon-Germanic and Norse-Germanic, Celtic and Germanic versus Christian—renders clear pantheons difficult to isolate. Furthermore, the lack of written records left by cultures that tended to transmit information orally leads almost inevitably to a coloring of earlier pantheons by more literate peoples. In the case of Britain, we have the Roman assimilation of British Celtic mythology that had begun on the continent. And both the Germanic and Celtic pantheons were reworked to varying degrees by Christian monks anxious to uphold Christianity even as they hoped to preserve local traditions for posterity. So it was that gods and goddesses of ancient Germanic and especially ancient Celtic pantheons were either destroyed or demoted if they could not be assimilated or converted in some way to the new religion.

Saxon and Norse Pantheons

Background and Sources of Germanic Mythology

Our information about Germanic mythology is only marginally more copious than that for Celtic mythology. The limited material available comes either from non-Germanic sources or from Christian Germanic sources because the pagan Germanic peoples didn't keep written records of any note. The most important of the texts containing Germanic myths include the sources most closely associated with the Norse traditions: Snorri Sturluson's *Prose Edda*, compiled by the important Icelandic chieftain and farmer around 1220 CE as a sort of how-to book for poets; the *Elder* or *Poetic Edda*, which contains a number of poems—mostly short—compiled in Iceland around 1270 CE, dealing largely with stories of the gods and of Germanic heroes; and the Skaldic verses—or Scandinavian court poems—handed down to us through Christian-era redactions from the ninth century on through the Middle Ages—often attributed to historical figures whose agendas are known to us and often written about contemporary events that may be independently verified. In addition to these major sources of mythic material we have a number of works that were written primarily as historical records. The most notable of these are the work of the twelfth-century historian Adam of Bremen and the *Gesta Danorum* of Saxo Grammaticus, a rabidly Christian Latin work of the early thirteenth century that is not forgiving to or indulgent of the pagan gods, as Snorri is. Finally, the Icelandic family sagas of the thirteenth century describe the events, culture, and beliefs of the major families of the island, and the *Landnamabok*—or "Book of the Settlements"—describes the lives of the earliest Icelandic settlers, which likewise contributes not a little to our knowledge of the early religion.

This handful of books tells us most of what we know about pre-Christian Germanic myth; as we shall discover shortly, however, Anglo-Saxon literature provides us with several additional works that illustrate the ways in which British Germanic Christianity interacted with the earlier material. These texts include the *Beowulf* manuscript, which contains *Beowulf* and the Old English version of *Judith*; the *Vercelli Book*, which includes the Old English *Andreas*, *Elene*, and *The Dream of the Rood*; and a number of other manuscripts, most notably the *Exeter Book* and the *Junius Manuscript*. These Anglo-Saxon sources are overtly Christian, yet they often combine pagan and Christian themes in uniquely British ways that promise to illuminate telling aspects of both traditions.

Germanic Ritual and Festivals

Most of the sources dealing overtly with pagan Germanic gods and the Germanic conception of the supernatural are Icelandic; this may be in part because the church was never very strong in that remote outpost. It also may be that Iceland—with its long, dark winter, its northern lights, its inexplicable mists and steams and boiling springs—is a natural breeding ground for tales of the otherworldly. In any case, these Icelandic records indicate that, like the Romans and the Greeks, the Germanic peoples left us many stories of their gods. Unlike the case of the Mediterranean traditions, however, relatively little has been preserved regarding Germanic religious rituals; this vacuum might be supposed to reflect the lack of a priestly caste. This lack, in turn, might be explained by the fact that, in Germanic society, the role of chieftain and that of priest were often conflated.

However much may be known about Germanic ritual, we do know the names and seasons of some of the associated holidays—names which have remained although with new meaning in a Christian context. It is clear that the coming of Christianity did not completely eradicate the pagan traditions brought to Britain with the Anglo-Saxons, however; this fact is most neatly illustrated by the survival of a number of overtly pagan terms in contemporary expressions, including two names that refer to the holiest times in the Christian calendar. Yule comes from the Old English *Iul*—cognate with the Old Norse *Jol*—and refers to the heathen festival of death and rebirth at the time of the winter solstice; indeed, even the tradition of the Yule log refers us back to a Germanic past. Easter itself, the holiest day in the Christian liturgical year, takes its name from the Old English *Eastre*, the goddess of the dawn, a deity of the birth of the day who was associated with a pagan vernal festival—at the birth of the new growing season—of the same name. Moreover, four of the primary gods of the Germanic pantheons survive to the present time in the Modern English names for days of the week. Tuesday is named after the Old English Tiw, who is equivalent to the Old Norse Tyr; Wednesday takes its name from the Old English Wodan, known to the Norse as Odin; the name Thursday comes from the Old English Thunor, or the Old Norse Thor; while that for Friday is derived from the Old English name Frige, who is equated with the Old Norse Frigg.

These four primary Germanic gods represent only a portion of the total pantheon, however, and it is noteworthy that the major fertility gods are excluded. We most usually would set the number of major Germanic deities at twelve; these are collectively known by such titles as "rulers," "binding powers," and "bright, shining ones." We will deal with only the most important of these, and specifically with those about whom we know enough to make archetypal comparisons. There were two distinct sets of Germanic gods, two tribes that were—according to Norse lore—at war early in their history. This conflict may well represent the tension between an earlier set of fertility gods that was supplanted by that of usurping war-gods; such a struggle may be replicated in Celtic mythology in the war between the Tuatha De Dannan and the Fomoiri. The usurpation of one cult by another may be indicative in turn of a cultural change that necessitated the ascendance of war-gods. In other words, the conflict between the earlier Vanir and the upstart Aesir might indicate a cultural shift from a more strictly agrarian way of life to a more violent one.

The Construction of the Pantheon:
The War of the Aesir and the Vanir

In the early days there were two sets of gods, the Vanir, led by Njordr and his children Freyr and Freya, and the Aesir, led by Odin, Tyr, and Thor. These tribes went to war, perhaps owing to an insult by the Aesir to a member of the Vanir. At first the Vanir took the advantage, pressing their attack on Asgard, the home of the Aesir, and destroying the protective walls around it. The Vanir were skilled in *seidr* and other forms of magic unknown to the Aesir and feared and loathed by them, and this magic may have been the secret to the early success of the Vanir. Eventually the Aesir seem to have proved to be the greater warriors, however, and battled the Vanir back to Vanaheim, their home. Neither group was entirely victorious, though, and eventually the two tribes sought peace.

According to some accounts, the gods determined to seal their truce with an exchange of hostages. Njordr and his offspring left the Vanir to live among the Aesir, while Honir and Mimir went from Asgard to Vanaheim. At first the exchange seemed an equitable one: Njordr and Freyr soon held high rank as priests among the Aesir, while Freya taught those who would learn the forbidden magic of *seidr*. For their part, Honir was honored as a powerful leader, while Mimir's advice was held to be peerless in its wisdom. It soon became apparent to the Vanir, however, that they had fared rather poorly in the exchange. While Hoenir was an able leader as long as Mimir was present to advise him, he was indecisive and ineffectual without his counselor. As it appeared that they had been duped, the Vanir decided to take their revenge upon Mimir; they cut off his head and sent it to Odin as a token of their displeasure.

Odin, however, always one to see the profit to be made from adversity, was far from discomfited by this grisly gift. Instead, he smeared the head with herbs and balms to preserve it, and whispered magic charms to give it speech. Henceforth Odin was never without the wise counsel of Mimir, and increased his own power, prescience, and wisdom through his acquisition of the bodiless head.

THIS MYTH CONCERNING the end of the conflict between the gods illustrates typical Germanic practices of truce-keeping through the exchange of hostages, as well as the price for duplicity. Hostages in Germanic culture were not prisoners in any modern sense; rather, they lived as honored members of the tribe to whom they were hostaged and would fight for that tribe to earn personal glory, and to reflect well upon the honor of their own nation. Moreover, the head-taking theme apparent here is one that we will revisit on a number of occasions. Head-hunting was common among Iron Age Northern Europeans, most notably the Celts, and ritual decapitation and/or strangulation was practiced by Germanic and Celtic tribes alike. There seems to have been a notion of a magical quality of the head as the repository of wisdom and power, a notion quite clearly exemplified by this myth and that might explain the ritual significance of decapitation.

Not all accounts, however, agree as to the way in which the peace between the gods was compacted; but although the narrative details of this next myth are fleshed out quite differently from those of the last one, both share crucial archetypal elements. The myth of Kvasir—like that of Mimir—illuminates folk understandings of the purposes of ritual human sacrifice. In both myths symbols of potency (the head of Mimir, the blood of Kvasir) are taken by force and the powerful wisdom represented by these symbols is harnessed through mystical charms and processes. Further, this second truce myth illustrates the importance of witnessing and the rituals of oath-taking in early Germanic culture, and also suggests a metaphorical link between literal and creative fertility.

The Pantheon United: The Truce Crock and the Mead of Poetry

When the gods of the Aesir and the Vanir decided to end the war between them, they agreed upon terms and then swore their oaths by spitting into a communal jar. The divine spittle of all the gods was allowed to mingle in this jar and then was formed into a man, who thereby provided a witness to their truce and who embodied the very spirit of the newfound friendship between the tribes. This man was called Kvasir, and he soon became regarded as the wisest of men. Kvasir was noted for his quiet manner and helpful, suggestive advice, advice he was willing to share with all who sought him out.

Kvasir's fame and equanimity proved his undoing, however, as Fjalar and Galar—unsavory brother dwarfs—conspired to gain his wisdom for themselves. They invited him to a feast in their subterranean home, after which they murdered him, bled him dry into two jars and a cauldron, mixed his blood with honey and water, and brewed a magical potion out of this grisly concoction. The resulting mead granted poetic inspiration and great wisdom to all who tasted it.

Fjalar and Galar managed to keep their ill-gotten brew a secret, but were forced to surrender it to the giant Suttung as recompense for the murder of his parents. Suttung locked the mead away in the base of the mountain Hnitbjorg, with his daughter Gunnlod left to guard it. Unlike his predecessors, Suttung was not at all discreet about his possession of this marvelous liquor, and Kvasir's fate and the existence of the mead brewed from his blood soon came to the attention of the gods, who vowed to win it from the giant. Odin took this task upon himself and took on one of his many disguises, that of a large man named Bolverk, or "Evil-worker."

Bolverk made his way to the lands of Baugi, the brother of Suttung, and through treacherous guile was able to set all of Baugi's hired hands upon each other, leaving them all dead and their employer with no means to take in his hay. Offering himself for the job, Bolverk imposed just one condition: a draught of Suttung's mead. Although noncommittal, Baugi agreed to act as an intermediary in return for Bolverk's labor. At the end of Bolverk's employment Suttung refused his request, but Bolverk coerced Baugi into drilling a hole for him into the heart of Suttung's mountain. As soon as the hole was completed Bolverk changed into a snake, slithering to the heart of the mountain an instant before Baugi, who had grown sick of his workman's swagger, could put an end to him.

Once safe within the mountain Bolverk changed back into a man before the eyes of the lonely and love-starved Gunnlod, who soon succumbed to his false-hearted words of love and his amorous caresses. After three passion-filled days and nights, the besotted Gunnlod granted Bolverk's request of three drinks of her father's mead. With those three draughts Bolverk emptied all three vessels; he then promptly changed himself into an eagle and made for Asgard. Suttung soon realized what had happened, transformed himself into another eagle, and gave chase. Hearing the commotion, the gods put all of their pots, pans, and other containers in the courtyard within their walls; Odin—cheeks bulging with mead—arrived just before Suttung could catch him and spat the precious liquid into the gathered vessels, although in his haste he spilled some along the way. The spilled portion is that which poets in this world drink from; it provides their inspiration. Suttung returned to Hnitbjorg empty-handed and furious, where he was greeted by Gunnlod, debauched, deceived, and humiliated. When the giants returned in force to seek Bolverk, Odin, now in his familiar form, swore on his ring that Bolverk was not in Asgard, and the giants were forced to accept this oath. Thus the gods gained and kept the mead of poetry.

AN UNDERSTANDING OF THE relationship between the creation of alcohol and a truce between warring gods is not limited to Germanic culture. In Indic myth, for example, a struggle between groups of gods similar to that between the Aesir and the Vanir reached its climax when Cyavana created the monster Mada (the name is significant, meaning "intoxication"; similarly, *kvas* denotes a fermented beverage), who coerced Indra into accepting his rivals. After peace was established Mada was divided into his component parts: alcohol, lust, gambling, and hunting. This example illustrates that there may have been an Indo-European Ur-myth about a divine struggle and the role of alcohol in the compacting of peace; in this culture, however, alcohol was a by-product of a monstrous weapon wielded to impose peace, while in Germanic myth its association was with the witness to an uncoerced peace, and its genesis links it with wisdom and divine inspiration. This distinction may explain in some small measure the difference in the moral perception of alcohol in each culture: in Indian culture alcohol was seen in relation to the other vices, while in Germanic (and Celtic) tradition alcohol became associated with divine inspiration.

In addition to the aforementioned concepts of potency, sacrifice, oath-taking, and witnessing, this myth also manifests an important relationship between literal and metaphorical fertility, as well as illustrating a number of crucial characteristics of the god Odin. First, both the brewing of alcohol and the composing of poetry were considered magical processes by many ancient cultures. Further, the creation of Kvasir from the spittle of the gods directly prefigures that of the mead of poetry from Kvasir's blood: saliva and honey both contain natural agents of fermentation, and thus both were seen as agents of spontaneous creation; both were therefore perceived by the ancients as having somewhat mystical qualities. More specifically, both acts of genesis serve to emphasize the conceptual link between the art of the brewer, through whom ordinary water and honey is mystically transformed into intoxicating mead, and that of the poet, through whom ordinary words and memories transcend the usual limitations of time, space, and language. Poets have traditionally been revered in oral cultures because of their function as a sort of communal memory, because of their power to create or destroy reputation, and because of their perceived role as a conduit through which divine inspiration may be accessed. Alcohol often played a sacramental function in early cultures because of its intoxicating properties, and thus likewise was viewed as a conduit to divine inspiration.

Finally, the myth of the mead of poetry provides us with a telling glimpse into the character of Odin, who is usually counted as the chief god of the northern pantheon. Odin is a war god and a chieftain of the gods, to be sure, but he is much more than that, as his role in this myth makes clear. Here we see the craft and guile we will come to associate with Odin illustrated several times: we note his love of disguise—an ongoing theme—here with a significant name, Bolverk, meaning "Evil-worker." In his clever murder of Baugi's field hands, enacted with no compunction whatsoever, we perceive the capricious nature of a god of battle and slaughters. But it is in his subtle coercion of Baugi and his seduction and abandonment of Suttung's daughter Gunnlod that we note elements of the trickster, that manipulative and self-serving figure to be associated more with the demonic than with the divine. Odin is as treacherous and false-hearted in love and in negotiations as he is in war; in this myth Odin is even represented as a troth-breaker who violated an oath upon his ring, the most sacred of Germanic pledging ceremonies. But in this myth Odin is more than trickster and war-god; he is also the god of poetry and inspiration. Odin thus conflates a number of elements that might be considered contradictory in other cultures, and it is fitting that we now turn our attention to the development and diversification of Odin, that most ambiguous and all-encompassing god of the Germanic pantheon.

Wodan/Odin

The treaty between the Aesir and the Vanir, however well guaranteed, seems to have been sufficient to end the enmity between the two groups, and soon the very notion that there ever was a conflict fades away. At this point a power structure becomes apparent. Although not always chief among the gods worshiped in Germanic Europe, Odin—known as Woden, Wodan, or Wotan to the Anglo-Saxons—is purported in Norse sources, and notably by Snorri Sturluson, to be the father of the gods and the wisest and most powerful of them. At times robust and warrior-like in aspect, Odin is most often depicted as one-eyed, with a gray beard (hence his nickname Harbard, which means "hairy bearded"). Odin's wife was Frigg, but in some sources he also was said to have been married to Jord, with whom he fathered Thor. The Norse Odin was multifaceted and wore many divine hats; according to the dialogue in Snorri's *Gylfaginning,* or "The Beguiling of Gylfi," Odin has as many names as he does mythic functions: he is "the all-father," "the father of the slain," "the father of victories," "the god of the captured," and "the god of the hanged," to name but a very few of the scores recounted. The first title refers to his rank in the Norse pantheon as the great god, while the next three refer to his function as a battle-god who brings the worthiest of his followers to his bosom; the final example alludes directly to the grisly nature of sacrificial victims rendered unto Odin; Adam of Bremen—among other sources—describes in graphic detail an eye-witness account of the sacrifices to Odin at the temple at Uppsala. Every ninth year the sacred grove surrounding the temple was filled with the hanging bodies of humans, dogs, and horses dedicated to Odin. Some saga accounts indicate that a common procedure was first to hang the victim and then to pierce the body with a spear. Indeed, it was a common practice for those in danger of dying in their beds to be "marked with the sign of Odin"; that is, ceremonial stigmata meant to represent a spear wound was applied to the man's side, thus ensuring that the bearer of the mark might be accepted into Valhalla. Such rites were modeled upon Odin's own mystical sacrifice of himself unto himself, to which we shall turn in our discussion of the dying-god. Other names for Odin take into account his physical characteristics or penchant for disguises, such as "the one-eyed god," or "the hooded one," while still others examine his behavior and moral fiber, such as "the evil-doer" and "the destroyer."

Generally, and especially when examining the specific manifestations of this deity as they appear in the Norse tradition, we will refer to this god consistently as "Odin"; when discussing the more general Germanic mythic context, however, we will use the West Germanic "Wodan." This system is not perfect, but it will allow the reader to distinguish between general and specific mythic traditions, and we will use analogous parallels when dealing with the other major Germanic gods. It would be fair to say, for example, that Odin is certainly the most volatile and interesting of the Aesir of Norse tradition, while the Germanic Wodan's very name denotes "rage," "possession," or "fury"—attributes that came to be associated with the votaries of this demonic warrior god.

ODIN'S BERSERKRS

Animal battle frenzy—a type of demonic possession involving an animal form and/or beastly ferocity—is the hallmark of the Odinic warrior, the fury of whom is most regularly associated with that of wolves and bears. Accounts of such individuals—and of the beastly homicidal rage they manifested—are legion in the Norse sagas, in the history of Saxo Grammaticus, and even in Icelandic law codes. The modern word *berserk* comes from the Old Icelandic, meaning "bear-shirted" and is indicative of the appearance of these frenetic, irrational warriors, who were associated both with animal disguises and with actual lycanthropy, or shape-changing. To cite but one famous example, Bodvar Bjarki was a noted Berserkr who, as we shall see, fought for King Hrolf Kraki in the form of a bear. The two main classes of such warriors who worshiped Odin were the *berserkir* and the *ulfhednar*, "bear-shirted ones" and "wolf-skinned ones," respectively, and they were noted for the onset of a battle fury that rendered them incapable of speech or reason, but that also made them cyclones of unfettered martial wrath, and all but invulnerable to mortal weapons. The physical contortions associated with these antics are reminiscent of the battle-warp spasm undergone by the Celtic hero Cuchulainn, and this resemblance may suggest an Indo-European mythic tradition concerning psychotic fighting frenzy. It also is of note that some Indo-European terms cognate to English "wolf" imply such bestial insanity. The story of one family of Berserkrs—that of Arngrim of Bolm, taken from the thirteenth-century *Hervararsaga*—illustrates eloquently several of the mythic qualities of this fearless and manic way of life.

The Legend of Tyrfing and the Family of Arngrim the Berserkr

Tyrfing was a magic sword forged by the dwarfs Dulin and Dvalin for Svafrlami, a grandson of Odin. Svafrlami caught the dwarfs out of doors by surprise, and coerced them into the task. They were forced to create the weapon according to his specifications, and thus it had a beautiful gold hilt, a blade that never tarnished, and an edge that would cleave iron like cloth. The dwarfs repaid his treachery with a curse, however; the sword was to kill whenever it was unsheathed, it was to perform three foul deeds, and it would be the cause of Svafrlami's death. The last prophecy soon came to pass. Arngrim the Berserkr lived on the island of Bolm, and often went raiding in the territory of Svafrlami. It happened one day that the two were paired in single combat, and Svafrlami struck at Arngrim and missed; the point of Tyrfing then stuck fast in the ground. Arngrim, seeing his chance, hacked off Svafrlami's hand, seized Tyrfing, and sliced Svafrlami in two with the man's own sword. To complete his victory, Arngrim carried off Svafrlami's daughter Eyfura, who subsequently bore him twelve sons.

The sons of Arngrim followed in their father's footsteps, and each was a bloodthirsty pirate and a full-blown Berserkr; the eldest was named Angantyr, who inherited the magic sword from his father. These brothers were such fearsome Berserkrs that, when the rage of Odin's divine frenzy fell upon them, they often killed some of their own men. In order to avoid such mischances, they learned in time that, when the frenzy began to possess them, they should leave their camps or ships and do battle with the rocks of the shore and the trees of the forest, thereby dispelling their wrath without harming their followers. Their madness and power was such that all were in awe of them, and no man sought them out—or indeed, crossed their path—if he could at all avoid it. Eventually Angantyr's lust was the cause of his downfall, as he and his brothers were slain by Hjalmar and his companion Orvar over a dispute concerning Ingeborg, the daughter of King Yngvi of Uppsala, although Hjalmar died at Angantyr's hand. Orvar buried the brothers in mounds where they lay, and Tyrfing with Angantyr.

Soon thereafter, Angantyr's wife Svava gave birth to a daughter named Hervor. Even in childhood this girl showed that she had Berserkr blood, and at an early age she dressed as a man and entered a company of Vikings. She soon decided to claim Tyrfing as her birthright, and sought out her father's grave. Terrified of the demon's wrath even in death, her companions soon deserted her, but she continued stouthearted. As she approached the barrows, they appeared to burst into flame, but she strode on, undeterred and unblemished by fire. She then spoke the spells that summoned her father and forced him to do her bidding. Threaten and cajole though he might, the shade of Angantyr was unable to persuade Hervor to depart without the sword. Finally he cast it out to her, and she caught the flying sword in her hand, heedless of her father's prophecy that Tyrfing would cause the death of all of those near to her. The girl then set off alone.

IT IS CLEAR THAT Berserkrs, as we have classed all such warriors generically, were fearsome adversaries: there are records of Berserkrs biting through shields, swallowing hot coals or passing through fire unharmed, and killing enemies by biting through their throats. Indeed, the supernatural powers of such creatures in their fury is underscored in *Egilssaga*, in which Egil was able to dispatch such a warrior—who could not be killed by weapons—only by ripping out his windpipe with his teeth. Unfortunately, as the story of Arngrim makes clear, it was not unusual for Berserkrs to turn their wrath on those near to them who were their comrades, and for that reason they were feared by all and hated by most; the historian Saxo, for example, tells of a Swedish Berserkr who killed six of his companions in the heat of his fury, which may help to explain the Icelandic codes outlawing such warriors. That Berserkrs were especially favored by Odin is clear from a number of sources, and it is perhaps especially noteworthy that his personal retinue at his son Baldr's funeral included a number of them in addition to the expected Valkyries. The association of Berserkrs with Odin underscores his complex and shifting divine nature: while the attributes of these followers may be indicative of Odin's demonic characteristics, his need for such warriors, as we shall see, underscores his role as a bastion against the forces of chaos that will gather against the gods at Ragnarok. The association of animal characteristics with warriors devoted to Odin should come as no surprise, however, and neither should accusations of shape-shifting; Odin himself, as we have seen, often took other forms in his trickster aspect, and his most commonly noted familiars were ravens and wolves, the Germanic beasts of battle.

Odin's Familiars

A wolf guards the westernmost door of Valhalla, Odin's home; an eagle circles above him. When he goes out of his hall into the world, the All-Father rides forth

on Sleipnir, the finest of horses, whose eight legs gallop faster than any mortal
steed. At home, sitting upon Hlidskjalf, his high throne, the One-eyed God can see
all that comes to pass in the worlds of gods and men. His spear Gungnir never fails
to find its target, and he wears the gold bracelet Draupnir; every ninth night eight
equally precious rings drop from this treasure. Although he survives on wine alone,
the Lord of the Slain feeds huge hunks of meat to his wolves Freki and Geri, but
they are never sated. Perched on his shoulders are Odin's ravens, Huginn and Muginn, and each day the king of the gods sets them loose to fly far and wide over
Midgard, to seek out the secrets and actions of men and to return to their master
with this knowledge.

ODIN'S ASSOCIATION WITH wolves and with birds of prey reflects an ancient
Germanic belief that these beasts betokened war and slaughters. We see similar associations in Old English poetry of the Christian period, and it is clear
that these animals—perhaps originally perceived of as scavengers, and thus
literally the beneficiaries of human battles—have become by this time imbued with metaphorical, totemic, and mythic qualities. No longer thought
simply opportunistic carrion eaters, Odin's wolves are seen as models of ferocity for those who would be his warriors, and their very appearance would
suggest an oncoming battle. *Freki* means "ravenous" and *Geri* can be translated "greedy"; Odin's wolves are not simply hungry for flesh, however, insatiable though they be. More than that, their boundless appetite for fresh meat
represents both the battle-lust of their master and his almost desperate desire
to fill Valhalla with the bodies of more and more slain warriors. The function
and names of Odin's ravens, moreover, help to account for the prescience attributed to ravens in the sources. Huginn ("Thought") and Muginn ("Memory") seek out intrigues and conspiracies every day to keep their master
abreast of the doings on earth; it perhaps should come as no surprise, then,
that the appearance of ravens quite often foretells the doom of many mortal
men. Wodan's association with the beasts of battle and the warriors who emulate them is central to his cosmic role, as it is his duty to provide the army
that will fight with the doomed gods against their enemies at the final cataclysm of Ragnarok; this role is more fully examined in the mythic descriptions
of Odin's home, Valhalla.

Odin's Home: Valhalla

Those who are unlucky enough to die from old age or disease may never pass Valhalla's doors, but are sent instead to Hel, the shadowy realm ruled by the goddess
of the same name, where they will wait for the end of days in its cold, dank embrace. Only the *einherjar*, the greatest of warriors, Odin's chosen host, are plucked
at their prime from the battlefield like ripe fruit by the Valkyries, the handmaids of
the God of Slaughters. Often these emissaries of Odin will show passing favor to a
champion so that he gains great renown for his martial prowess, only to strike him
down when they deem that the time is right. The greatest of the chosen are greeted
by gods or senior *einherjar* and presented by them to Odin. The host of chosen
warriors spend every day on the open field before Odin's hall, doing battle and

practicing their feats of arms; they find great sport in these daily exercises, and each tries every day to kill the dearest of his comrades. They treat this activity as practice for their real purpose, which is to fight on the side of the gods against their combined enemies at the apocalypse of Ragnarok. One of the three cocks that will crow upon the day of that apocalypse resides in Valhalla; its name is Salgofnir. In the meantime, at the end of each day's practice battle the dead rise up again, all are made whole, and the entire host returns into the hall to feast and make merry throughout the night; they are served by the Valkyries. The cook Andhrimnir prepares their feast in his mighty cauldron Eldhrimnir: each day he boils up the great boar Saehrimnir, who is magically made whole again on the morrow. To wash down this hearty pork stew, the warriors swill endless gallons of mead drawn from the teats of the magic goat Heidrun; these teats fill a huge barrel daily. Odin himself drinks only wine, however, and this he may share with those he wishes to show special honor. Heidrun feeds upon fresh shoots from the tree Lerad and lives on the roof of Valhalla. On the roof of this hall also stands the hart Eikthynir, who gnaws on Lerad. The Hall of Heroes itself is hard to mistake: its outer gate is named Valgrind, and the river Thund rushes by just beyond it. Its roof is made of shields, and its rafters are spears. Valhalla has five hundred and forty doors, and on the last of days the warriors will march forth from them, shoulder to shoulder, eight hundred from each door; some count this number of doors to be six hundred and forty, and claim that nine hundred and sixty warriors issue from each. Valhalla is considered a sacred sanctuary by the gods, and thus no blood may be spilled there in anger.

THE ENGLISH NAME Valhalla comes from the Old Icelandic *Valholl*, meaning "Hall of the Slain." The fact that this hall is peopled by slain warriors who at one time were favored by Odin—only to be betrayed by him upon the field of their last battle—is indicative of the mercurial nature of his favor, and of the paradox that to be Odin's man promised a warrior ultimate death, as well as great prowess in the meantime. This paradox was not lost upon the very warriors who dedicated themselves to the fickle God of Battles: "gone to visit Odin in Valhalla" was a common euphemism for death in battle, and a warrior challenging an enemy to mortal combat commonly invited him on a "journey to Valhalla." Likewise, when two armies met it was common to hurl a spear over the heads of the advancing enemies, dedicating them to Odin much as one would those to be sacrificed to him at his temples. This tradition has as its source Odin's own hurling of a spear over the advancing Vanir at the onset of the war between the gods. Moreover, fallen warriors, buried in their barrows or about to be put to the torch on their pyres, were commonly commended to Odin in similar terms. The funeral ode to King Hakon the Good of Norway (*Hakonarmal*), composed around 960 by his court skald, Eyvind, illustrates such a fate from the fallen warrior's point of view: chosen by the Valkyries to die, Hakon chastises them for their wavering favor; they answer him that his prowess was the result of their good offices from the start. Hakon seems less than convinced, however, and the modern reader will hardly blame him. Odin's point of view is more forcefully articulated in *Eiriksmal*, the saga of Erik Blood-Ax; when the god Bragi asks his father Odin why he did not grant victory to this, the greatest of warriors, the Lord of Hosts replies that it is far safer for the gods to surround themselves with such in Asgard, rather than to favor them in Midgard. The mortal warrior Ragnar Lodbrok takes such a traditional Odinic view in his twelfth-century *Krakumal*, in which he vows not to enter Valhalla with cowardly dying words or thoughts. Odin's association with his Valkyries, and the method by which he chooses the champions who are brought to Valhalla, is descended from the Germanic concept of the wild hunt—the pack of ghost riders in the sky who seek mortal quarry upon the battlefields of earth. The name Wodan is significant in this context, and its original meaning becomes clear. Here we see evidence of early belief in a death-god at the head of a "raging army"—rendered literally, in Old High German, the *Wutanes her*—of corpses, their passage causing violent storms: their hooves and feet the thunder, their clashing arms the lightning, their maddened howls the screaming wind. The tradition of the wild hunt has Celtic counterparts and is to be found in various forms throughout the medieval period.

Tiw/Tyr

Tiw was the protector of judicial assemblies; this fact is attested by a Roman inscription in Britain to "Mars Thingus," who watched over legal proceedings, which were held on his day (Tuesday) of each week. Later Icelandic traditions likewise link the Norse Tyr with the Thing, or national assembly. The association of the god of war with matters of law and oath-keeping also may explain why the trial by combat was consistently popular with the Germanic peoples (even reentering England as late as 1066 with the invading Normans, who brought it as part of their Scandinavian heritage); indeed, this fact may shed some light on why the *holmganga*, or sanctioned duel, was held close to the Thing in medieval Iceland, and why Germanic warriors traditionally swore oaths on their weapons. Trials by ordeal and by combat were central to Germanic concepts of justice, and we shall discuss the mythic consequences of such a conception presently. Suffice it for now to note that the straightforward and trustworthy Tiw presents an altogether different face of the god of war than does Wodan.

Tyr is the Norse name for a late and marginalized version of Tiw. In the one major myth about Tyr still in existence, his function as lord of troth is central, and the fact that he forswears himself is significant in the context of the process of his mythic conflation with Odin; Odin's demonic craftiness and guile in combination with Tyr's steadfast courage and reputation for integrity help the gods out in the short term, but the knowledge that Tyr's sacrifice (physical and moral) will do no good in the long run emphasizes the pathos surrounding Odin's increasingly desperate attempts to stave off the inevitable at all costs, even if only for a little while.

The Binding of Fenrir

Loki—although married to Sigyn—fathered three monstrous offspring by the giantess Angrboda. These were Fenrir the wolf, Jormungand the serpent, and Loki's ghastly daughter Hel; this last one—although human in form—stood out in a crowd as much as her brothers did. A normal and healthy woman from the waist up, from her waist down her flesh was rotten and blackened, and her expression was ever grim. The gods, warned of trouble by prophecy, hastened to cast Jormungand and Hel out of Asgard. Thus the serpent was thrust into the ocean around Midgard, where it grew and grew until it encircled the world, taking its own tail in its mouth. Likewise was Hel exiled to Niflheim, where she was granted sway over those who died of sickness and age. Fenrir, however, was allowed to remain in Asgard, the better to keep an eye on him. He grew larger and more fierce by the day, however, and Tyr alone of all the gods was brave enough to feed him huge hunks of meat, which Fenrir swallowed whole, bones and all. Finally, the gods decided that they must rid themselves of the menace in their midst, but they were loathe to despoil the sanctuary of Asgard with blood spilled in anger. The course of action they resolved upon, therefore, was to bind the wolf. The gods attempted to hide their purpose in the guise of a contest, and appealing to Fenrir's vanity they challenged him to break the strongest bonds they could devise. The first two times the gods bound Fenrir in great fetters, the second more massive than the first, but both times the wolf burst his bonds with ease. Driven to the point of desperation, the gods bargained with the dwarfs to devise a bond strong enough to hold Fenrir. After some time the dwarfs produced a slim and silky cord that they made of six substances: the noise of a moving cat, the beard of a woman, the root of a mountain, the sinew of a bear, the breath of a fish, and the spit of a bird. Although the gods couldn't help but doubt that this thin ribbon would succeed where mighty chains had failed, they invited Fenrir to sail out to an island in a lake, where they approached him a third time with their challenge. Suspicious of this turn of events, Fenrir at first refused to be bound by the cord; he was persuaded only when Tyr agreed to place his arm in Fenrir's mouth as a surety of the good faith of the gods. As soon as the cord was tied around him Fenrir began to struggle, but this time his bonds only tightened with every movement. As his predicament became clear to him, Fenrir bit down upon Tyr's arm, severing it at the elbow. Now the gods tied the cord to a mighty chain, which in turn they looped through a large stone; this stone they drove well into the earth, topping it with another boulder. Finally, the gods drove a sword through Fenrir's two jaws, gagging him. Thus the three bastards of Loki and Angrboda were cursed and imprisoned by the gods, powerless to free themselves until the day of Ragnarok, when they would join their father in the overthrow of their keepers. The price for the imprisonment of Fenrir was the loss of the strong arm of Tyr, as well as the smirching of his honor.

THE STORY OF TYR'S loss of one hand is similar to myths in a number of other Indo-European traditions, notably the Iranian, the Roman, and the Irish. In Iranian myth, Jamshid retrieved his brother Taxmoruw from the anus of the demon Ahriman, but his hand withered as a result of its unholy contact with the rectum of the devil. The Irish Nuadu lost his arm in battle against the Fir Bolg, and the Roman Mucius Scaevola heroically burned off his right arm as a result of his own act of deception. Perhaps most suggestively, the priests of Dius Fides, the Roman god of troth, symbolically bandaged their right hands to the very fingertips. Tyr's archetypal relationship with Odin has similar parallels in other Indo-European divine pairs, most notably in Indic and Celtic myth. In Mitra and Varuna, the Indic tradition also pairs a relatively benign oath-keeping god with a more chaotic and less trustworthy one, while the Irish Nuadu and Lug evoke Tyr and Odin through similar physical characteristics.

The consistent pairing of these mythic archetypes may tell us something about conflicting pressures within the societies in which they arose. In simplest terms, perhaps Wodan replaced Tiw because he represented a fuller range of characteristics valued in Germanic society. Tiw's courage as a god of battle may not have been sufficient to offset the detriment posed by his sense of justice, a notion of fair play being an unfortunate occupational hazard of a god of troth. The Norse Odin's demonic volatility and capriciousness make him a more ideal war-god: he is violent and chaotic, he fights dirty, and he does whatever it takes to get the job done. Therein lies his chief appeal to a warrior society: while Odin is often not at all morally superior to his enemies, he usually is more clever, more cutthroat, and more efficient, and while such attributes might not endear him to philosophers, idealists, and those who depend upon justice and fair play, successful warriors tend to be a pragmatic lot. Wodan may have usurped Tiw in the Germanic pantheon precisely because his moral ambiguity reflected such pragmatism.

Thunor/Thor

After the supplanting of Tiw by Wodan, Thunor provided a much needed counterweight within the Germanic pantheon. Thunor is predictable, dependable, and steadfast in his hatred and persecution of the giants, the sworn enemies of the gods. Thunor's steady nature made him popular among the settled, the stable, the weak, and the threatened. After the demise of Tiw from any major active role, Thunor became a god of justice and of troth, and it was in his name (and with his hammer, called in the Norse sources Mjollnir) that marriages were consecrated and justice dispensed. In fact, up until the year 1000 CE the Icelandic Thing—the primary legal and legislative assembly, held annually—was opened with an invocation to Thor, the Norse version of this god; after that year, the invocation was to Christ as well as to Thor. Thunor was always popular in times of crisis, and during periods of Christian conversion was vastly more popular than his father. Thunor is a classic sky-god whose name is commonly translated "thunder." The thunderer armed with a hammer might be equated with the Roman Hercules, but Adam of Bremen associated Thunor with Jupiter, and indeed, Thunor's day of the week was equated by the Romans with that of Jove, and hence Thursday falls on the fourth day of the work week. Thunor was associated by the Germanic peoples with mighty groves of outsized oaks within the primeval forest, and moreover the Baltic tribes, Celts, Greeks, and Slavs all likewise associated the god of thunder with these sacred trees. On Iceland, which lacked great trees of any kind, this sacred relationship was transferred to holy wooden posts dedicated to the thunder-god. To this day, some Anglo-Saxon place names in Britain denote "thunder-groves."

Thor's father is Odin and his mother is Fjorgyn or Jorth, meaning "earth." Thor is described as huge in size, appetite, thirst, and anger, with a large red beard and fiery eyes. Thor's fuse is short and his wit—according to Loki—is as blunt as his hammer. Besides his hammer and his chariot, Thor's notable possessions include his iron gloves and his girdle of power. Thor's hall is called Thrudheim or Thrudvang, both meaning "home of power"; his daughter is named Thrud, and hence his offspring represents physical might. Thor's wife is Sif, who had the most beautiful hair of all the goddesses; this hair was shaved by Loki as a prank, and subsequently replaced with a wig of spun gold created by the sons of the dwarf Ivaldi. These same dwarfs forged Odin's spear Gungnir and Freyr's ship *Skidbladnir*. Sif has been said to be a fertility goddess whose hair represents ripened wheat; Thor's genesis as the son of the sky-father and earth-mother might be significant in this context. Thor was thus associated with fertility, but his role as thunderer also placed upon him the mantle of weather-god, and so many travelers made sacrifice unto him even after the conversion to Christianity was nominally complete. Indeed, Thor was said to have appeared to Christian sailors in dreams, threatening doom to those who forsook him.

THE TEMPLES OF THOR

There remain many records of images of Thor, and there appear to have been more temples to Thor than to any other god. Statues of Thor usually included a hammer, mace, scepter, or other symbol of his role as thunderer, and some of his temples included elaborate chariots that ran on wheels fitted into runners in the floor; evidently, one could do homage to Thor by pulling the chariot along this fixed course, which the Christian king of Norway Olaf Tryggvason learned to his chagrin. Having been tricked into this act of obeisance by a pagan guide named Skeggi, Olaf had men ransack the temple; Olaf reserved for himself the privilege of unseating the idol of Thor from the offending chariot. In temples that served several deities, Thor often was granted precedence. Sacrifices of bread and meat were common tributes to Thor, while some temples contained a ritual bowl in which was caught the blood that flowed from sacrificial beasts. The saga of Thorolf the Bearded of Most (recorded in part both in *Landnamabok* and *Eyrbyggjasaga*) describes some elements common to temples to Thor, as well as rituals associated with founding such sanctuaries.

Thorolf Mostarskegg Establishes a Temple to Thor

Thorolf Mostarskegg was a great friend to Thor, as his first name implies; his surname informs us that he hailed from the tiny island of Most off of the west coast of Norway, and that he had a great beard, as well befits the followers of the thunderer. When Harald Fairhair was consolidating his control over that kingdom, many freedom-loving landholders who were used to going their own way departed Norway for new homes abroad. Thorolf was one of those who had a mind to try his luck elsewhere, so he consulted his friend Thor as to his best course of action. Thor gave his follower a sign that he should leave Norway for Iceland, and Thorolf then dutifully packed his household for the trip. Along with his family's possessions and wealth, Thorolf took great care to disassemble his ancestral shrine to Thor, taking special pains to include the sacred pillars and the tamped earth from under the platform where the idol of Thor had been situated. When he reached the coast of Iceland, Thorolf threw the pillars overboard, determining to stake his claim wherever Thor might see fit to bring them to shore; Thorolf had not long to wait, and he did as he had intended, marking out his new property around the coast indicated by the beached posts; having determined the extent of his holdings, Thorolf sanctified his claim by walking the boundaries of his estate with Thor's sacred fire. After completing these ritual aspects of land-taking, Thorolf set himself to the task of constructing a new farm and house, and he did not stint his divine companion, either: Thorolf raised for Thor a fine new sanctuary close to his own house, built in part over the sacred earth brought from the old temple on Most, and complete with sacred posts, holy nails, holy ring, ritual bowl, and images of Thor and other gods.

A SACRED RING IS mentioned in *Eyrbyggjasaga*, and many of Thor's temples are said to have contained such a holy ring; as we learned in the discussion of the mead of poetry, swearing a vow upon a sacred oath-ring was the most solemn of pledges in the Germanic world, while forswearing such an oath was the vilest of crimes. Several English and Irish accounts confirm that this practice was widespread in Britain, and indeed the truce enacted between the English under Alfred and the Danes under Guthrum was sanctified by the Danes upon such a holy ring. The Althing in Iceland began on Thor's day with an invocation to the thunderer, while Adam of Bremen records the presence of a statue of Thor at the place of assembly at Uppsala in Sweden; these facts, in addition to the relationship between Thor and sacred rings, argue persuasively that Thor had completely supplanted Tiw/Tyr as god of troth by the heyday of the Viking period. Saga and chronicle accounts and the archaeological record both suggest that such rings were more like neck torques or armbands rather than like finger rings, and some are said to have weighed around twenty ounces; the Cuerdale Hoard unearthed in Lancashire and the ship burial found at Sutton Hoo both contained examples of such large rings on British soil.

Common to many temples to Thor were sacred posts—such as those revered by Thorolf—situated on either side of the high seat; often one of these posts would be carved with an image of Thor, and sometimes a holy iron nail would protrude from one of these posts. Later Lappish traditions might suggest that the holy nail most logically would be set in the side of the carved head of the god on the post, where it would be struck with flint to tinder the sacred fire dedicated to Thor. Such a practice might well be associated with the myth of Thor and Hrungnir the giant recounted below. Further, the practice of transporting soil hallowed by the seat of Thor to a new temple, and the ritual of sanctifying the boundaries of the new farmsteads with Thor's holy fire, both serve to underscore Thor's relationship to his mother the earth. Moreover, many centuries after the tradition of sacred posts had faded from common memory in Britain, the folk practice of raising a branch on a new house continued in England; records attest to this practice at least into the twentieth century. The function of this practice originally may have been to appease the god of thunder and thus to protect the dwelling from lightning, and it has been argued to have had its genesis in the tradition of the sacred posts.

THOR'S CHARIOT

Thor's wagon might well be thought to be constructed of wood or of wicker, with iron wheels and silver reins. These reins are laced about the horns of the two goats that draw the chariot across the sky. These goats are called Tanngnost—"Tooth-grinder"—and Tanngrisni—"Gaped-toothed." The rumbling of the iron wheels as Thor moves through the heavens causes thunder, while the sparks that fly from these wheels when they clash with mountaintops seems to us to be lightning. At the beginning of the myth of Utgard-Loki in the *Prose Edda*, Snorri Sturluson describes an enlightening episode concerning Thor's chariot, his hammer, and his goats. Of special note in this description are the theme of resurrection and the sanctifying role of Mjollnir. Thor's visit to Utgard-Loki is one of the most famous and beloved of the Norse myths, and it is the longest single tale spun by Snorri: we will turn to the crux of this tale later, in our discussion of Thor and the Midgard serpent. At this point we will examine the prologue to that main event; in this passage Snorri records several fascinating tidbits concerning Thor's mode of transport.

Early one summer morning Thor determined to depart from Thrudvang to Utgard— a great fortress city in Jotenheim, the land of the giants—in his chariot, with Loki at his side. In Utgard, the thunderer meant to find sport. Tanngnost and Tannrisni quickly were set in harness, and Thor took the silver reins into his hand. All morning the god and the trickster passed through Asgard, and by the afternoon they had left the abode of the gods and rumbled through Midgard, the land of men. By evening they had come to a solitary spot, empty of any habitation save one rundown, turf-roofed cottage. Here the gods thought to stop for the night. Climbing out of the chariot, Thor greeted the trembling family that awaited him, and asked for shelter and hospitality for the night. The farmer, his wife, and their son and daughter could offer their divine guests shelter and meager rations, but no meat. Hearing this, Thor turned without another word and slaughtered his goats, skinning them and quartering the carcasses. This meat he thrust into the family's cauldron, but the skins he set carefully on the ground, well away from the fire. The god then enjoined the family to eat their fill of flesh, but he warned them gravely to place all of the bones upon the skins.

It had been many years since these poor crofters had shared such a feast, and the temptation to suck the marrow of a juicy bone proved too much for Thialfi, the farmer's son. While Thor was distracted Thialfi cracked and sucked a leg bone, quickly hiding it under others in the pile. After this hearty feast they all went to bed and slept soundly. Thor woke early, left the house, and raising his hammer Mjollnir over the goatskins, he hallowed and rejuvenated them. At once both Tanngnost and Tanngrisni leapt to their feet, bleating and pawing the ground. But although they were both healthy and happy, Thor noticed that one goat was lame in his rear leg. At this sight the thunderer's eyes flashed and his rage was ignited. Rushing back into the house, Thor demanded to know who had disobeyed him. Seeing the panic of the family, however, Thor forgave them and took Thialfi and his sister, Roskva, to be his servants. Leaving goats and chariot with the farmer for safekeeping, the four travelers continued their journey to Utgard afoot.

THOR'S HAMMER

Images of a sanctifying hammer or ax are of ancient provenance in the far north, and Bronze Age rock carvings may suggest that some such implement has hallowed weddings in Scandinavia for time out of mind. Whether or not this is the case, it is doubtless true that Germanic peoples from earliest historical times seem to have utilized sacred hammers to bless weddings, to acknowledge newborns, and to sanctify funerals. Such rituals continued into the Christian period, and indeed, practices such as making the sign of the cross and wearing crosses were often conflated with pagan equivalents throughout the Viking world. Moreover, ritual hammers and related symbols continued in use in Lappland for many generations after the conversion of lower Scandinavia. The conception of the mystical powers of smiths—to heal the sick, to perform marriages, and the like—may be related to these traditions, and therefore it may be noteworthy that smiths could perform marriages at Gretna Green in southern Scotland well into the modern period. Archeological finds in Denmark suggest that some smiths traded in both Christian and pagan amulets (sometimes even utilizing the same mold), and finds in England confirm that Thor's hammers were popular talismans through much of the Anglo-Saxon period. As late as the twelfth century a temple of Thor in Sweden is recorded to have contained huge bronze hammers with which it was believed that thunder could be ritually replicated. The hammer of the ancient god Thunor was equated by the Romans with the club of Hercules, and Germanic mercenaries fighting for the Romans worshiped their deity by both names because of this association.

Thor's hammer is called Mjollnir in the Norse sources, and Thor used it by hurling it through the air; his girdle of strength made it a devastating missile, as did its capacity to return to the thrower (who then caught it with his iron gloves). The association between this flying weapon and thunderbolts seems obvious, as does its phallic connotations when placed in the lap of a new bride. The image of Thor's weapon spinning end-over-end through the heavens is captured in art as a swastika symbol (common in Indo-European art, and indeed beyond); this symbol is—as one might expect—widespread in Scandinavia, but it also is common on Anglo-Saxon grave goods of the pagan period, notably in East Anglia and Kent. Hammers and swastikas thus were associated with most of the major rituals of life and death, and the totemic power of the hammer seems to have been evoked both to harness the awesome power of the thunderbolt against enemies and to hallow and protect kith and kin. If Thor's hurling of his hammer against the skulls of giants represents a mythic embodiment of the former quality, his resurrection of his goats with the same instrument represents a mythic understanding of the latter power. Mjollnir thus had two primary functions, functions which in the myths can seem more literal than metaphorical (at least to his enemies). Thor's hammer was used to sanctify the good (law giving, justice, marriage) and to destroy the evil (giants, dwarfs, monsters).

The association of such a weapon with a sky-god is an Indo-European commonplace, as is the use of a thunder-weapon in the battle against the chaotic and the demonic. Perhaps the most familiar—at least to those steeped in Western European traditions—of these sky-gods is the thunder-bolt-wielding Zeus of the classical pantheon. Some distance east of Mount Olympus resided another manifestation of this archetype: the Iranian *Book of Kings* describes Feridun, who possessed Gurz, a cow-headed cudgel clearly drawn from the Indo-European tradition of the thunder-club. To the far north, the Baltic thunder-god Perkons—whose name originally meant "Striker," but which came to denote "Thunder"—carried Milna, which may be linguistically linked to Mjollnir, as are indeed the Russian word *molnija* and the Welsh term *mellt*, both of which mean "lightning." Further, Thunor's role as thunder-wielding, chaos-fighting demon-bane is paralleled by that of the Greek Zeus in his battle against the Titans, as well as by those of Indra and Thraetaona, in the ancient Indian and Iranian traditions, respectively.

THOR AND THE WORLD SERPENT

Although the Norse Thor may be most closely associated with giant-killing, in Germanic myth the greatest archetypal example of the sky-god with thunder-weapon battling demonic power is manifested in Thor's struggle with Jormungandr, the world serpent, a struggle which does not reach its climax until the final cataclysm at Ragnarok. In this conflict Thor manifests the Indo-European patriarchal sky-god who battles evil incarnate in an attempt to protect humankind; we well might say that in this archetypal opposition Thor represents life and light, while Jormungandr represents death and darkness. Myths concerning such polarized battles between the forces of life and those of death are particularly well suited to mid-winter, when rituals related to them also may take place. This association may be especially true in the far north, where darkness and cold always threaten the delicate balance of subsistence; it is Thor, in the Germanic pantheon, who stands between his followers and the frigid abyss. The thunderer's battle with the world serpent, then, carries mythic overtones regarding ancient and widespread concerns about agricultural fertility. Two familiar comic Norse myths provide the context for this particular manifestation of that struggle, which turns starkly serious at the time of the apocalyptic battle between the gods and their foes. Our first glimpse of Thor's conflict with the great serpent comes from the saga of Utgard-Loki told by Snorri; we pick up the tale shortly after Thor has taken Thialfi and Roskva into his service as recompense for the lameness of his goat.

Thor and Utgard-Loki's Cat

After leaving his chariot and goats with the farmer and his wife, Thor continued his journey into Jotunheim, accompanied by his new servants, Thialfi and Roskva, as well as by Loki. All day they walked across gently rolling farmland, until at nightfall they were on the shore of the sea; across the water they could see the thick and misshapen hills of Jotunheim. That night they slept in the dunes, and they crossed the water in the morning in an old boat they found pulled up on the beach. Landing on the far shore, they walked until they entered a mighty forest that stood between them and the mountains; plunging into the woods, they walked on until night fell, and as the light failed they found themselves in a clearing, empty save for a mighty hall into which might fit all the homes of the gods. Large as this was, it was entirely empty, and so they took up lodging in it for the night.

The travelers were so weary that they dropped to the floor immediately and went to sleep without eating a morsel. In the middle of the night, however, Thor and his companions were jolted out of their repose by a horrible roaring so mighty that it caused the entire hall to quiver and shake. Fearing earthquake, the four started to make their way out of the hall just as the tumult ceased. They then decided to remain indoors for the night, but moved into a room that jutted off from one side of the main hall; Thor stood watch at the entrance to this room, Mjollnir in his grasp. Here they stayed for the rest of the night, not that they slept much; they were awakened several times by crashing roars, although none quite as horrible as the first. Feeling his way out in the earliest dawn light, Thor soon found the cause of their disturbed slumber: a massive giant lay stretched out in the clearing, snoring so loudly that the very trees shook and swayed with his every breath.

Never one to stand on ceremony in the presence of giants, Thor shifted his grasp on his hammer and made ready to strike. Before he could bring home the blow, however, the giant woke and leapt to his feet, and he was of such a mighty stature that even the great giant-killer himself was astounded; he could barely make out the features of his adversary through the topmost branches of the highest of the trees at the edge of the clearing. The giant recognized Thor at once, introduced himself as Skrymir, and offered to join them on that day's journey; he also asked if Thor and his companions had thought to borrow his glove. Looking back over his shoulder in the clear light of day, Thor saw his fellows emerging from the great opening that they had taken to be a mighty dwelling. Now it was clear that they had spent the night in the thumb of Skrymir's leather mitten. When Skrymir offered them breakfast from his own ample rations the others quickly assented to his company for the day, and soon all were sated and all of their rations were tied up into the giant's huge rucksack. Without further ado the group set off together, and they traveled in this wise all the day long.

Thanks to his long shanks, the giant often strode far ahead of the others; still, because of the racket he made, Thor's group followed his trail easily. At dusk they found him sitting under a great oak tree at the edge of the forest. Skrymir pleaded fatigue and tossed his rucksack to Thor; soon he was snoring as loudly as ever. Although Loki and the others soon kindled a fire, Thor had no luck undoing the cords around the giant's baggage and soon became enraged by the notion that Skrymir had so intended. Losing his temper, Thor strode to the massive prone form of the giant and slammed Mjollnir down upon the broad forehead before him. Skrymir seemed unhurt by this blow, although he woke and asked if a leaf had chanced to fall upon his pate. Thor, chastened, quickly made his way back to the others, and all went to bed with rumbling bellies. Twice more that night Thor, driven mad by the giant's snoring, brought his hammer down upon the sleeping giant's head, and each blow was more powerful than the last; the result was ever the same, however, as the giant woke to ask, first, if an acorn had dropped upon his brow, and second, if bird droppings had rained down on him. Thor was ever the more perplexed, and more than a little afraid.

Now Skrymir took his leave of the others, warning them against pride in the court of Utgard-Loki and advising them to go home instead; when they refused to heed this advice, he pointed them in the direction of their goal and stomped off on his own errands. Well rid of their surly guide, Thor and his followers trekked on toward Utgard with the forest at their backs, first climbing a saddleback hill with three square valleys and then moving down into a great open plain with a huge citadel at its center. Though they thought to have reached the end of their journey at this point, it soon became apparent that Utgard was much farther away than it seemed. By the time they finally reached the gates the day was near its end, and they could barely see the tops of the turrets of Utgard from their vantage at the base of the walls. No gatekeeper deigned to answer Thor's bellow for admittance, and once more his strength availed him not; it was up to sly Loki to show the others how to gain entrance with the dexterity of a thief, and again straightforward Thor had to swallow his pride as he finally forced his way between the bars of the gate.

Once within the stronghold, Thor led his friends into the main hall and between the many benches, right up to the high seat of the lord of Utgard. Their host was unimpressed by his guests and less than civil in his greeting to them, however, and bluntly asked what skills each traveler had to earn a place at the tables of so mighty a company. Loki was known in Asgard for his gluttony, and so offered to compete at eating; but although he met his opponent Logi at the center of the trencher, Loki had eaten only the meat, while Logi consumed meat, bones, and table, and thus took the victory. Thialfi was the fastest of men, and so desired a race; but fleet as he was, Thialfi could not keep up with Utgard's champion, Hugi. Thor, at his wit's end with frustration, tried three tasks: he drank from Utgard-Loki's great horn; he tried to lift Utgard-Loki's cat; and he wrestled Elli, Utgard-Loki's ancient nurse. In the first instance, Thor's three drafts, although great, only lowered the level of the horn a few inches; in the second, struggle as he might, Thor was only able to lift one of the cat's paws from the earth; in the third, the old crone withstood Thor's best throws, and soon enough brought the Lord of Thunder to one knee. At this last humiliation Utgard-Loki called an end to competition, refusing to demean his followers further in contest with such small talents. Thor's group was offered a more gracious welcome now, and given places at table and all of the food and drink they could ask for; soon enough they were sated, and beds were made for them on the floor with the rest of the company.

Thor was the first to stir, and soon roused his companions; they thought to leave Utgard without further embarrassment, and so made their way toward the door. Utgard-Loki woke before they made an exit, however, and insisted on breakfasting with them. Transformed, as it were, into the very soul of gentility, their host himself led them from the hall, through the gates, and out into the plain beyond. Here Utgard-Loki revealed himself to be one and the same as their erstwhile guide and companion Skrymir, and admitted that his magic had deceived Thor every step of the way. Skrymir had substituted the saddleback hill for his own head when Thor thrice had brought his hammer down upon it in wrath, and the three square valleys the journeyers traveled past the next day stood as testament to the god's power.

Loki's all-consuming opponent Logi was "fire" itself, and Thialfi had tried to race against Hugi, who moved at the speed of "thought." Elli was "old age," which brings even the greatest to his knees, while Utgard-Loki's drinking horn dipped its end into the very sea itself, which because of Thor's thirst lapped its shores some feet lower than the day before. Finally, Utgard-Loki's cat was none other than Jormungandr the World Serpent, and Utgard-Loki and his thanes had quaked with terror when they saw how high Thor thrust it into the sky. Having seen Thor's power Utgard-Loki was glad to have him safely out of his kingdom, and he himself vanished before Thor could take vengeance upon him. Thor then turned to lay low the stronghold of the giants, but behold! Nothing greeted him but the whistling of the wind through an empty plain. Thor turned to make his way home without another word, Thialfi and Roskva close on his heels, Loki laughing silently behind.

LOKI'S PARADOXICAL DUAL role as boon companion to and mortal enemy of the gods is discussed in detail below. It is sufficient here to note that Utgard-Loki is a parallel trickster figure and shape-changer, and that some sources may conflate the two. It is also noteworthy that the straightforward head-basher Thor seems quite at a loss in a world of illusion in which his father would feel quite at home. Finally, this myth sets the stage for the next confrontation between Thor and his reptilian nemesis, and indeed, provides a comic prefiguration for the tragic final struggle between the powers of divine order and those of demonic chaos on the battlefield of Ragnarok.

Thor's Fishing Expedition with Hymir

After his humiliation at the hands of Utgard-Loki, Thor was anxious to avenge himself upon the world serpent Jormungandr. Soon he disguised himself as a young rambler and made his way from Asgard afoot and alone. When he had traveled some ways, Thor came upon the dwelling of the giant Hymir, who was known for his fishing. Without making his true identity known, Thor asked for and received the hospitality of Hymir's hall, and passed the night there. In the morning Hymir was up early to go out for fish, and Thor asked if he could accompany the giant. Hymir replied rather caustically that a slip of a lad like Thor wasn't apt to make much of a match for Hymir in rowing, and he was likely to find himself chilled if he were to go out in a boat as far as the giant was accustomed to journey. Thor was angered at this reply, and made it known in no uncertain terms that he was hardly likely to be the one most anxious to return to port; in fact, Thor was so enraged by Hymir's effrontery that he hardly had the will to restrain from teaching the oaf a lesson in courtesy with the iron end of Mjollnir. Thor calmed himself with the knowledge that he had bigger fish to fry, however, and he swallowed the indignity of Hymir's scorn.

Thor next asked what sort of bait the giant tended to use, but Hymir answered that his guest should look to his own devices on that score. This notion Thor took literally, and scanning the area he sighted a herd of Hymir's oxen, the greatest of which was a mighty beast called Sky-bellower. Thor then repaid Hymir's rudeness by slaughtering his host's prize ox and taking the head for bait. Thor rushed back to the boat and jumped in just as Hymir was casting off. Settling himself in the boat, Thor took up a pair of oars and rowed along with the giant. Soon they came to a set of shoals where Hymir said he was often wont to try his luck for flat fish; Thor replied that he wanted to go a bit farther out, and his host assented. Before too much longer, however, Hymir complained that they were entering dangerous waters, and that Jormungandr the World Serpent inhabited the area. Not discomfited one whit by this news, however, Thor said that he'd like to go out a bit farther; Hymir was none too pleased by the prospect, but for once he held his peace.

Once he had settled on a spot, Thor shipped his oars and made ready to fish: his line was mighty and heavy, and his hook was none the less so. Thor baited his great barb with the giant ox's head, cast it over the side, and let out line until his rig was scraping the seabed. Now Thor had his vengeance upon Jormungandr, for when the great serpent spied that tasty morsel its mouth watered for it, but as soon as it bit down upon the bait, Thor heaved hard upon the hook, and soon the serpent writhed in agony and wrath. So powerfully wriggled the worm, moreover, that Thor's knuckles were skinned against the gunwales, and the god's anger was incited in turn. Now Thor pulled with all of his divine fury, and indeed, he set to so forcefully that his feet plunged through the bottom of the boat until his boot heels were buried in the bed of the sea. Thor then pulled Jormungandr up until their heads were level, and it has been said that one does not know true terror who has not seen those two enemies eye to eye, the snake boiling venom, the god in his wrath.

Then Thor raised Mjollnir for the kill, but Hymir—pale and shaking—cut the line at that moment, and the world serpent sank back into the depths. Some say that the god hurled his hammer after his foe, shattering its skull then and there, but I think not. Surely the snake slid back to the seabed, waiting and watchful for that day when it should meet Thor again, on the final battlefield of Ragnarok. For his part, Thor bashed Hymir in his great stony head so that the last he saw of the giant was his backside as he broke through the waves. Then the god himself waded to shore, Utgard-Loki's prank requited, but his own rage unsated.

IN THIS MYTH Thor has his revenge upon Jormungandr for Utgard-Loki's trick, and in taking this vengeance Thor reasserts those qualities of literal mindedness, wrath, and straightforward power with which audiences were most familiar. It is probably in part for these reasons that this was and remains one of the most popular and enduring myths of Thor. It is also, in this version by Snorri, a finely told and funny story. There are three other versions of this myth known to exist, and this myth was most certainly known in England during the Viking period: the Gosforth Slab shows Thor fishing with an ox head, while the Gosforth Cross contains an illustration of Thor fighting Jormungandr; both are from Gosforth churchyard in Cumbria, and both are from ca. 900 CE. In comparative terms, Thor's bait—the ox head—recalls Feridun's Gurz, and this association may suggest the early and archetypal origin of this late Norse version of an Indo-European myth; further, the ox's name ("Skybellower") might indicate a faint cultural recollection of Thor's archetypal identity as protector sky-god. Finally, this myth has been persuasively associated with the medieval tradition of Christ catching Leviathan on a hook. Laughter aside, however, Jormungandr proves to be—quite literally—Thor's nemesis, and with this foreknowledge the comedy of this myth has a ring of pathos. Thor's last battle with the monster and their mutual destruction underscore the final failing of the old gods of the North; when Thor falls, the forces of order have lost their greatest part:

Thor and Jormungandr at Ragnarok

On the dawn of the day of the final struggle, when Heimdalr has sounded his horn and thus announced the approach of Ragnarok, Thor will strap on his girdle of strength, put on his iron gloves, take up Mjollnir, and mount his chariot. Thor will ride into battle at the hand of his father, who will be the first to engage the enemy in the form of the great wolf Fenris. Before Thor can turn to Odin's aid, however, he will be attacked by Jormungandr, and their struggle will be mighty and fearsome to behold. Thor's power will prove the greater at the last, but in its death throes the great worm will spew forth rivers of venom so potent that even the thunderer's vigor will be overcome. Thor will stumble back nine paces and fall, stricken by the serpent's poison. The battle will rage on without him, but the hopes of the gods die with Thor.

THOR VERSUS THE GIANTS

Thor's constant warfare with the giants takes several different mythic forms, three examples of which we will pause to examine. First, some of the myths of Thor's undying emnity for giants are classic types of a savior figure doing battle against the elemental and chaotic forces that constantly imperil mankind. Thor was after all a god of troth and stability, and it is logical that his myths reflect this role as a stabilizing and protective force standing between mankind and the mythic personifications of a hostile environment; further, surely his role as weather-god underscores his ability to master the power of the natural world. Second, many of the Norse myths of the thunder-god's battles are comic rather than epic in tone; in the light of these cases it is not unreasonable to assume that some of the humor associated with Thor in the later tradition was injected by the Christian compilers of the stories, scribes who surely could take no pagan god—and certainly not the primary Germanic competitor of Christ—too seriously. Third, some of Thor's most embarrassing episodes might well have been told for the pleasure of recounting the distress and discomfiture of an old and dear friend who seems to live his life falling from one scrape into the next.

The following stories contain a wealth of mythic details that, viewed together, form a mosaic or a composite portrait of Thor's archetypal identity. For example, the myth of Hrungnir helps to elucidate Thor's role as champion of order and civilization against the giants, who represent the forces of the chaos of the natural world; moreover, Thor's treatment at the hands of Groa after this battle is in itself worthy of comment. Next, the myth of Thor, the river Vimur (the river of blood), and the giantess Gjalp combines coarse humor with an echo of ancient folkloric practice that survived in Britain into the modern period. Finally, the myth of Thor as the bride of the giant Thrym inverts traditional Germanic gender roles and sexual mores for the sheer

entertainment value of this inversion; gender-bending, which is morally suspect behavior and evidence of a transgressive nature in Loki—or even
Odin—is merely the vehicle for high comedy when it is imposed upon the
ultra-masculine (and hypersensitive) Thor.

Thor's Duel with Hrungnir

One fine day when Thor was off hunting trolls and their unsavory kin, Odin despaired of the amusements in Valhalla and thought to seek adventure abroad in
Jotenheim. Donning one of his host of disguises, the Allfather leapt upon the back
of Sleipnir and galloped off to the home of Hrungnir, the greatest, stoniest, and
most dangerous of all the giants. Hrungnir saw Odin riding toward him for some
way across the plains, and his curiosity, such as it was, was piqued. The giant com-
plimented his mysterious visitor on the lines and speed of his mount, but received
only boasts and taunts in return. When the stranger's insults turned to the subject
of Hrungnir's own horse Gold Mane, the giant could bear them no more and hurried into the saddle himself to take off after his visitor, capture him, and teach him a
lesson. Odin's taunts were not without merit, however, for although Gold Mane
was swift, Sleipnir was the swifter, and before he knew it the giant found himself
no longer in pursuit, but rather the cornered quarry himself: he had followed Odin
right through the gates of Asgard.

Hrungnir grew anxious for himself when he realized his predicament, but it was
his luck that Thor was off elsewhere that day, and Odin offered his giant adversary the
sanctuary of hospitality. Soon Hrungnir was drinking from Thor's own horn, filling the
vast Hall of the Slain with hot air as he repaid his hosts with nothing but taunting
words: boasts of his own prowess, threats and curses for the gods and the fallen heroes surrounding him, and promises of amorous attention to the beautiful goddesses
Sif and Freya. The company quickly tired of the lout's drunken ramblings, and Odin
quietly sent for Thor. The thunderer soon appeared, and his rage was the mightier
when he noted the drunken giant ogling Sif while Freya herself waited upon the churl-
ish oaf. When Thor reached for his hammer, however, Hrungnir sobered up enough to
remind the god of his own sacred status as a guest, and an unarmed one at that. Thor
relented when his honor was questioned, and he quickly assented to Hrungnir's invitation to single combat; no foe had ever dared issue such a challenge to the thunder-
god before. A date was set and a place—the House of the Stone Fence, on the border
between Jotenheim and Asgard—and the drunken giant made his exit.

The other giants thought that Hrungnir had won great honor through his challenge of Thor, but they also feared what might happen to them all if their champion
should fall. To hedge their bets, then, they determined to create a massive giant
out of clay; this creature was the biggest giant by far—taller even than Hrungnir
himself—but he was made only of clay, not of stone, and he had for a heart only
that of a slaughtered mare. They named their creation Mist Calf, and they commanded him to await Thor at the appointed place. On the chosen day the thunderer mounted his chariot with Thialfi by his side, and his passage was tempestu-
ous: lightning flashed, thunder crashed, sparks flew from the wheels of Thor's cart,
and the very earth itself seemed to roil and buckle with the god's anger. Mist Calf's
terror was such that—as the god approached—a cascade of urine flooded from the
trembling clay giant; Thialfi's ax made short work of Hrungnir's second.

Hrungnir himself was more steadfast and determined, however, and he cast his mighty whetstone at Thor just as the storm-god sent Mjollnir end-over-end toward his foe; the two weapons intersected with a mighty cataclysm, and the whetstone was pulverized into a thousand fragments. Those pieces that landed in Midgard are the sources for whetstones even today. A large chunk of stone also found its way to Thor, who was knocked off of his feet by the force of the impact; stunned and bleeding profusely, Thor soon discovered that he had a great piece of lodestone imbeded in his head. His wound and mighty headache were not the end of Thor's problems, however; although his hammer had found its mark and ended Hrungnir's boasts and insults forever, the giant had fallen over the body of the god, and Thor found that he couldn't budge. Thialfi could not help either, and so he brought the gods, who all likewise failed in the task of shifting Hrungnir's corpse. Finally Thor's bastard Magni—his son by the giantess Jarnsaxi—was allowed to try, and he lifted the giant off of his father with ease. For this Thor gave Gold Mane to Magni, although Odin chafed at this gift, as he had coveted the horse for himself.

Once home, Thor sent for Groa, the wife of Aurvandill, a woman of uncommon powers and mystical gifts. Groa worked her magic on Thor's wound, saying spells over him and using charms to work the stone out of his skull. Toward daybreak the sorceress had almost completed her magic, the stone was nearly out, and the pain had all but completely faded away. To show Groa his gratitude for her services, Thor took her out to view the dawn sky, telling her that her husband—whom she had long presumed lost—would soon rejoin her. Thor knew this to be the case because he himself had helped Groa's husband to escape from Jotenheim, nearly frozen but quite alive. As proof, the god pointed to a new star he had formed from Aurvandill's frostbitten big toe. No good deed goes unpunished, however; Groa's joy at this news was such that her spells went out of her head and her arts failed her. Thus Thor in his first single combat had his victory over Hrungnir, and the giants lost their greatest champion; but the whetstone remained forever lodged in the thunderer's head.

THOR'S ARRIVAL AT THE DUEL at the center of a tempest of thunder and lightning sparked from his rumbling chariot is a classic example of how the thunder-god's mode of transport is linked to the tumult and destructive power of electrical storms. It should also be noted in passing that Hrungnir's challenge to Thor and his eagerness to accept it might best be understood as a folkloric echo of the initiation of young warriors into manhood through the rite of single combat. Perhaps most significantly, through this myth we gain insight into one of the most interesting facets of the worship of Thor: the whetstone fragments in Thor's head may explain the function of the holy nails in the high seat pillars of Thor in many temples; flint would be struck against these nails to ignite the holy fire, thus underscoring Thor's role as thunder/sky/fire god. The parallels between the sparks struck off of the sacred nails and the natural phenomenon of lightning associated with Thor seem obvious. Hrungnir's use of a whetstone as weapon might not make sense otherwise, but in this context the iron of Mjollnir might be said to spark divine fire from the flint of the whetstone. As late as the end of the seventeenth century, some Lappish clans still worshiped a thunder-god shaped out of a block of wood, holding a hammer, with iron nails and sometimes flint imbeded in its head. The association of the thunder-god with sacred fire such as might be sparked in this way seems to have been a commonplace throughout the Baltic region and Scandinavia, and was exported abroad with the Germanic migrations.

In this myth the giants represent forces that are associated with those natural phenomena that can destroy agricultural fertility, and with it, civilization. Seen in this light, the material about Groa and her husband Aurvandill—although it may seem tangential to the main plot of the narrative—is hardly incidental in mythic terms. Indeed, this episode may participate in an ancient Indo-European tradition of fertility; his name may be rendered something like "swamp-wand" and thus may have phallic implications, while her role as fertility figure is literally underscored by her name: "Growth." Here Groa practices upon Thor the forbidden arts of *seidr*, which clearly associate her with the fertility gods of the Vanir. Further, the "big toe" to which Thor refers has been associated with the frozen phallus of the captive Aurvandill; here the giants represent the chaotic and ruthless forces of nature in the form of arctic cold, and it is only through Thor's intervention that Aurvandill's fertile power may escape their icy clutches.

It seems clear that various versions of this mythic material were known throughout the Germanic world (e.g., the Langobard *Auriwandalo*, the Frankish *Orentil*, and the Middle High German *Orendel* are all cognate to *Aurvandill*); indeed, some elements were well known in England after the Christian conversion. In Anglo-Saxon England the morning star was called Earendel, commonly taken as a form of *Aurvandill*, and usually glossed with Latin *jubar* and translated "effulgence" or "shining brightness." Further, the story of Groa working her charms upon Thor may have been memorialized upon the heads of three eleventh-century stone crosses preserved in the Chapter House of Durham Cathedral in Northumbria; in the center of each cross face are three figures, one with its head in the lap of the central one, which holds a looped wand or implement over the head of the other. The third figure looks on. Finally, it has been argued that Aegil was another name by which the Anglo-Saxon mythic figure Earendel was known; this is an intriguing possibility, as the seventh-century walrus ivory Franks Casket contains a scene in which the archer Aegil—brother of Weland the Smith—wards off foes. The artisan went so far as to inscribe the episode with Aegil's name. The Franks Casket is a prime example of the many wonderful Anglo-Saxon artifacts that conflate pre-Christian and Christian mythic elements, some of which we already have discussed; this series also includes the Gosforth Slab and Cross, the Ruthwell Cross (which we will touch upon in our examination of *The Dream of the Rood*), and the Durham Chapter House crosses. We will explore the significance of the Franks Casket more fully when we talk about Weland the Smith of the Germanic gods.

Thor and the River of Blood

Once more Thor and the trickster traveled together toward Jotenheim; on this journey they made their way to the dwelling of Geirrod the Giant, but the full tale of

that adventure must wait until another day. Midway between the house of the giantess Grid and that of Geirrod, the travelers found themselves upon the banks of
the river Vimur. The stream had burst its banks that day, a swirling, muddy rush of
foam and flotsam the color of blood. The bed of the river was strewn with mighty
boulders, and the force of its torrent sent smaller rocks crashing against the larger
ones fixed in its bed; the crossing looked to be unpleasant at best, and certainly
deadly without luck and proper care. Strapping on the belt of strength given to him
by Grid, and feeling his way with her staff, Thor plunged into the rushing river and
soon was waist deep in the treacherous flood, slipping and sliding and barely keeping his feet; Loki, meanwhile, was only just keeping his chin above the flow. As
they made their way to the midpoint of the stream, Thor found himself neck deep,
and Loki held on to that neck for dear life, his legs paddling uselessly behind him as
the current attempted to pull him off and cast him downstream against the waiting
rocks; the riverbed was deepest at that point, but the water level seemed to be rising of its own accord, as well. Thor cursed the river then, and vowed that, high as it
might rise, he would rise the higher.

Pausing for breath, Thor glanced upstream for a moment, and what he saw
then both quenched his curiosity and roused his rage. A short distance upstream,
standing bowlegged across the course of the river, Geirrod's daughter Gjalp was dis-
charging blood in a mighty gush; this crimson cascade was the cause of the force
and fullness of the flood. Muttering that a river must be dammed at the mouth,
Thor reached down into the streambed and grasped a suitable plug, flinging it with
all of his power at the source of the raging flow; he found his mark, and Gjalp
screamed and fell backward. Lamed, she made her way back to her father's stead,
where soon enough the Thunderer would deal with her again. Meanwhile, the force
of his effort threw Thor off balance, and he and his unhappy passenger found
themselves tumbling head over heels downstream. The Norns smiled upon them,
however, as Thor was able to catch hold of a rowan tree that leaned over their path,
and with the help of this tree the travelers made their way to shore, where, after a
brief respite, they continued on their way to the home of Geirrod.

THE APPEARANCE OF THE rowan tree in this narrative has direct connections
to well-known British traditions, and these insular beliefs are part of a wider
European context. Although Sif is the goddess to whom Thor is married in
the Norse sources, some interesting associations between Thor and the rowan
tree surface in Lappish and Finnish ancillary traditions, where the spouse of
the thunder-god has a name associated with that tree. The rowan has folkloric qualities throughout much of northwest Europe; it commonly was held,
for example, to be a bane to witches, and rowans utilized for such purposes appear in several English literary contexts. Moreover, it was an age-old custom
in the Highlands of Scotland to plant rowans outside of dwellings, and this
practice continued well into the modern period. The river itself represents
both life and death, and in its association with menstrual flow it has shamanistic associations; the monthly cycle of the seeress is tied in many cultures to
her ability to prophesy. Such relationships are mythic and folkloric common-
places, and Gjalp in her earliest manifestation well might have represented a
respected natural force, one which was worshiped and emulated. However, in
the late Germanic traditions, as we have seen, this type of magic and its asso-

ciations with fertility clearly mark it as *seidr*—"dirty" or "woman's" magic—
and as such anathema to all of the Aesir (excluding, of course, Odin). Such
magic is inextricably bound up with the forces of nature, which Thor is ever
attempting to constrain and bend to his (and his followers') patriarchal purposes. His damming of Gjalp's flow, therefore, is quite suggestive of Germanic
conceptions of hierarchies of power and of associated taboos. This discussion
of gender roles and taboos leads us to our final myth of Thor, which subverts
these for comic effect.

The Wedding of Thor and Thrym

One luckless morning, the thunderer awoke with a sense of foreboding; he reached
for his hammer, but horrors! Mjollnir was not there. Thor searched high and low for
his weapon, but to no avail. Finally he consulted Loki, telling the sly-one that no
one among gods nor men had seen his hammer, and that he feared the worst. Thor
then asked Loki to search throughout all the worlds until he uncovered some hint or
rumor of the trusty skull crusher; Loki agreed, but on the condition that Freya lend
to him her magic plumage, so that he might fly. Thor and Loki quickly made their
way to the goddess, who just as quickly assented to their request. Loki donned the
suit of feathers, and in the wink of an eye he was soaring through the clouds,
headed for the mountains of Jotunheim. From far off he saw Thrym the Giant sitting upon a great mound, grooming his horses and weaving collars of gold for his
horrible hounds. Loki landed near to the giant and greeted him; hearing Loki's errand, Thrym chuckled, and Loki asked the giant if he had stolen Mjollnir. Thrym
laughed the louder and admitted that it was he who had secured the bane of giants
well beneath the surface of the earth, hidden that hammer in a craggy crevass eight
miles below the sun-kissed surface; further, his price for its return was high: no less
than that Freya, fairest of the goddesses, must be his bride and be brought to his
bed. Seeing Loki's discomfiture at his demand, Thrym's mirth increased, and Loki
departed for Asgard with the giant's mocking laughter in his ears.

The trickster returned to the home of the gods as quickly as he might, and
soon he had told Thor the terrible truth; the two of them then confronted Freya together, and by this time Loki was beginning to enjoy the humor of the situation.
When Freya refused Thrym's demand on the grounds of her honor, Loki nearly
laughed out loud, while even Thor seemed amused by her protestations of virtue.
Refuse she did, however, and Freya became so angry at the thought of selling herself for Thor's hammer that the chain of the priceless Necklace of the Brisings burst
as her sinews bulged in wrath. Thus stymied, all of the gods were called into conclave to discuss what course of action to pursue. No one could come up with an
idea until Heimdalr suggested that Thor dress as Freya and go in her place; not long
before, Thor had been quite willing to give Freya over to the giant's lust, but now
the shoe was on the other foot, and all of the gods and goddesses laughed at the
thought of Thor in the guise of a woman. At first Thor refused, stating that his
good name and honor would ever be tarnished by such an unmanly act, but the
gods were unswayed, and finally Loki himself declared that there was no other
course of action if the gods were to be saved from the impending invasion of the giants. Thor assented, although he grumbled all the while, and soon he was kitted
out like a comely young maid, complete with dress and veil, keys at his waist and

Necklace of the Brisings upon his throat, bedecked with jewelry and rings, and crowned with a fitting and fashionable cap. All the gods joined in the joke, and as soon as Thor's conversion was complete he departed for Jotunheim in his cart, with Loki at his side in the garments of a bridesmaid. Thor's wrath and his rage at this humiliation were made manifest through the tumult of his coursing: lightning flashed, thunder roared, and great fissures opened in the surface of the earth over which the son of Odin passed.

Meanwhile, Thrym awaited his bride with longing. He numbered his many treasures and possessions—herds of golden-horned cattle, bulls as black as pitch, mountains of jewels and gold—but he counted himself penniless without Freya, the treasure of the gods. Now that he was about to possess the object of his desire, he shouted at his servants to ready the banquet, the sooner to claim his prize. When his bride finally arrived it was evening and time to eat. Thrym himself led his veiled betrothed to the benches, where he seated her next to his own high seat; her bridesmaid quickly scuttled to a place at her far side. Thrym's joy soon turned to confusion, however, as he watched his bride-to-be devour a whole roasted ox, accompanied by eight large salmon and all of the dainties set aside for the entire troop of giantesses. Such feasting is thirsty work, and Thrym's wonder was doubled as he saw his longed-for Freya wash down her meal with three huge beakers of mead. When Thrym gave voice to his amazement, Freya's lady in waiting announced that the goddess was famished, as she had not eaten in eight whole days and nights, so great had been her desire for her bridal bed. Restraining himself no longer, Thrym lifted the veil to kiss his bride; he jumped back, however, when he saw two red-hot coals peering back at him. When he shouted out his alarm at her aspect, Freya's bridesmaid announced that the goddess was exhausted, as she had not slept for eight whole days and nights, so great had been her desire for her bridal bed. At this point the giant's kinswoman strode forward, demanding a dowry and tribute for her love.

Thrym could contain his lust no longer; he called for the hammer to sanctify his union with the goddess, so that he might quench the fire in his beloved's eyes. At this command, Mjollnir was brought forth and placed between the knees of the bride, as custom dictated; seizing his hammer and opportunity, Thor cast off his veil and revealed his identity, and quickly avenged himself upon those who had forced him to dishonor: Thrym had thought to claim Freya by placing his own hammer in her lap; what he won for his lust was Thor's hammer in his head. Thrym's kinswoman had sought gold for a dowry; what she gained for her greed was hard iron. No giant left Thrym's hall alive, and thus Thor regained his hammer.

THOR'S HAMMER WAS used to hallow marriage rites, to be sure, but more than that, the phallic symbolism of placing such an object of masculine force and might into a virgin's lap cannot be overlooked. The fact that Thor, stripped of this power, is forced to dress as a woman and give himself over to his enemy to be his bride underscores Mjollnir's phallic functions: the ritual of the hammer sanctifies the troth of the newlyweds, of course, but more than that, in this myth Thor's hammer both symbolizes and embodies his physical power. Moreover, Freya's role in this myth has interesting parallels to Thor's. While Thor thought nothing of asking Freya to whore herself to regain his hammer (much as she did to gain the Necklace of the Brisings) Thor shrinks from taking on her role himself. Indeed, we may infer that it is only because he knows that Mjollnir will be placed in his lap at the climactic moment that Thor grudgingly goes along with the plan. In simplest terms, Thor rebels against dressing as a bride both because cross-dressing was taboo and would permanently besmirch his honor, and because—until the moment he reclaimed his masculinity by grasping the hammer placed between his knees—he would be as powerless and vulnerable in Thrym's clutches as would Freya. The hammer makes the man: just as Mjollnir symbolizes masculine might, his bridal garb symbolizes Thor's womanly weakness.

Cross-dressing such as described in this narrative has several Indo-European parallels, notably in Indic and Greek myth. The humor of the Norse myth, however, derives from the comic role reversal and gender-bending imposed upon a horrified and humiliated Thor. This imposition is comic precisely because it both draws upon and inverts the unwholesome *seidr* and transvestism willingly practiced by the Vanir, by Odin, and by Loki. Norse culture was extremely unforgiving to sexual and gender transgressors, which explains in some part why mythic practitioners such as Loki were seen as unnatural and untrustworthy. Seeing the hypermasculine and shamefaced Thor forced to cross-dress is therefore funny exactly because his role-playing is neither transgressive nor voluntary; Thor wants nothing more in the world than to grab his hammer, get out of his bridal gown, and reclaim his masculinity. The fact that Loki willingly plays the role of bridesmaid to Thor's unwilling bride seems particularly noteworthy in this context, and we shall turn to Loki's penchant for gender-bending shortly; next we examine some of the Vanir, and note how the rigid rules of gender and sexual activity that constrain the war-god Aesir do not apply to these fertility figures. Finally, it should be noted in passing that this myth may have been known in Britain; it has been suggested that an allusion to this story is to be found in an eleventh-century Norse runic inscription in England.

Nerthus/ Njordr

Njordr is the Norse form of the Germanic god Nerthus; in examining his role as the father of Freyr and Freya and chief of the fertility gods of the Vanir we may uncover some aspects of sexuality that stand in stark contrast to Thor, the epitome of the Aesir war deities. Njordr is identified in Norse myth as the god of the sea, and as the father of Freyr and Freya; he is one of the Vanir who were subsumed into the Aesir as part of the peace treaty between the two groups. The most famous myth involving Njordr involves his marriage to the giantess Skadi as partial compensation for the loss of her father. The preoccupation with feet in this myth smacks of Cinderella-like folkloric elements, and resonates with the Roman practice of *nudipedalia*; meanwhile, the marital strife between the bride and groom caused by their differing lifestyles might reflect the social tension between a primeval nomadic hunter-gatherer culture and the later agricultural and mercantile cultures that supplanted it.

The Marriage of Skadi and Njordr

Skadi was a creature of the mountains and the scree, of the tundra and the vast wastes; she was a huntress beyond compare, and she brought death and destruction gliding silently across the snows. Skadi was the daughter of Thiazi the Giant, who with the aid of the ever-duplicitous and self-serving Loki kidnapped Idun, the keeper of the apples of youth precious to the gods; it was Thiazi's hope to defeat the gods through their own age and decline. His plan went awry, however, and the gods finished him, instead. His daughter waited for him at home in vain, and soon enough it became apparent to her that the gods had gotten the best of her father. Arming herself with the choicest of her father's arms and armor, Skadi plotted vengeance. Smoldering with rage, the snowshoe-goddess made her way to Asgard.

Having regained their eternal youth and savoring the bounty of life as never before, the gods were anxious to avoid further conflict and death. Thus when Skadi came upon them in anger, the Aesir made haste to sue for peace. Skadi had already inherited her father's vast wealth, and so was in no mood to take gold for his blood. She did, however, lack a husband, and she no longer took joy in life now that her father was gone; therefore she stated these terms to the gods: the price for peace was to be marriage and mirth. She wished to pick a husband from among her foes, and she demanded that one among them make her laugh as she had never laughed before in her life. These terms seeming both just and easily accomplished, the gods agreed. The wily Odin put one condition upon this pact, however: Skadi was to choose her mate by the beauty of his feet, and his feet alone.

Skadi quickly assented to Odin's condition, reasoning that Baldr, the most beautiful of the gods, surely walked upon the comeliest feet. The gods were then arranged before the giantess, but with a screen concealing them from their ankles up. It took but a little while to determine her choice, for to Skadi one pair of feet was clearly superior to all the rest; these she took to be Baldr's, and she chose he who possessed them. Skadi was soon disillusioned, however, as when the screen was lowered she found herself looking into the eyes of Njordr, lord of the sea and its fruits. Skadi complained that she had been duped, but it was too late, for the vow had been sworn and her choice made. Still, Skadi had not yet laughed, and she quickly reminded the gods that their arrangement would be null and void if she didn't receive her full measure of mirth.

At this point Odin called Loki over, knowing well that if anyone could accomplish this feat, it would be the trickster. At first Loki proclaimed his ineptitude; he said that he could not make Skadi laugh until he had related the tale of his morning's adventure with a billy goat. Loki then produced a thong, which he proceeded to tie to the beard of the goat. The god had been leading the goat to market in this way, he explained, but as his hands were full of other goods, he had had to make use of his scrotum to anchor the tether; this part of his tale told, he proceeded to tie himself to the goat in this manner by way of illustration. Loki then made a loud noise, mimicking the sound that he claimed had startled the goat on the way to market. At this clamor the goat leapt forward, and the god and the goat began a protracted and farcical tug-of-war. Finally, with a last sharp thrust of Loki's hips the goat lost its purchase on the turf and flew back into the trickster, knocking him over and into Skadi's arms. At this sight the giantess laughed long and loud, and for a moment she forgave Loki and the gods for her grief.

Leaving Asgard together, Skadi and Njordr each wished to live in the way to which each had grown accustomed; therefore they agreed to divide their time between their domains. For nine nights they would sleep in Skadi's fastness of Thrymheim in the icy north, with the cry of the arctic wolf for a lullaby; the next nine nights they would pass in Njordr's harbor home of Noatun, where the gulls and swans would lull them to sleep. Thus they lived together for some time, each at home in turn; but their lifestyles and tastes proved too different, and they soon had to live apart. Njordr could not stand the silence or the barrenness of the icy mountains and flat tundra, and Skadi for her part detested the bustle, activity, and constant noise of the busy port. Though they remained married, then, they went their separate ways, and the frigid wastes of Skadi's heart—which had warmed a bit with the love of the god of the fertile sea—froze solid once more. Thus the love of the giantess was like the brief but spectacular growing season of her homeland, which thaws with the midnight sun of high summer, but freezes again quickly with the early onset of autumn, and is all but dead in the darkest months of winter.

NJORDR IS THE GOD of the sea in the Norse pantheon, as the name of his hall—Noatun, or "shiptown"—makes clear; he survives into Norwegian folklore as the seagoing merchant Njor. Njordr is not the original sea-god of the North, however; Aegir came before him, and this displacement may be worthy of examination. It must not be forgotten, moreover, that Njordr is of the Vanir, a fertility god, and the father of both of the great Norse fertility figures. Considering the reliance of the northern peoples upon the bounty of the sea, the relationship between sea-god and fertility figure is a natural one. The Vanir were all fertility gods, of course, and as such they represented far more than the bounty of nature: they were associated with a sense of sexuality unbounded by moral principles. They practiced incest, for example, and we are told in the Norse sources that Njordr's first wife, and the mother of his children, was also his sister, but one assumes that this unfortunate mate fell by the wayside after Njordr joined the more prudish Aesir. Skadi, then, becomes Njordr's lawful wife in Asgard, and an odd but significant couple they are. Skadi's name is likely cognate with Old English and Old Norse words for either "shadow "or "scathe," and indeed may be related to both: it seems logical that this demi-deity called the "snowshoe goddess" by Snorri should be associated with the cold and dark of the frigid wastes, as well as with the destructive power of the icy north. Here we are confronted with a giantess who is the embodiment of the natural forces so apparent and dangerous in Scandinavia. The symbolic pattern that links the giants with natural forces is repeated here, and in the marriage of such a power to a fertility figure we see a classic union of light and dark, of order and chaos, of production and destruction, of life and death.

The Vanir are not the only figures in the Norse pantheon who deviate from accepted sexual norms. It is surely worth noting that in this myth Loki, whose sexuality is ever ambivalent, so readily risks his testicles for a laugh. It is also apparent that Loki's moral character is every bit as changeable as his sexuality. Loki had played both sides against the middle yet again in his dealings with Thiazi, and it was Loki's treachery that betrayed that giant at the last, just as the trickster had betrayed Idun to Thiazi in the first place. In the present myth Skadi forgives Loki for the time being, but at the binding of the trickster it is the daughter of Thiazi who indeed has the last laugh: it is she who mounts the serpent above Loki in the cave, the serpent which drips its venom upon the trickster's face until the time of Ragnarok.

DIVINE SEXUALITY

The straightforward and rather uninteresting identity of Njordr represented by his Norse form, however, just scratches the surface of the gender-bending and the ambiguous and incestuous fertility traditions that he and his children represent. Sexual appetite may have run rampant among the Aesir, but deviation from firmly established sexual norms did not. Thus while the forced cross-dressing of the humiliated super-masculine Thor may have been an occasion for mirth, a tale of such behavior was acceptable precisely because it was ridiculous and wildly unlikely. The Aesir were primarily war-gods, and as such were not associated with the many and various facets of sexual nature to be associated with fertility cults and rites: incest, homosexuality, and ambiguous gender—common and acceptable among the Vanir—were strictly taboo among the Aesir.

Sexual transgression of any kind was swiftly and savagely punished in warlike late Germanic society, long before Christian moral values were superimposed upon the Anglo-Saxon and Scandinavian cultures; such puritanical sexual mores were projected onto mythic characters as well, which explains why any sexual ambiguity on the part of Odin would be viewed as simply another example of his shifting and untrustworthy nature, and why Loki's gender transformation and feminine fertility are so significant in the context of the aftermath of the war between the Aesir and the Vanir (see the myth of Loki and Asgard's wall). Such sexual ambiguity clearly marks one as suspect among the Aesir; just so the gender-bending and incest associated with Njordr call to the fore his identity as a member of the Vanir. Njordr's sister was said to have borne him his children Freyr and Freya, and no discernable shame seems attached to this union. Further, as we shall see, Njordr was himself a gender-bender of sorts; he seems (both etymologically and thematically) to have evolved from Nerthus, an early Germanic goddess whose rites closely correspond to those of the Norse Freyr.

THE RITUALS OF NERTHUS, THE EARTH-MOTHER

Tacitus translated Nerthus as *terra mater*, or "earth mother," and told of the association of this goddess with a sacred grove on an island. Periodically an attendant priest took the goddess on a tour of the country in an oxcart shrouded with curtains; as she was a deity of peace and plenty, during this time warfare was prohibited and weapons were locked up. After the travels of this mysterious veiled goddess, her corporeal image was removed from its cart and ceremonially bathed in a hidden lake; the slaves who performed this function were ritually drowned immediately thereafter, thus taking her secrets to their graves.

Nerthus was the earlier, female form of Njordr, and perhaps this shift in gender explains the myth of the incestuous union that produced Freyr and Freya: if Nerthus and Njordr are indeed different faces of the same godhead, then this hermaphroditic deity might be said to be both mother and father to the Norse fertility gods. It has been argued that Nerthus reached her apex in very ancient times among a matriarchal agricultural people of whom the earth-mother was the chief deity; her conversion to a male sea-god, then, could be said to illustrate a shift in the Northlands to a patriarchal society that depended more on the bounty and mobility offered by the sea than on the sustenance and stability to be coaxed from the soil. In any case, as we shall see, Nerthus—or a demigoddess related to her—survived in Britain in a Christian and stylized form well into the medieval period. That the great goddess and the dying god took on Christian trappings after the conversion of the Anglo-Saxons is a subject of another section.

Freyr

The Norse Freyr is a classic fertility god, usually represented in the form of a male figure with a massive erect phallus. Freyr was called Fricco by Adam of Bremen, and he eventually came to be the most highly regarded god among the Swedes. Freyr was said to be the son of Njordr, and this myth of descent may be attributable in part to the fact that the myths and rituals associated with the Norse fertility god seem to have been born from those of the Germanic Nerthus. Freyr certainly was a deity of peace and plenty like Nerthus, and he also traveled the country in an enclosed cart in the company of a single attendant, in his case a priestess. Furthermore, human sacrifices were made unto Freyr, and these victims were drowned in sacred wells in a manner not unlike the execution of the slaves of Nerthus. The similarity between the early ritual of Nerthus and the later one of Freyr is more than coincidental; the shift of gender is the single greatest contrast between the two deities and their ceremonies. Freyr thus may be supposed to have inherited an already well-established ritual some time after his cult and status eclipsed that of Nerthus, who subsequently underwent a change of station and of gender. The mythic status of Njordr as the progenitor of Freyr, however, illustrates that some intimate relationship between the two was understood, as was the fact that Njordr antedated Freyr. Freyr in various guises and by various names is always associated with peace, prosperity, and plenty, even in later, Christianized accounts of his myths, in which he has been demoted to a human king.

The Legend of Frodi, the Dead King

It is said that when Odin, the mighty king of the Aesir (also known as the Asians), led his people to the Northlands from their ancestral home in Asia Minor, he placed Freyr on the throne of the Swedes at Uppsala. Here he was known as Yngvi-Freyr, and the Swedish dynasty of the Ynglings sprang from his loins. Sweden was so blessed with peace and plenty during the reign of Yngvi-Freyr that even after his death tribute was paid to him in his barrow. The story goes that Freyr's son Fjolnir ruled in similar prosperity until he was drowned in a vat of mead. Some tales, however, have it that this Yngvi-Freyr was actually named Frodi, and that he was lord of the Danes instead of the Swedes, and thus the progenitor of the dynasty of the Scyldings. The tellers of this version of the tale would have one believe that Frodi traveled the length and breadth of his domain yearly, and that this practice was credited with the wealth and stability of his realm. Indeed, when King Frodi died, legend has it that his counselors hid this fact for three years, and that the mummified corpse of Frodi was carted about in his stead to ensure that peace and prosperity would continue.

THE CHRISTIAN-ERA LEGEND of King Frodi still clearly displays elements of his mythic origins in the pagan god Freyr (the cart reference is obvious, but note also the echoes of Freyr's human sacrifice in the drowning of Fjolnir; indeed, the sacrifice of ceremonial kings to ensure harvests is also well attested!) Freyr, however, was fundamentally a fertility god, and although peace and plenty are certainly to be associated with a god of harvests, fertility gods are most closely concerned with sex and sexual attributes. It comes as no surprise, then, that the most famous pre-Christian myth associated with the god Freyr runs the gamut of sexual and romantic imagery: lovesickness, reckless lust, central elements that overflow with phallic and vaginal symbolism, and references to Freyr's dominion over sexual fecundity. At the end of this myth Freyr does indeed receive the pleasure of the body of his intended, but at a cost that leaves him effectively castrated and powerless at the final battle at Ragnarok.

Skirnir's Journey

One day Freyr trespassed upon Odin's sacred high seat Hlidskjalf, which was situated within the great hall Valaskjalf; only Odin and Frigg were accorded this privilege, and Freyr was to pay dearly for his presumption. Far across the worlds of gods and of men he gazed, well into Jotunheim, the home of the giants. In the midst of a dark plain he saw a shimmering light: it was Gerd, the daughter of Gymir, emerging from her hall. Her beauty was such that she seemed to light up the sky around her, and Freyr was struck down by the desire to possess her. He could not take his eyes off of her, and only stirred from his perch when she had returned into her house and darkness had recaptured the sky above Jotunheim. Silently Freyr made his way from Valaskjalf, in equal parts besotted by lust, ravaged by despair, and chastened for his intrusion into the all-father's domain.

Freyr was no stranger to desire, but his longing for the bright flesh of Gerd knew no bounds: he could not sleep, and he had no wish to eat or drink; he desired no company but that of his memory of his sight of the loveliest of giantkind. Freyr was all but consumed by his lust for Gerd, but he knew that the gods would never agree to his union with her, and so he kept his peace. Thus no one knew what ailed Freyr, but that he was afflicted was plain to all. Finally Njordr, fearing for his son's well-being, approached Freyr's servant Skirnir and commanded him to ferret out what troubled his master. Skirnir therefore strode boldly before Freyr, and what was bluntly asked soon was bluntly answered. Then all of Freyr's anguish was made clear to Skirnir, who soon agreed to court Gerd in Freyr's stead; the god commanded his vassal to bring the giantess to Freyr's bed, by fair means or force. Skirnir's price was twofold: his master's finest steed, which could find its way through pitch of night and which would not shy at fire or magic; and that greatest of blades, Freyr's giant-slaying sword that magically fought under its own power. Freyr quickly agreed to these terms; Skirnir leapt into the saddle just as quickly, and commenced his journey to Jotunheim.

Skirnir rode all day, and he came to the river bordering Jotunheim at dusk; he then crossed over as quickly as he might, and galloped onward into the gathering gloom of Giant Land. In the middle of the night, as he entered a mountain pass, Skirnir was confronted by a wall of fire that ringed Gerd's valley; his horse didn't seem to notice the flames, however, and Skirnir soon left this barrier behind him. At dawn the god's messenger cantered into a bowl-shaped dale covered with dismal gray grass; in the midst of this bowl stood Gymir's hall, and his daughter's hard beside it. Gerd's house was ringed by a fence, and two ferocious dogs stood guard. A herdsman sat crouched on a hill across the way, and Skirnir approached him; but the shepherd's words were full of doom and gloom, and so Skirnir made his way to Gerd's gate unaided. Meanwhile, alarmed by the baying of her hounds, Gerd sent a servant to investigate Skirnir's approach. Unaccustomed as she was to visitors, Gerd commanded her servant to treat Skirnir with courtesy and to bring him before her, even though she discerned that her caller might have slain her brother.

As Skirnir entered the hall he noticed that it was uncommonly cool within, and he shivered as he drew his cloak more tightly around himself. Brought before the giantess, Freyr's trusted retainer explained his errand, and offered Gerd eleven shining apples of youth plucked from Idun's basket; but the daughter of Gymir proclaimed that she was unwilling to sell herself at such a price. Likewise she refused the offer of Draupnir, the magical golden bracelet that dropped eight like rings from itself every ninth night. Gerd next scoffed at Skirnir's threat to behead her, and answered his challenge with one of her own: the giant Gymir was not accustomed to allowing Gerd to receive visitors from Asgard, and might slay Skirnir more easily than Skirnir might take Gerd's head. Finally Skirnir brought forth a magic staff, and waved it before the giantess. With that staff he threatened her with a curse: he marked her out as barren, desolate, and untouchable; he threatened her with eternal loneliness to be measured only with the yardstick of her misery and burning lust; he promised her a future of wasting and despair and unconsummated desire. Broken by her terror of such loveless isolation, Gerd yielded before a curse as she would not to bribes or physical force. As tears welled in her eyes, she agreed to give herself to the God of Plenty in the wood of Barri in nine nights. Skirnir returned to his master in triumph, although Freyr shuddered at the thought of the eternity of nine nights stretching between him and the fulfillment of his desire.

MYTHS OF HIGH PLACES with the virtue of granting all-seeing powers to those who visit them are common to many mythic traditions; closest in the Indo-European mythologies are Zeus on Ida and numerous references in Welsh and Irish sources. Perhaps the most notable British parallel is one that also combines mystical vision and sexual union. This example comes from the Welsh *Mabinogion*: Gorsedd Arbeth is the mound where Pwyll Prince of Dyfed is foretold to receive a vision or a beating, and from whence he first glimpses his future bride Rhiannon. In the myth at hand, Freyr sees a vision of loveliness indeed, but he pays for his transgression with a twofold "beating": first through his nearly fatal bout of lovesickness, and second through his sword-less battle with Surt at Ragnarok.

Here Skirnir seems to act as an alter ego for Freyr, a fact underscored by the servant's name: Freyr was often described as *skirr*, or "shining," which seems to be the root of *skirnir*. Other names in this myth are likewise telling: Gerd's name means "earth," while *barri* is the root of the term for "barley"; clearly, then, the union between Freyr and Gerd parallels that between Njordr and Skadi. In both cases the giantess represents the frozen earth, while the god is the life-giving force that brings forth plenty from the seed cast upon what seems to be barren soil. Further, parallel Celtic myths of golden apples and coursing through magic flames—together with the obvious relationship between any Norse reference to golden apples and Idun, and the reference of the gentleman caller as brother's killer—suggest that Idun and Gerd may in fact have had a common mythic origin.

A god who embodies life-giving force is often represented by an erect phallus, and thus it hardly comes as a surprise that phallic imagery abounds here. Freyr buys his bride with his sword, a bargain which clearly leaves him unmanned and vulnerable in his final confrontation with the fire demon who consumes him, and with him all fertility. Skirnir's threat to decapitate Gerd with this sword clearly evokes images of the forcible taking of the maiden-head with the penis, while his final threat of barrenness is likewise accompanied by a phallic symbol, in this case a magic staff. Thus the ring of fire through which Skirnir rides—and indeed the very topography of Gerd's valley—serves as a vaginal complement to Freyr's phallic symbols. Finally, the threat of infertility combined with insatiable lust seems most appropriate to the relationship between the god of fecundity and the womb of soil he covets, as the bare and rocky fields of Gymir and the coolness of Gerd's hall both help to illustrate; the coming of the God of Plenty will both warm this inner sanctum and cause life to sprout from the earth.

Freya

Like her brother Freyr, Freya has the earmarks of an archetypal fertility deity, including a lack of sexual inhibition and an association with the magic of fecundity, the *seidr* so disparaged in the masculine Norse world. Such magic was related to women—most likely because, on an archetypal level, all fertility magic is associated with the ability of the female to bring forth life. Freya is closely associated with Odin for several reasons that help to illuminate the tension between fertility rites and warrior cults in the later Germanic period. It is Freya who teaches the arts of *seidr* to Odin, therefore underscoring the mythic volatility of his moral and sexual ambiguity; Freya is often confused with or conflated with Frigg, Odin's wife; Odin openly lusts after Freya, and is at times insanely jealous concerning her; Freya, like Odin, takes home with her a share of the battle dead, thus both associating herself with the war-goddess Valkyries, and illustrating the archetypal relationship between sexuality and death, and the mythic tension between the rituals of fertility and those of war. Perhaps the most famous myth concerning Freya illustrates best her wanton and covetous nature, her relationship with Odin, and the interplay between all of the conflicting and yet complementary attributes of her nature.

The Necklace of the Brisings

One morning before the sun had risen in the east to bathe Asgard with the dawn, Freya made her way from Sessrumnir, her still and silent hall, and soon left the abode of the gods behind her. She went afoot, and left her chariot and her cats at home; she traveled silently, and none took notice of her save a shadowy figure skulking about in the last hours of night on its own vile errands: this was none other than Loki. Sensing the profit that only the trickster might gain from mischief and discord between the gods, Loki pulled tight his cloak and followed the retreating figure of Freya, her ghostly figure discernable through the morning mist only by the form and motion of her swaying hips. Soon she had passed over Bifrost, and as the day began to brighten she made her way across the rock-strewn plains and mountain passes of the land of the dwarfs. Throughout the course of the day she continued on past ice, stone, and snow, never slackening her pace and ever driven on by her lust for gold; her watcher glided silently after her. By nightfall she had found the passage she sought, and threaded her way down a path that led into the bowels of a mountain. She moved on in the subterranean darkness until she saw the flash of the forge and heard the clash of hammer on anvil. Freya stepped into the light; he who followed stood in darkness.

Freya blinked in the brightness of the smithy; it was as if the sun had risen again under the mountain home of Alfrigg, Berling, Dvalin, and Grerr. Everywhere the goddess looked she was dazzled by the blinding beauty of gold and more gold, silver beyond reckoning, and unmatched gemstones. Most beautiful of all was a necklace of cunning artistry, bright as the sun at noonday, and shimmering and shifting like a rushing river of liquid gold; Freya's heart leapt in her heaving bosom. This necklace was all she could desire, and more. But the goddess had not entered unseen; just as Freya stood fixated and salivating with her eyes upon the shimmering object of her lust, so too did the ugly dwarfs gaze upon the flesh of the goddess, inflamed with the need to possess her shining body. Collecting herself as well as she might, Freya offered the dwarfs mountains of treasure for the necklace; they were curt in their refusal. Gold and silver they possessed in mounds; the sweet treasure of her body was the only price that they would take, each to share the pleasure equally, one night apiece. At first the goddess recoiled from this disgusting offer, noticing as if for the first time the horrible, twisted features of the dwarfs. Soon, however, she reconsidered: foul as the dwarfs might be, the necklace was far more fair. What were four nights of submission set against the eternal pleasure of commanding that which she treasured most? The goddess consented; each dwarf possessed her in turn, until they were paid in full.

Freya was without shame as she left the bed of the final dwarf, and she held her head high as her doting lovers bestowed the necklace upon her, fastening it around the nape of her neck. She walked back the way she had come, returning to Asgard under cover of darkness; but though she thought her deeds were secret, she did not walk alone. As Freya fastened tight the doors Sessrumnir behind her, a shadow scuttled past on its way to the hall of Odin. Loki's joy at witnessing Freya's whoring ways was matched only by his delight in recounting the sordid tale to the all-father, whom he knew to lust after the bright goddess most jealously. But Loki's wicked pleasure turned quickly to terror as the wrath of the one-eyed god was turned upon the trickster; Loki ran for his life that night, commanded not to return until he brought the ill-gotten treasure of Freya to the king of the gods. The shape-shifter tried his wiles for some time at Sessrumnir, finally inching his way through a gap in the gable in the form of a crawling insect. Then he flew on the wings of a fly into Freya's bedchamber, where she was asleep, still bedecked with her treasure; she lay with the clasp under her neck. Loki turned then into a flea, and in this form he walked upon her breasts, over the necklace, and across her neck until he sat upon her cheek. Then he bit. Freya moaned and turned, and soon the trickster had pocketed her ill-gotten gain. He left as quickly and quietly as he had come, rushing back to Odin with the treasure.

When Freya awoke, her first thought was of admiring her glorious adornment; as her hand moved to her throat, however, she discovered the horrible truth. Shock and dismay soon turned to anger and a thirst for vengeance, however, as Freya quickly surmised who the thief must be, and who had sent him. Fuming with rage, the goddess quickly came before Odin and demanded the return of her necklace. The all-father returned wrath for wrath, however, and condemned Freya's illicit bargain. Moreover, for the return of her necklace to Freya, Odin demanded his own price: war, hatred and strife in Midgard, bloody battles between mortal kings, and Vanir spells and charms to bring dead warriors back to life to fight again. As quickly as Freya had agreed to the terms of the dwarfs she consented to those of the all-father; thus the Necklace of the Brisings was bought with flesh and ransomed by blood.

THE THEME OF transgressive desire that drives this myth recalls Freyr's lust for Gerd; in both cases it is clear that fertility figures are driven by their basest desires, and in this they clearly symbolize human frailty. Plainly put, the Vanir do not represent the more intellectual facets of human nature. Unlike Freyr, however, Freya transgresses not by trespassing upon Odin's turf but by acting behind his back. In both cases the deity in question is overcome by lust for an object of desire only glimpsed in the first place because of a furtive, taboo act of searching. Sight is often decried as the precursor to lust, and in both of these cases the act of seeing is a secret and forbidden one. Further, gold lust is clearly linked to carnal desire in this myth, and thus Freya's covetousness provides the perfect context for the amorous lust of the dwarfs. Archetypically, moreover, the relationship between Freya's material avarice and the jealous rage of Odin helps to explain the relationship between greed and blood lust, and between sexual arousal and a sense of mortality: reproduction is always inextricably entwined with demise, and thus the little death of orgasm is always a reminder of the great death of the grave. Loki's roles as agitator and sexual intermediary recall the trickster's mythic relationship to sexuality and mortality.

This myth was known in Anglo-Saxon England: the Necklace of the Brisings is mentioned in lines 1197–2000 of *Beowulf,* and the allusive nature of this reference is compelling evidence that the early English took tales of Freya and of her adventures for granted. Freya traditionally takes a share of the battlefield dead, and thus the spells she weaves at Odin's command perhaps result in the magic reincarnation each evening in Valhalla. We cannot say for certain, however, as we have no sense of when this myth takes place in the order of cosmic events.

Freya comprises aspects of the earth-mother, and has been conflated with Odin's wife Frigg, as well as compared to a great many earth-mother figures, not least of which include the classical Demeter and the Near Eastern goddess Ishtar. The Necklace of the Brisings is the symbol most commonly and strongly associated with Freya, and this association serves to underscore her identity as earth-mother goddess: In the early Northland the goddess Nerthus was the most powerful version of the great goddess, and she is sometimes depicted wearing a torque or necklace such as described in this myth.

Heimdalr

Heimdalr is the watchman of the gods: he can hear wool and grass growing, he can see for great distances in light or dark, and he guards the entrance to Asgard at the edge of wavering Bifrost. Heimdalr's most precious possession is Gjallarhorn, the trumpet upon which he will blow the blast announcing Ragnarok, and which he keeps in Mimir's spring beside Odin's bartered eye; through various associations Heimdalr etymologically and thematically is linked to mystical hearing. The watchman has no weapon but his head, and his name itself—perhaps denoting "tree" or "fruit tree"—connotes the butting ram's head. Heimdalr will be the last of the gods to be consumed at Ragnarok, where he will kill and be killed by his mortal enemy, Loki. This animosity plays itself out in several ways in the Norse tradition, and is in fact alluded to in Anglo-Saxon literature: it has been argued that the "Hama" mentioned in *Beowulf*—he who returns the Necklace of the Brisings to the "Bright Burg" from whence it was stolen—is none other than Heimdalr himself. It is probable that Heimdalr is a very old deity who had been almost entirely supplanted by the Norse period. Though he is not known to have a wife, Heimdalr was born of nine mothers, perhaps daughters of the sea-god Aegir. In this association he is to be linked with the Indic sky-god Dyaus, and it has been posited that both represent an ancient Indo-European tradition of the sky born from the waves. The most important myth of Heimdalr in the Norse tradition concerns the genesis of the human race, and in its sets of threes and its rhythmic repetitions we hear the echo of a folkloric source.

The Song of Rig

One fine spring morning, at the start of the sowing season, Heimdalr left his post at the edge of Asgard and walked across the Bifrost bridge into Midgard. All day the god walked, and as evening fell he came to a humble, turf-walled shack; a thin stream of smoke made its lazy way out of a hole in the roof. Hunching nearly double to make his way through the entrance, he almost thought he had entered a cave: the inside of the house was dim and smoke-filled, and he could just discern two wizened shapes by the side of the smoldering fire. These were Great Grandfather and Great Grandmother, and they soon made their visitor—who called himself Rig—as welcome as they might. They offered him the best place by the fire, and they gave to him the finest portion of their dry, crusty loaf and their thin gruel. When time came to sleep, Rig soon convinced his hosts to grant him the warmest spot in the bed, in the middle between Great Grandmother and Great Grandfather; and in this wise Rig spent three days and nights in the turf shack; the days his hosts spent in mindless drudgery, the evenings in speechless torpor. At dawn on the fourth day the god left, but he would not be forgotten: nine months later Great Grandmother bore a son, ugly and twisted but strong and healthy, with black wiry hair and a dark, blotchy complexion. This son Great Grandmother and Great Grandfather named Thrall, and when he had grown he found a kindred mate, and from their loins sprang the race of slaves.

Meanwhile, Rig had made his way to the nearest farm, which he approached as evening was falling. This house looked sturdy and dependable, if lacking in artistry and grace. Knocking on the solid door, the god had soon made his way into the main room, where he found his hosts in their persons to be as cleanly, sensibly, and stolidly attired as their house would suggest. These were Grandfather and Grandmother, and they soon made their visitor—who called himself Rig—as welcome as they might. They offered him the best place by the fire, and they gave to him the finest portion of their hearty brown loaf and their butter, of their boiled meat and their beer. When time came to sleep, Rig soon convinced his hosts to grant him the warmest spot in the bed, in the middle between Grandmother and Grandfather; and in this wise Rig spent three days and nights in the solid farmhouse; the days his hosts spent in the useful industry of animal husbandry and farmwork, the evenings no less so in practical tasks such as whittling and spinning. At dawn on the fourth day the god left, but he would not be forgotten: nine months later Grandmother bore a son, solid and broad and strong and healthy, with brown curly hair and a ruddy complexion. This son Grandmother and Grandfather named Karl, and when he had grown he found a kindred mate, and from their loins sprang the race of peasants.

Meanwhile, Rig had made his way to the nearest farm, which he approached as evening was falling. This hall was fair and fine, wide and tall. Knocking on the broad and finely carved doors, the god had soon made his way into the main room, which was spacious and airy. Here he found his hosts in their persons to be as finely, elegantly, and nobly attired as their great hall would suggest. These were Father and Mother, and they soon made their visitor—who called himself Rig—as welcome as they might. They offered him the best place by the fire, and they gave to him the finest portion of their well-milled white loaf and their cheese, of their broiled meat and their wine. When time came to sleep, Rig soon convinced his hosts to grant him the warmest spot in the bed, in the middle between Mother and Father; and in this wise Rig spent three days and nights in the fine hall; the days his hosts spent in the management of their estate, and in the pastimes of hunting and of embroidery; their evenings were given to feasting and to drinking, to conversation and to chess. At dawn on the fourth day the god left, but he would not be forgotten: nine months later Mother bore a son, quick and cunning and strong and

> healthy, with blond wavy hair and a fair complexion. This son Mother and Father named Jarl, and when he had grown he found a kindred mate, and from their loins sprang the race of lords.

THE "RIG" FROM whence this myth takes its name is clearly identified in the source as Heimdalr, and the use of this alternate name suggests a number of associations with Celtic mythology. *Rig* is the Irish term for "king," and surely this wandering deity's role as sire to the human race earns him this designation; moreover, Manannan, the Irish god of the sea, also participates in a sexual peregrination during which he moves from one cottage to another, siring offspring as he goes. This possible Celtic connection has intrigued generations of scholars, and some have gone so far as to argue that the poet who composed the single extant source for this myth (the *Rigsthula,* in the *Codex Wormianus*) lived in the western part of the British Isles. However, whether this myth is the result of the conflation of Germanic and Celtic mythic elements or whether it is an example of parallel development within distinct mythic systems, "The Song of Rig" certainly illustrates a mythic attempt to justify social stratification. Moreover, this attempt recalls similar origin myths in other Indo-European systems.

Thrall is an English term as well as a Norse one, and means "slave," just as *karl* is equivalent to the English "churl" and denotes a nominally free peasant; *jarl* is the Norse form for the English title "earl," which generically may be rendered "noble" or "aristocrat." Thus in this myth we find a template for a tripartite socioeconomic system with possible racist origins, or at least the overtones of physical stereotypes regarding class divisions. Such a caste system clearly was common across Indo-European cultures, and cultural practices often are validated through such mythic origins. Mythic conceptions of social hierarchies perhaps reach an apex in the Indic system, but are hardly exclusive to that system. Moreover, most Indo-European cultural systems—including the Celtic culture current in Britain during the period that produced this myth—would include at least a fourth (sacramental) caste. The social stratification suggested by "The Song of Rig" mirrors traditional Germanic structures, however, and in its lack of a distinct priestly caste reminds us of the conflation of secular and religious authority found, for example, in the form of the Icelandic *godar.*

Baldr

Baldr is the most beautiful of the Norse gods, with brilliant, shining white hair and visage; he is kind and gentle, and is noted for his wisdom. There are not very many myths in which Baldr is the central figure, but those that exist are among the most important of the entire Norse cycle. As might be supposed from his characteristic wisdom and forgiving disposition, Baldr has many attributes in common with Christ, and after his unjust and untimely death the mythic function he serves is very similar to that of Christ. The myths of Baldr's death and the events that follow it will be treated in the section concerning the mythic archetype of the dying god and that of the rebirth, return, and apotheosis of the hero; it is more appropriate at this point to recount the myth that foretells his doom, and that concurrently foreshadows the end of the Norse pantheon as a whole. In the myth of Baldr's dream we encounter perhaps most explicitly in Norse mythology the pagan Germanic conception of *wyrd*; the most notable references to *wyrd* in English literature occur in *Beowulf* and in some of the Old English elegies. Somewhat like the Christian concept of Providence or the classical vision of Fate, *wyrd* represents an immutable, inexorable destiny that even the gods themselves cannot withstand.

Baldr's Dream

Baldr thrashed and sweated as he did battle with his dreams; each time he awoke the nightmares glided away before he could remember the worst of them, but each time he drifted off to sleep they haunted him anew. Soon the god's shining hair was soaked and matted, and his bright fair face was lined with anxiety and fatigue. Baldr no longer rested easy in his hall Breidablik, and his nightly torment struck fear and concern in the hearts of each of the gods. They gathered together each day, as was their custom, but there was no joy now in Gladsheim: each asked how the most beautiful, gentle, and beloved of the gods could be so cursed, and for what reason; but none could offer an answer. Finally Odin, chieftain of the gods and the father of Baldr, volunteered to seek out the reason for his son's suffering. Without another word, the all-father mounted Sleipnir and rode to the gates of Hel, passing by horrible monsters and over fearsome obstacles without thought or a backward glance.

Now Odin dismounted, and although he ignored the shades clustered around Hel's doorway, he noticed the shining ornaments within and the bustle of preparation. The one-eyed god made his way to Hel's east gate, where the mound of a seeress rose in the gloom. Muttering ancient words and working forbidden runes as he spoke, the spell master raised the seeress from her damp, cold grave. Though she was bound by frost and disabled by rot, and though she protested at every turn, Odin wrenched words from the wretched wraith. Identifying himself allusively as *Vegtam*, "he who knows the way," son of *Valtam*, "he who knows battle," the all-father asked why Hel's palace was adorned as never before; the seeress answered that Baldr was expected soon, and that mead had been brewed and the hall decorated for this most noble of guests. Again the god pressed the shade, asking who would slay Baldr, and who would avenge the god's death. She answered that Hod would be his brother's killer, and that death would be repaid with death by Vali, son of Rind and Odin; but she offered no more than that. Finally, seeing through the wanderer's ruse, the seeress called Odin by his true name and mocked the coming sorrow of the gods as she glided back to her rest. She would rise no more, she foresaw, until Loki the trickster would loose himself from his confinement to meet the gods at their final doom at Ragnarok. Odin in turn realized that the seeress was not whom he thought her to be, and was in fact an enemy of the gods, and the mother of three monsters. Having found what he came for—though it was not much to his liking—Odin mounted Sleipnir and spurred home in silence and despair.

MORE AKIN IN THIS respect to their Greek and Roman counterparts than to the Christian Almighty, the Norse gods are subject to fate just as mortals are, and the dream of Baldr prefigures not only his personal demise but that of the entire pantheon. The finite nature of the power of the gods is likewise presaged through Odin's impotent encounter with the seeress; just so the innocent and beautiful Baldr is soon to be lost, and though the gods will have the power to punish the responsible party, retrieving their loved one will prove beyond their ability. We may push this parallel still further, as the unnamed seeress herself—both through her mocking tones and through the mention of her monstrous offspring—ultimately reminds us of Loki, who is soon to become the villain of this drama.

In this myth we also see yet again Odin cast as the magician, the necromancer, he who conjures the dead and consorts with evil itself in his quest for forbidden knowledge. In the gleeful response of the demonic seeress whom he invokes we hear the satisfaction of the forces of chaos that for so long have been lapping like an incoming tide at the feet of the complacent gods. Through her words we also begin to realize that Loki's role within the pantheon is about to take an evil turn, and that Odin's friendship with him—and Odin's own ability to stave off the victory of the forces of darkness by manipulating them to his own ends, which his relationship with Loki symbolizes—is at an end.

Loki

Loki is neither Aesir nor Vanir, is a shape-changer and a gender-bender, is the off-spring of giants, and can be charming as well as cunning. In a word he is demonic, as his three children by the giantess Angrboda, discussed in reference to "The Binding of Fenrir," should make clear. Loki's loyal and long-suffering wife is the goddess Sigyn, who plays no major role in the Norse myths until she serves as her husband's nursemaid during his confinement by the gods; in any case, marriage serves as no barrier to Loki's promiscuity, and he manages both to sire and to whelp a number of bastard offspring. Loki is doubtless the most interesting character in the Norse pantheon, perhaps because evil makes for a much more compelling narrative than does good. Loki is the god of fire and of mischief, and is a classic trickster figure; his mythic function as such will be discussed on page 88. His volatile relationship with Odin—and all the subtext associated with such a relationship—is discussed elsewhere at some length, and likewise need not be reiterated. Loki is a central figure in the unfolding of the fate of the Norse gods, however, and it is necessary to pay special attention to him as we discuss the working out of the events leading up to the final battle between the gods and their enemies.

Loki personifies the forces of chaos constantly challenging the authority and structure of Asgard, and by taking a seat among the Aesir, Loki represents a type of the traitorous Fifth Column working to destroy order and civilization from within. If Loki is—on the one hand—an archetypal representation of the forces that will gather against the gods at Ragnarok, he also is—on the other hand—the actual agent who actively brings about that final conflict: It is Loki who provides the deadly mistletoe dart and who guides Hod's hand in the murder of Baldr; it is Loki who—disguised as a crone—discovered Frigg's lapse concerning the mistletoe in the first place; it is Loki who—this time in the guise of a giantess—refuses the tears that would restore the shining one to Asgard. Finally, in "The Flyhting of Loki," the trickster drops his duplicity altogether, telling the gods what he really thinks of them, boasting of his hand in the loss of Baldr, and leaving the hall with a final curse that evokes the horrors to come. At this point Loki flees Asgard, knowing full well that he will never again be safe there, but at the same time relishing the coming conflict that will bring low the citadel of the gods forever.

The Binding of Loki

Fleeing the vengeance for Baldr's death that he knew was soon to come from the gods, Loki swiftly made his way from the glory of Gladsheim to the most desolate mountainous wastes of Midgard. Loki ran and ran until he reached a steep valley falling away from the mountains toward the sea. Here there were mighty waterfalls pounding the rock at their base and a wide pool that flowed into a river and down a short, narrow shallows into the sea. Loki thought to spend his exile here, in a house cobbled together from the stones blasted free from the riverbed by the force of the falling water. This house he fashioned to be low and flat, so that it blended perfectly into the rubble at the base of the falls; no one would notice this house unless tripping over it. He built his house with four doors—one in each direction—so that he could keep watch for his pursuers both night and day.

Each day passed without any sign of pursuit, and yet Loki's nerves were soon frayed ragged by anxiety; every tiny sound he took to signal the approach of his enemies, and he spent his time trying to think of ways to outwit them for as long as he could. Each morning he ran from his hut to the base of the waterfalls, where he leapt into the pool, changing himself into the form of a salmon; even at the bottom of his pool, however, surrounded by the force of the cataracts and shielded from prying eyes, the trickster never felt safe. His nights he passed in sleepless worry in his low house, turning from door to door to watch for pursuers. He also spent his evenings thinking of ways the gods might catch him, and trying to think of how he might escape such attempts. Meanwhile, back in Asgard, the rage of the gods kindled as their sorrow grew colder; those who mourned Baldr now thought to temper the bitter taste of despair with a sweet draught of vengeance. From his high seat of Hlidskjalf, Odin searched the nine worlds, and what at first seemed just a pile of rocks in a remote corner of Midgard soon drew his attention; the all-father spied a shape leaving each morning to dive into the pool at the base of the thundering falls. Soon a party of gods left Asgard to capture the miscreant.

That evening Loki was amusing himself by lacing threads across one another, forming a loose weave such as a spider might make. Loki was well pleased with his invention, a net with which one might well catch a fish. He studied his creation for a long time, looking for flaws through which quarry might escape. Suddenly, he heard the sound of approaching feet and voices; casting his new net into the fire, Loki ran out of his hut and down to the pool, splashing away in the form of a salmon long before his visitors were close enough to see him. As the gods entered the empty hut, they had no idea of Loki's whereabouts; peering into the cooling embers of the fire, however, Kvasir discerned the pattern of Loki's net in the ashes. Realizing at once the potential of this invention, Kvasir set himself the task of weaving a fishnet of his own; the other gods soon pitched in, and before they slept they had fashioned a long, rectangular net.

The next morning the gods divided their party into two, and each group took one end of the net. Dropping the bottom of the net into the end of the pool at the base of the falls, the gods dredged the stream, forcing Loki before them. Right before he was pushed into the shallows, however, the trickster found a hollow in the streambed between two stones, and so the net passed right over him, although it scratched his back. When the gods reached the shallows they brought up an empty net, but all agreed that they had felt a fish being dragged for some distance. They then decided to refine their method, and they weighted down the bottom edge of the net with stones. This time as they proceeded downstream Loki could not elude them by hugging the streambed, and so, right before being forced into the shallows, the trickster reared up and leapt over the net, swimming madly upstream.

This time there was no doubt: the gods all had witnessed the colorful flash of the salmon's leaping escape, and they discussed how best to capture such a wily and powerful fish. Finally, Kvasir suggested that they drag the bed a third time, but on this occasion Thor would wade down the stream in the wake of the net. This agreed to, the gods moved up to the base of the falls and began again. This time Loki was trapped, and he knew it; he didn't dare to try his luck in the shallows, and so, as he was pushed to the far edge of the deep water yet again, he tried once more to leap to safety. His luck had run out, however; Thor was there to greet him, and though Loki the salmon was wet and slick, and though he wriggled as much as he might, the Thunderer clenched ever tighter with his mighty grasp, until the very tail of the salmon was crushed into a tapered shape. The trickster was caught; he lay limp and silent.

Back on dry land, Loki reverted to his normal form. The gods gathered around him, eager for vengeance; although—even in the heat of their anger and the depths of their despondency—they had been loathe to sully the sacred soil of Asgard with the trickster's blood, here they felt no such compunction. They took him to a cave nearby, dripping and dank and dark. Then they fetched Loki's two sons by Sigyn; they transformed Vali into a wolf, and they laughed as he ripped the life from his brother Narvi, and ran off into the darkness. The gods then completely disemboweled Narvi, and it was with his son's own entrails that Loki was bound in the cave; these hardened and tightened as they were tied, and soon held the prisoner more fast than steel. The trickster's quick wit and saucy retorts he kept to himself now. The gods set three great slabs on end, and bound Loki's shoulders to the first, his waist to the second, and his knees to the third.

Then Skadi, the giantess, had the last laugh on Loki: she found a deadly viper and fixed it in the roof of the cave so that its venom streamed down into the trickster's face. So the gods left Loki to pay for his crimes, with Sigyn at his side weeping, mourning the loss of her sons and the pain of her husband; a bowl she holds over his face to catch the venom of the serpent, but each time it fills she must leave him to empty it, and then he has no protection: the snake's poison drips into his eyes, and he howls and he writhes; when this happens, the very earth shakes with his pain, his anger, and his hatred. This then, was the vengeance of the gods for the death of Baldr: Loki lies in pain and anguish in the dark, with the hiss of the snake and the drip of the venom his only music, and his loyal wife his lone companion. There he remains until Ragnarok, when he will arise to take his own vengeance.

THE IMAGE OF A fire-god chained in punishment for his sins has obvious resonance with the classical story of Prometheus, just as, in a Christian context, it reminds one of Satan bound in the depths of the pit. It is possible that the binding of Loki is related to the former narrative through some common Indo-European ancestor, but it is even more probable that the story of the punishment of the Norse demonic trickster was influenced by the latter tradition through direct contact with Christianity. Furthermore, the relationship between a dark, forbidding subterranean god and the phenomenon of earthquakes—while something of an archetypal commonplace—might also suggest folkloric influences, just as the details about the first fishing net and the reason for the form of the salmon's body do. Moreover, Loki is the representative of the chaotic forces of nature contained by the gods (albeit narrowly and only for a time) to the benefit of mankind; thus it does not seem at all strange that he would be associated with one of the most powerful physical manifestations of those forces.

This myth is known to have been current in Norse Britain, as a rendering of Loki's imprisonment and Sigyn's ministrations to him appear on the Gosforth Cross; once again, such a depiction does not merely prove that the myth was known but also illustrates how fully a great deal of Germanic pagan material was incorporated into early British Christian symbols and motifs. Loki is the last of the major figures of the Norse pantheon, although there are a number of important lesser figures; most notable among these are the Norns and the Valkyries, both of which have resonance with Anglo-Saxon mythic figures and concepts, and which therefore help to illustrate the relationship between Anglo-Saxon Christianity and earlier Germanic beliefs. The final figure we will discuss in this section, however, is a paradoxical one: Weland the Smith might be said to appear everywhere and nowhere in the Germanic myths that have come down to us, and he appears provocatively—if allusively—in a number of British contexts. In this conflicted way Weland has much to tell us about the body of mythic material we have lost.

Weland/Volundr

It seems fitting to conclude our discussion of the Germanic deities with Weland—known in the Norse sources as Volundr—because in Weland we find a stunning Anglo-Saxon example of the type of mythic synthesis that this book strives to illuminate. Weland is an important Germanic deity in some ways, but in terms of volume of extant mythic material his significance is almost negligible; indeed, it is through only the sheerest of luck that any Anglo-Saxon references to him survive, or that we may claim with assurance that Weland is the Norse Volundr (or the German Wieland). Weland was the smith of the Germanic gods, lame in one leg, and as such is naturally to be compared with Vulcan/Hephaistos of the Romans and the Greeks; moreover, as his saga makes clear, he has indeed much in common with Daedalus, that master craftsman of classical mythology.

The heroic saga of Volundr was known in Britain, and we will tell it in the appropriate place; here we will pause only to note that images of Weland with hammer and tongs in his smithy, or defending a house with bow and arrows, are common throughout the Scandinavian world, and appear also in Britain, notably on a number of stone crosses and perhaps most impressively in the form of intricate carvings on a whalebone ivory box known as the "Franks Casket." Now housed in the British Museum (except for one side), the Franks Casket combines scenes from pagan Germanic myth with some from classical antiquity and from the Bible, and betrays its Germanic heritage still further through the runic inscriptions running along the sides. These scenes include one of Weland in his smithy, as well as depictions of Sigurd/Siegfried, Romulus and Remus, the siege of Jerusalem, and the gifts of the Magi. It is perhaps particularly evocative that the Magi are clearly labeled in their illustration with Germanic runes.

Several allusive references to Weland survive to us in Old English poetry. Weland is mentioned in *Beowulf* as the maker of a fantastic coat of mail, while the *Waldere* poet credits him with the creation of a choice blade. In *Deor*, a poem about alienation, exile, and suffering, the poet alludes directly to the epic of Weland, and cites the great smith as an example of one to whom such terms had real meaning.

Thus in Weland we find a paradox: his name appears in a number of Old English texts and representations of him appear in various artistic contexts, quite often in combination with Christian motifs; here is a god who was clearly known and revered in pagan and early Christian England (as well as in the rest of the Germanic world), whose name has remained current in English literature almost until the present day; yet we know only the barest outline of one of Weland's sagas. Indeed, it has been argued persuasively that Weland the Smith was so well known, and so many tales accrued about him, that allusions to him were often made without any attempt to flesh out the all too familiar stories.

The stories of Weland's family are likewise both tantalizing and frustrating. Weland's father was the giant Wade; Wade's mother was named Wachilt. A number of stories concerning Weland's genealogy are related to Irish mythic traditions, and specifically to the nine sea maidens mentioned in reference to "The Song of Rig." It has been suggested that this relationship stems from the antiquity of a common mythic source for Wade, who—it has been posited—was originally a sea-giant from the Baltic region transplanted with early Germanic settlers of Britain. According to the thirteenth-century *Didriksaga*, a mysterious woman appeared to a king, first in a forest and then holding on to the gunwales of his ship. On this second occasion she informed him that she would bear his child, and so he took her home with him. She disappeared after the birth of Wade, but later saved Wade's grandson Widia from enemies on his heels by transporting him to her undersea dwelling. This association with water seems important, and it should be remembered that Weland himself is reputed to have carried his son on his shoulders through water nine yards deep. In the Norse world Weland's oceanic heritage was remembered and celebrated, but in Britain somewhat less so, and in those islands Weland's father Wade came to be most closely associated with ancient stone structures of mysterious provenance, and with the roads left behind by the Romans. Wade was known in England throughout the Middle Ages, and Chaucer mentions him in "The Merchant's Tale" and *Troilus and Criseyde*.

The Celtic Pantheons

Background of Celtic Mythology

The question of Celtic pantheons must inevitably begin with an attempt to identify the Celts themselves. Scholars argue as to the origins of this very rough ethnic grouping. There are those who trace the Celts to the early Indo-European Urnfied and Tumulus Late Bronze Age cultures of the second and third millennia BCE. More often, early Celts are associated with the iron-weaponed Hallstatt culture of the eighth century BCE in northwestern Europe and the Second Iron Age La Tene culture that followed it. The Greek historian Herodotus tells us that by 500 BCE the Celts were a significant force in Central and Western Europe, and we know that in 387 BCE they were powerful enough to defeat and sack Rome. There are archeological evidences of Celtic migrations to Britain in the fifth century BCE. By the third century BCE there appears to have been a strong Celtic presence in Ireland. The migrations continued into the first century BCE with the arrival of the Celtic Belgae in Britain. Meanwhile, by the first century BCE the continental Celts had deteriorated in importance. Their land was, in effect, limited to the three parts of Gaul defeated by Julius Caesar in the Gallic wars (58–51 BCE). Caesar attacked the insular Celts of Britain as well, but with only limited success. It was not until one hundred years later, in fact, that the Romans were able to conquer Britain. The Roman conquest and the Norse-Germanic invasions that followed it eventually pushed the Celts to restricted areas of Ireland, Scotland, Wales, and Cornwall. These remaining Celts were divided into two linguistic families that had been established by the sixth century BCE—the Goidelic Celtic of Scottish Gaelic and Irish and the British or Bythonic Celtic of the Welsh and Cornish, which was essentially the same as that of their continental cousins, the Bretons.

The Transmission of Celtic Culture

Celtic culture was transmitted orally until the contact with the Romans and later with the Christian monks. Again, it must be emphasized, our knowledge of Celtic pantheons largely is filtered through the writings of these two groups, each of which operated under its own agenda. First came the politically motivated Julius Caesar and later conquering Romans, who saw Celtic gods as reflections of Roman ones. Much later, Christian monks in Britain were anxious to document local traditions and to write down the old tales, but they also strove to assert the superiority of their own faith, sometimes even going so far as to insert aspects of Judeo-Christian mythology into their retellings of Celtic stories. It can be said, however, that through the druidic bards, the Brahmin-like *filid* (*filidh, fili*), the Celtic tradition as practiced in Ireland was reasonably well preserved until the final success of Christianity in the sixth century CE. The monks of the second half of the sixth century who wrote down the old texts at least worked, therefore, from accurate and full narratives. But much of this material was eventually destroyed. What we depend on for source material, therefore, are monastic compilations of the twelfth century such as *The Book of the Dun Cow* and *The Book of Leinster* and other books of later centuries, including *The Great Book of Lecan*, *The Yellow Book of Lecan*, *The Book of Lismore*, and *The Book of Fermoy*, and, perhaps most importantly, the twelfth-century *Book of Invasions*, or *The Taking of Ireland* (the *Leabhar Gabhala Eireann*). The sources for Welsh mythology are the still later *Mabinogi* or *Mabinogion* and *The Triads of the Island of Britain*, the late fourteenth-century *White Book of Rhydderch* and *Red Book of Hergest*, and poems questionably attributed to the semi-mythic sixth-century poet-prophet Taliesen, whose Irish equivalent was Amairgen, the poet-warrior. In connection with Celtic mythology in the British Isles, it might well be suggested that, given the length of time between the formation of early Celtic mythology on the continent and the written expression of insular mythology, we are on much firmer ground when we speak of Irish and Welsh mythology rather than Celtic. The stories of the Ulster cycle and *The Mabinogi* are Irish and Welsh rather than Celtic, just as the plays of Shakespeare are English rather than Germanic.

Celtic Ritual and Festivals

Historical records indicate that there were four primary festivals in the Celtic year, each of them linked to important seasonal and agricultural cues. Samhain—or Samain—came at the end of October, and was the festival marking the coming of winter and the beginning of the Celtic New Year. At this time the livestock were rounded up, and the choice was made of which animals to slaughter and which to keep for breeding. This was also a spiritually volatile time of year, and potentially dangerous: it was neither summer nor winter, and this ambiguity made it an ideal time for communication and transportation between worlds. Thus the gods and spirits might walk the earth, and conversely, men might enter into the otherworld. Such practices are hazardous, however, as the denizens of the otherworld have little regard for men or for their values and codes, and therefore usually are to be avoided. Notions of the volatility of such ambiguity survived well into the medieval period, as evidenced, for example, in the romance *Sir Orfeo*. The holiday of Samhain itself lives on in the tradition of Halloween and All Saints' Day, and vestiges of an understanding of this festival as a threshold to the otherworld live on in practices such as "trick or treat."

Imbolc—or Oimelc—was the next festival in the Celtic year; it was a fertility festival, and fell at the beginning of February, when the ewes and cows began to lactate. *Imbolc* seems to denote something like "purification" and was related to fire, as were most Celtic rituals and holy days. The goddess Brigid was the central figure at this holiday; she was sacred to poets, smiths, and brewers, and was associated with seers. Perhaps most notably in the terms of the festival of Imbolc, Brigid was associated with childbearing and medicine, and also had powers over fire. Brigid entered the Christian canon almost without effort, and her connection to Imbolc may have eased this transition, as it fell close to the day reserved for the Feast of the Purification of the Virgin. Imbolc itself became known as the Day of the Festival of Brigid, and like the goddess before her, the saint was said to have special powers over fire. Throughout the Middle Ages, nineteen (or nine) virgins were said to stand over her sacred flames at Kildare, keeping it ever burning and all men away from sight of it. In Scotland Brigid was revered as the midwife to Mary—clearly adding one of her pagan functions to a Christian role—and Christ was known as her foster son. Indeed, well into the modern period believers called upon the powers of the saint by reciting her lineage, and butter churns in Ireland were made in the image of a woman and dedicated to Saint Brigid.

Beltene—or Beltain—was a festival of the time of pasturing and sowing, and took place in early May; its name means "bright fire" or "fire of Bel." Like Samhain, this was a hazardous time, as the young crops and livestock were at risk, and disease and poor weather could strike down whole fields and herds as if by magic. Recalling Imbolc, this was a festival concerned with ritual purification in the form of sacred fire; here fire represents the burgeoning power of the sun to give and to protect life. Priests ignited two large fires, and animals were herded between these to cleanse them. The lighting of sacred fires was an important Druidic rite, and St. Patrick is said to have used this fact to his advantage when he set a huge bonfire on the eve of the Beltene festival at Tara, thus co-opting druidic power and prestige. Bonfires are still ignited each May in parts of Cornwall. Food often plays a role in sowing rituals, and food sacrifices associated with Beltene continued to be offered in Scotland through the eighteenth century. Further, the fertility figure known as the Green Man continued to grace British country festivals at this time of year well into the modern period, often accompanied by unbridled passion in the fields. Sacrificial sexual union in newly plowed fields certainly may have been a Celtic rite, and is a common component to fertility rituals. We will return to the Green Man in our discussion of *Sir Gawain and the Green Knight*.

Lughnasadh—or Lughnasa—was a month-long harvest festival that took place in August. It was named after the god Lugh, who was said to have founded it. This festival included feasting, horseracing, and ritual battles. It was also an occasion for legal and political assemblies, meetings that often took place at sacred places on hills or near water sources. Lughnasadh was replaced by the Christian church with Lammas, the "loaf-mass"; the eponymous loaf was made of the first grains of the new harvest, and thus Lammas served some of the same functions as a harvest festival, as did its pagan forebear. It has been noted that a modern potato festival known as Garlic Sunday—celebrated on the last Sunday of July—has its roots in Lughnasadh, as do a number of (now) Christian pilgrimages and conclaves, which take place at places similar or identical to those used for assemblies by the Celts. These Christian assemblies are sometimes dedicated to Saint Patrick, who may have co-opted Lugh's mythic and ritual role in these cases.

Many Celtic festivals involved sacrifices, both of animals and of humans. Human sacrifice among the Celts was attested by the Romans, as was ritual head-hunting; the material record confirms that there was a basis for these claims, and we shall turn to this topic in detail in our conclusion. Animal sacrifice clearly was more common in Celtic culture, and cattle, pigs, dogs, and horses all seem to have been deemed appropriate. Sacrifices accompanied the most important rituals, and often involved dedicating the head and feet to the gods and feasting upon the meat. Hence, many Celtic religious festivals must have contained feasting, an element that must have translated nicely into a Christian context that included "feast days" for nearly every saint and holiday on the liturgical calendar. Some sacrifices must have been more situational, however. For example, the Celts believed that a herd struck by disease might be saved by the ritual sacrifice of one or more of their number; thus the few die so that the many may survive. This is a notion that dies hard, and the practice of killing a designated individual during an outbreak in an attempt to save the herd survived in Scotland and Wales well into the eighteenth century, and might have persisted still later. It is ironic that church records decrying this practice are among the documents that attest to its survival. The Celts also sacrificed objects, and are rather famous for the practice. They seem to have conceived of their relationship with their gods as contractual, based upon bribes and mutually profitable arrangements, rather than on mutual love and trust. They therefore sacrificed food and valuable objects in pits, as their otherworld existed beneath the ground. This practice of throwing away valuables in order to store up divine credits might be likened to the modern practice of throwing coins in fountains or wishing wells.

Romano-Celtic Deities and Insular Celtic Counterparts

It is from the Roman sources that we must attempt to begin to recreate the Celtic pantheons, which, not surprisingly, take various forms according to linguistic, geographic, and political realities in the various parts of the Celtic world, including the British Isles. Julius Caesar commented primarily upon those Celtic gods of Gaul in whom he detected a kinship with the deities he himself worshiped; thus he claimed that the Gauls revered "Mercury" the most, followed by "Apollo" and some others. Some time later Lucan reported that human sacrifice was common among the Gauls, and cited sacrificial groves where victims were offered up to Teutates, Esus, and Taranis. This triad reflects an ancient Indo-European set of gods, and also may be equated with Germanic counterparts: *Taran* is a Celtic form of a root for "thunder," and thus this god shares common ground with Thunor/Thor. Sacrifices to Esus, meanwhile, were made by hangings in sacred groves, while those to Teutates were drowned; these practices recall those dedicated to Wodan/Odin and Nerthus/Freyr, respectively.

MERCURY-LUGH

Like the later Christians, Caesar inevitably attempted to assimilate the Celtic deities into his own religious tradition. He noted, for instance, the presence of a god to whom he gave the Roman name Mercury, thus associating him with the messenger of the Greco-Roman pantheon. As in the case of other Romano-Celtic deities, clues to this god's real Celtic identity lie in aspects that make him different from his assigned Roman counterpart. He is, for instance, often three-headed, and he usually has a consort, whose name is Maia or Rosmerta. Furthermore, Caesar describes him as the inventor of the arts. This "Mercury" seems to most scholars to be, in fact, the Gaulish Lugus and insular Celtic god known as Lugh in Ireland and Lleu in Wales. In a work named *The Battle of Magh Tuiredh*, for instance, Lugh identifies himself as the master of all the arts and crafts.

Lugh is also the young David-like hero who destroyed his evil one-eyed Cyclopean grandfather Balar. This killing had long been prophesied, and Lugh had been rescued as a baby from Balar, who had intended to kill the child to prevent the fulfillment of the prophecy. Lugh had been brought up by the sea-god Manannan Mac Lir or, some say, by the smith-god Goibhniu. This story suggests incidents in the biography of the Hindu Visnu avatar Krsna rather than that of Mercury. In Hindu mythology, the evil king Kamsa received a prophecy that he would be killed by the son of his relative Devaki, but the gods saw to it that the sacred child Krsna was rescued and brought up by the rustic cowherd Nanda. It is of interest to note, in this connection, that the great songs of Taliesen in Wales and Amairgen in Ireland bear some resemblance to Krsna's all-subsuming songs of the Hindu *Bhagavadgita*.

In *The Baile in Scail* ("The God's Prophecy") Lugh is seen as a sacred solar king and king of the otherworld, associated with Rosmerta, who is herself a kind of personification of Ireland, sometimes known as "the Sovranty of Ireland." Lugh followed Nuada as king of the gods in Ireland, and was—with the mortal Dechtire—the father of the great hero Cuchulainn. Lugh assisted a weakening Cuchulainn in the Tain war, and he once appeared with "the Sovranty of Ireland" out of the mist as a godly horseman, a "son of Adam," who revealed future Irish kings to King Conn. After the early gods, the Tuatha De Danann, were forced underground, Lugh became popular in Ireland as Lugh-chromain, or "little stooping Lugh" or "leprechaun." Eventually Christians would assimilate him, making him Saint Lughaidh.

APOLLO-MABON-AONGHUS

Caesar's Gallic Apollo seems to be at least in part an old Celtic solar-god Belenus, and perhaps a combination of Grannus, the god of thermal springs and a sacred youth who became Maponos and later Mabon in Wales, son of the great mother Modron or Matrona. In Ireland, Mabon was Mac ind Og or Aonghus Og (Angus or Oenghus), son of the god known as the Dagda (Daghdha) and the sacred river Boann. Aonghus was a handsome lover and trickster. Four birds accompanied him, symbols of his magical kisses. In a famous dream, Aonghus met and fell in love with the swan maiden Caer Ibormeith. Using his great powers, he was able to identify her from among 150 other swans and to win her love.

ROMANO-CELTIC GODDESSES

Caesar associated many of the Celtic goddesses with the Roman Minerva (Greek Athena). In fact, many of these goddesses had little in common with Minerva. Her closest equivalent emerged in Ireland as Brigid, daughter of the Dagda, who with her sisters of the same name formed the typical Celtic triune deity—in this case goddesses of healing and craftsmanship, as well as fertility. Brigid is perhaps related to the British Briganytia, herself the probable source of the later Britannia, and sometimes she seems to be an embodiment of the great goddess, the mother of the gods, Dana. Under Christian influence Brigid became the very popular Saint Brigid of Kildare of the monastery of the Sacred Oak—itself suggesting the Celtic druidic tradition of the sacred oak. Brigid in both her original and Christian forms was associated with poetry and fruition.

VULCAN-GOIBHNIU-GOFANNON

The Romano-Celtic Vulcan (Greek Hephaistos) was in all likelihood originally the Celtic smith known in Ireland as Goibhniu and in Wales as Gofannon son of Don. As Goibhniu killed Ruadan, who was famously lamented by his mother Brigid, Gofannon killed his nephew Dylan Eil Ton, the blond twin of Lleu. Dylan's role as a sea-god is reminiscent of the similar role of the Hindu Krsna's brother Balarama. Goibhniu required only three strokes of his hammer to make a spear, and his magic beer served in the otherworld had the power to heal and to overcome death. He would come to be seen as the architect of the earliest Christian churches in Ireland. To this day smiths, like this god, are believed to have certain healing powers.

HERCULES-OGMA

Lucian tells us in the second-century CE that the Gauls referred to Hercules as Ogmios; this figure was sun-burned, bald, and old. There is an Irish strongman god named Ogma, who was also a god of eloquence and poetry. A son of the great god the Dagda, he directed souls to the otherworld and he invented Irish script.

DIS PATER-DONN-BILE

Caesar wrote that the druids believed they were descended from a god of the dead called Dis Pater. An Irish equivalent is the dark god Donn, whose House of Donn was the resting place of the dead. Other possible cognates are the

Irish god Bile and the Welsh Beli, both gods of death. Beli was usually considered to be the husband of the great-goddess Don. He was also known as the father of Lludd (Nudd) and Llefelys, rulers of Britain and Gaul, respectively. According to the twelfth-century Welsh-Breton cleric and historian Geoffrey of Monmouth, author of *The History of Kings of Britain*, Lludd was the builder of London and, with his brother, the destroyer of the supernatural sources of plague. Geoffrey notes that a temple to Lludd stood in London, presumably reached by Lludd's Gate, the present-day Ludgate, near St. Paul's Cathedral. The Irish Bile was also sometimes considered the husband of the Irish great goddess, in this case Dana. One of his jobs was to escort the dead to the otherworld. Sometimes he is called the father of Milesius of Spain, "Spain" serving as a synonym for the otherworld and Milesius being one of the early invaders of Ireland.

Irish and Welsh Pantheons

THE FAMILY OF DON

In the Welsh tales collectively known as *The Mabinogi* or *Mabinogion*, we learn of the family of Don (not to be confused with Donn). In Ireland we have the equivalent Tuatha De Danann, the people of Danu. Danu/Don is the great goddess whose reign stretches far back into pre-Celtic Britain and beyond that to Indo-European roots in ancient India, where Danu—the mother of the demon Vrtra—mourns the death of her offspring at the hands of the patriarchal god Indra.

In Wales, Don is a daughter of Mathonwy, the ancient founder of the House of Don and, as noted above, is sometimes said to be the wife of the god of death, Beli. Another child of Mathonwy is Math, the god of wealth who requires that his feet rest on a virgin's lap unless he is at battle. When his virgin/footstool is corrupted by his nephews—Gilfaethwy and the storyteller Gwydion—Math turns the young men into wild animals for a year. Gwydion apparently fathered the great Lleu with his sister, the dawn-goddess Aranrhod, whose loss of virginity was revealed when she was brought to Math as a replacement for his corrupted footstool. As she stepped over Math's magic wand to test her supposed virginity, two boys, Dylan and Lleu, emerged from her. Dylan escaped to the sea, and Lleu was protected and reared by Gwydion.

Besides Gofannon, Gwydion, Gilfaethwy, and Aranrhod, the children of Don include, among lesser figures, the god Lludd, described above, and Penardun, who with her husband Llyr (the ocean-god Lir in Ireland and probably the source for *King Lear*) parented Manawydan, the sea-god. By another marriage Penardun was the mother of the peacemaker Nisien and the strife-maker Efnisien. Llyr fathered the famous Bran and Branwen by another wife.

Bran, whose Irish equivalent is also Bran, a god of the otherworld, leads an army into Ireland to protect his sister Branwen, wife of the Irish king Matholwch. Branwen's safety had been threatened by the malicious behavior of her half-brother Efnisien. After a terrible battle, only five pregnant women remained in Ireland to form a new population, and only seven Britons—including the great poet-warrior Taliesen—returned home, led by the head of the dead Bran, which remained magically alive and talking.

THE TUATHA DE DANANN, THE FIRBOLG, THE FOMORIANS, AND THE INVASIONS OF IRELAND

The Irish version of Don is Danu (Dana), the great-mother of the Tuatha De Danann. It was said that the Tuatha De Danann had come to Ireland originally from Greece or from a hole in the sky, that they had been protected by a magical mist, that they had once lived in the ancient cities of Findias, Gorias, Murias, and Falias, and that they were expert at magic and enchantment. It was they who brought druidry to Ireland.

The Tuatha De Danann had to fight for the control of Ireland with the terrible sea-born demonic giants called the Fomorians (Fomorii, Fomors, or Fomhoire) in the north and the dark Firbolg (Fir Bholg) in the south. The Fomorians are traditionally associated, like the ancient Greek Titans and the Vedic Asuras, with forces of nature that stand against order; in the Germanic traditions this role is played by the giants. The Fomorians are often depicted as misshapen, with one eye or one foot. The Firbolg were said by some to be descendants of the Nemedians, who had preceded the Firbolg and the other early peoples in Ireland and were led by Nemed (Nemhedh), son of the king of Scythia in Greece. They had come to Ireland in search of the gold of the Fomorian king Conann. Most of the invaders were drowned, but Nemed was able to establish a foothold, and he built forts and cleared land. The Nemedians were known as great artisans.

In their craftsmanship the Nemedians resembled the Partholonians, who, under their king Partholon, had come to Ireland before them, had fought the Fomorians—led then by the footless Cichol Grinchenghos—and had been destroyed by a plague. Partholon had murdered his father and mother in an unsuccessful attempt to take power in his original homeland. As in the case of King Arthur, Partholon's history was marred by the story of his wife Dealgnaid's affair with one of his servants, Togda. The Partholonians themselves, according to the twelfth-century Christian writers, had been the second invaders of Ireland, the first being pre-Flood followers of Noah's granddaughter Cesair or, according to others, the Irish eponym Banbha. Of this group, only Fintan, (the "Old White One") survived to live for many centuries and to bear witness to the past.

As for the Nemedians, much of their energy was spent in wars with the Fomorians, and eventually Nemed and 3,000 of his people died of a plague. After Nemed's death, the Nemedians were controlled by the Fomorians, who demanded excessive tribute of them. But with the help of Greek allies, the Nemedians, led by Nemed's son Fergus, were able to defeat their enemy. It was Fergus who killed the Fomorian king Conann. But few Nemedians survived an attack from the sea by another Fomorian king, Morc, son of Dele. After this battle, the Nemedians scattered in three groups. One group went to mainland Greece where they were enslaved and made to transport bags of soil on their backs from fertile land to rocky terraces in the hills. Thus the name Firbolg, or "bag men."

Along with other early peoples, the Gailioin and the Fir Dhomhnann, the Firbolg would eventually, upon their return, institute in Ireland the idea of the association of the sacred kingship and the fertility of the land. It was they who divided Ireland into provinces or "fifths." Another group of Nemedians, led by Fergus's son, escaped to Britain. The final group, led by Beotac, went to the northern Greek Islands. This group set about learning the mysteries of creation, including magic and druidry. According to some, a few of these people became so knowledgeable that they were deified as the Tuatha De Danann.

The rulers of the Tuatha De Danann when they came to Ireland were King Nuada (Nuadhu) and his warrior queen, Macha. They established their court at Tara. Nuada Argetlamhor is known as Nuada of the Silver Hand, whose Welsh counterpart in this aspect is the Lludd cognate, Nudd of the Silver Hand. Nuada was so named because after he lost his hand in a defeat of the Firbolg at the First Battle of Magh Tuireadh, the medicine god, Dian Cecht, replaced the lost limb with a silver version. It was the loss of the hand that led Nuada to transfer his crown to Bres, the handsome son of a Tuatha De Danann woman and the Fomorian king Elatha, and the husband of the fertility-goddess Brigid. When Bres's tyrannical ways led to his dethronement, he turned to the Fomorians for help.

Nuada was restored to the throne, but he gave up power to Lugh, who used his slingshot at the Second Battle of Magh Tuireadh to kill the much-feared Balor, a glance from whose "evil eye" could destroy armies. As Balor's eye was opened, Lugh cast his missile with such force that the eye was driven back through the skull of Balor, and thus its destructive power was unleashed upon the Fomorians. By that time, however, Balor already had killed Nuada as well as Macha, the warrior-goddess queen. With the defeat of the Fomorians, the Tuatha De Danann could afford to spare Bres in return for his teaching them the arts of agriculture. That Bres was so clearly related to fertility suggests that the myth of this war might have been derived from the same Indo-European theme of divine conflict as was the Norse myth of the battle between the Vanir and the Aesir. Hence the Fomorians seem to constitute at one time both the productive powers of fertility and the fearsome forces of destruction that exist side by side in nature.

The relationship between the one-handed Nuada and the battle-god Lugh calls to mind that between the Norse Tyr and Odin, and as examined in the discussion of that pantheon, this relationship seems to have very old roots. Further, several similarities between Odin and Lugh imply that both have some common Indo-European ancestor: Lugh was part Fomorian, just as Odin was part giant, and the name *Lugh* itself may well come from a Gaulish word for "raven," an animal explicitly linked to Odin. Finally, the association between Nuada and Lugh also may be the genesis of the Arthurian story of the fisher-king; *Nuada* may be derived from a word meaning "fisher," and the original myth seems to have had to do with a powerful war figure who comes to the aid of a maimed king.

Two other deities stand as particularly important figures in the Irish pantheon, figures of whom other tribal gods and goddesses were in some sense emanations. These primary deities are the Dagda as the tribal father and the Morrigan as the earth-mother/war-goddess, who was associated in triple form with Macha—a figure descended from the Gaulish horse-goddess Epona and one related to the British mare-goddess Rhiannon—and Bodb. The Dagda, father of Brigid, was a primary leader of the Tuatha De Danann; he was the protector of a magic cauldron of prosperity that had been brought from the city of Murias. The Dagda was known as "the Good." As the story goes, before a great battle the gods held a council of war during which each god announced his particular powers and intentions. When the Dagda's turn came he said, "I will do on my own all that you promise to do." In short, he is "the Good" because he was good at everything, assimilating the positive qualities of all the gods.

As for the Morrigan, she brings together the fruitful elements of a fertility goddess and the fear to be associated with a battle-goddess. Like her ancient Indian ancestor the goddess Devi she is at once mother and destroyer, goddess of life and of war. Celtic goddesses often exhibit voracious sexual appetites, and the Morrigan combines such amorous lust with bloodlust. The story is told of how Morrigan made sexual advances toward the Irish hero Cuchulainn, advances to which he did not respond; at his death she took vengeance for this insult by perching on his shoulder as his life blood flowed from him. This story resembles the incident in the ancient Sumerian epic of *Gilgamesh*, in which the advances of the great goddess Inanna or Ishtar are refused by the mortal hero Gilgamesh. The combination of fertility and destructive power manifested in the Morrigan is associated with the identification of goddess and "sovranty" in Irish mythology; cropfields and battlefields both do their part to make up the country, and the Morrigan has power over both.

THE MILESIANS

The Tuatha De Danann were not to reign forever over Ireland. In the land of Spain, a man called Ith saw Ireland from his father's tower. He sailed there with ninety of his followers and was met by Mac Cecht, Mac Cuill, and Mac Greine, who asked him to mediate their attempt to divide the rule of Ireland following the death of Nuada. When the Tuatha De Danann suspected that Ith himself wished to rule, they killed him and shipped him back to Spain. In Spain, Golamh—better known later as *Milesius* (meaning "soldier"), Mil, or Mile of Spain—led a force to Ireland with his wife Scota when he learned of the death of his nephew. Mil died on the way to Ireland and Scota was killed in battle there. The defeat of the Tuatha De Danann was to be accomplished by the sons of Mil. These invaders are said to have been the first Celts in Ireland.

At first the Milesians were prevented from landing by a cloud of mist conjured up by the Tuatha. They circled the island three times and finally were able to land at Inber Stainge on the Thursday before the first of May in the Year of the World 3500. The sons of Mil proceeded to Tara. On the way they met the three queens, who were eponyms of Ireland—Banbha, Fodla, and Eiru—who convinced the invaders to preserve these names of their island forever. This the sons of Mil promised before meeting with the three kings, Mac Cuill, Mac Cecht, and Mac Greine, at the royal court of Tara. It was decided that the Milesians should return to sea and invade again, and that the defeated party would depart and not return. As the Milesians attempted their second landing, the Tuatha used their druidic magic to cause a great storm and mist, and many of the invaders died. But, led by three sons of Mil—Eber, Eremon, and the poet-warrior Amairgen (Amergin, Amhairghin)—the Milesians defeated the Tuatha. Mil's wife Scota died in the battle of Sliab Mis, and the three Tuatha queens and kings were killed at the battle of Tailltiu. The Milesians then divided Ireland; Eber ruled the south, Eremon the north.

In *The Book of Invasions*, the coming of the Milesians is made somewhat biblical. Their journey involves a movement from Scythia to Egypt and then to Spain and Ireland and is reminiscent of the Book of Exodus. But Irish tradition prevails once the story of the landing begins. We are told that it was the power of the poet-warrior-judge Amairgen that was able to overcome the druidic power of the Tuatha. It is he who first touched Irish soil and he who sang the song of the new Gaelic Irish order, a song in which he took all the universe into his Gaelic self. He arrived from the sea of nonexistence and sang into existence Irish history itself.

Although defeated, the Tuatha De Danann were given the "lower half" of Ireland, which has been taken to mean that they retired under the leadership of the Dagda to underground homes in mounds and hills called *sidhe*. For himself, the Dagda took the Brug na Boinneon on the river Boyne in Leinster. The Tuatha are said to exist still in Ireland as *sidhe* or fairies or earth-spirits. Mostly invisible now, it is said that sometimes they can be seen by mortals on Midsummer Eve. The fairies of later Irish and British traditions seem to have been derived in part from myths related to this tale of the banishment of the Tuatha De Danann to their new home under the earth.

2

DEITY TYPES

The pantheon of any given mythology is composed of gods and goddesses who should be recognizable as mythological types—in at least some of their aspects—to followers of other systems. The supreme being, the great goddess, the trickster, the dying god, the thunder-god, and several other archetypal deity figures are found in the mythologies of Greece, India, Egypt, Mesopotamia, and elsewhere. They also are found in Northern Europe and the British Isles, and we shall examine Celtic and Germanic manifestations of such archetypes that have as much to tell us through their central common features as they do through their superficial differences.

The specific and varied characteristics and actions of particular deities reflect the different cultures from which they spring; the underlying similarity between gods of one culture and those of others, however, suggests an archetypal significance, a set of spiritual or psychological tendencies that, like our universal physical characteristics, express what it is to be human. For instance, when Jews, Christians, or Muslims confront the Hindu concept of Brahman—the absolute which informs and transcends existence—they find themselves in a complex and foreign mythological system involving apparently bizarre embodiments of the absolute such as the bloodthirsty Kali or the cosmic, sleeping Visnu who contains the universe in his mouth. Yet those who look more carefully cannot help recognizing in Brahman something of the sense of the ultimate reality expressed in their own concept of god. In short, that mystery of the absolute—the ultimate source which is impossible to know or to understand—is expressed mythologically in the particular cultural masks or metaphors provided by Hinduism or by the Abrahamic religions, or indeed, by those of the ancient Greeks and the Norse people.

Brahman belongs to Hindus, just as the Great Mystery belongs to the Plains Indians of North America; but the sense of mysterious existence—unknowable and unending—that is the archetype, and that gives rise to these masks and metaphors, belongs to the species as a whole. It makes sense, therefore, in a comparative cultural study of the very ancient and very foreign deities of the British Isles, to make use of an archetypal framework as a basis for perspective and as an aid to recognition.

The Supreme Being

The supreme male deity emerged as the creator and king of the universe concurrent with the establishment in the human world of a strong political and social patriarchy. This father-god is a metaphor for the dominance of the father in the home and of the male in the marketplace, on the battlefield, and in the palace. In many parts of the world, he is associated with the dominant heavenly body, the life-giving but sometimes brutal and unapproachable sun. He is Zeus, Indra, and Yahweh. Sometimes he is the sky itself, the thunderbolt-bearing moisture provider. His wife is usually the earth-mother—once perhaps the dominant deity, now distinctly subservient to her husband—on whose receptive fecundity the sky-god sprays his life-giving seed. The sky-god's home on high suggests "higher laws," and it is these laws that the authoritarian and often punishing father-god imposes upon his human and sometimes wayward "children."

Celtic Supreme Beings

THE DAGDA

In the British Isles, several versions of this Indo-European supreme being are identifiable. The primary Irish version is the god known as the Dagda, the "good god," the Eochaidh Ollathair or "Father of All." The son of the great-goddess Danu of the Tuatha De Danann, the Dagda is the god of fire as well, and his priests are the druids. He is perhaps the same as the Romano-Celtic Dis Pater from the continent, although it may well be that the Irish equivalent of Dis Pater as a god of death would be, as suggested above, the god Donn or the god Bile. The Dagda carries a huge club, one end of which rests on wheels. He plays a magic harp, the harp being always a symbol of the power of the arts and music and of Ireland as a nation. When the Tuatha De Danann were defeated by the Milesians, the Dagda sent his surviving followers to the *sidhe*, where they would evolve into fairies. The Dagda himself gave up his position as supreme deity and disassociated himself from the world.

CERNUNNOS

An equivalent of the Dagda in parts of Britain and Gaul was Cernunnos, known as the "horned god," the bull or stag god, who also carried a large club and was associated with the care of animals. There is perhaps a connection between this figure and Pan and the satyrs of the Greco-Roman world, as well as with the horned huntsman of later British folklore and even the white-horned bull of the Irish epic, the *Tain Bo Cuailnge*. The horn in most Indo-European mythologies suggests the phallus and fertility—especially when associated with the hunt and animals.

Germanic Supreme Beings

ODIN

When the Scandinavians came to the British Isles, they brought with them the Norse high god and "father of all," Odin, clearly a development or close mythological relative of the Germanic Wodan. With the goddess Jord, he produced the great god of thunder, Thor, a god who seems to share some of the qualities of the supreme god, reminding us, like Odin, of other Indo-European divine patriarchs such as Indra and Zeus. Odin's tryst with Jord is of particular note from a comparative perspective, as *jord* means "earth," and thus here we see the common archetypal union of warring sky-god with the agriculturally based earth-goddess. Odin was a lusty god, and he took many lovers and concubines, notably the giantess Grid and the goddess Rind. Odin is—in various sources—specifically noted to be the father of at least ten divine sons (Thor, Balder, Vidar, Vali, Heimdalr, Hodr, Bragi, Tyr, Meili, and Hermod), and in various sagas many heroes and kings were said to have descended from him.

Odin is a god of war. His companions are the Raven and the Wolf, who eat those killed in battle; his servants are the Berserkrs, who fight in frenzy and without fear, and his handmaids are the Valkyries, the choosers of the battle slain. Dead heroes are welcomed to and live with Odin in Valhalla. Odin had particular favorites among heroes. To Sigmund the Volsung he gave a magic sword, thrusting it himself into the tree support of the hero's hall. At the time of Sigmund's death, Odin caused the sword to shatter and be remade into a sword for Sigmund's great son Sigurd. Odin was a "hands on" god; he advised his human vassals in battle. One time, in remarkable similarity to the

Visnu avatar Krsna of the Indian *Bhagavadgita*, he became the guiding battle charioteer of a human hero, in this case the Danish King Harald Wartooth.

In the Norse poem *The Havamal*, or "Words of the High God," Odin reveals a less warrior-like aspect, telling how he was pierced by a spear and hanged willingly on a tree in a sacrificial rite leading to wisdom. This high god thus reveals shamanistic qualities, and indeed, Odin's thirst for secret knowledge was such that his behavior borders on the demonic; these aspects of his character will be detailed in our discussion of trickster gods. Spears, hanging, and fire often were associated with Odin, especially in Scandinavia. Apparently the burning of those heroic dead who were destined for Valhalla was important to worshipers of Odin, as, according to some reports, were ritual stabbings and the sacrifice by hanging of both humans and animals. Odin was sometimes called the God of the Hanged. The self-sacrifice hanging aspect of Odin's own story—including the mention of the spear—is, of course, of particular interest to Christians.

TIW/TYR

It would be profitable to mention at this point that the Odin of Norse myth was something of a usurper in the Germanic pantheon, and to note that by the historical period the later, demonic trickster god Odin had supplanted fully the primeval Germanic sky-god Tiw. Tiw is an ancient diety of counsel and troth, far older than Wodan, but almost entirely eclipsed by the younger god by the time that Germanic myth came to be recorded. A one-handed god was worshiped in the North from at least the Bronze Age. Tiw is known to have been worshiped in Britain by Germanic Roman soldiers, and the etymological relationship between "Tiw" and "Tuesday" has significant parallels in a number of Northern European languages. Tacitus remarks that Tiw is to be associated with Mars, the Roman god of war, which explains why the Roman Dies Martalis became the Old English Tiwesdaeg ("Tuesday"). The early Germanic name Tiwaz is cognate with the Greek Zeus, the Latin deus, the Sanskrit deva, the Lithuanian dievas, and the Old Irish dia, all meaning "god" and all thought to derive ultimately from an Indo-European term *dieus* or *deywos*, meaning "god," "sky," and "daylight." Hence Tiw is descended from the original Germanic form of the most powerful deity, god of sky and of battle as well as of law and of troth.

THOR

It is important to keep in mind that, although Odin was called the father of the gods, he was not always and in all places regarded as the most important of the Norse gods, nor did he comprise all aspects of the supreme being. There is evidence that the fertility figure Freyr was considered the chief god among the Swedes, for example, and it is without doubt that Odin's son Thor was more popular than his father in certain regions and constituencies. The Norse Thor certainly was considered to be the primary pagan competitor of Christ

during the conversion of the Scandinavian peoples, and a number of tales illustrate this adversarial role: the Christian Norwegian King Olaf Tryggvason
was said to have engaged in a battle of strength with Thor, while one Icelandic devotee of the god of thunder delivered to a Christian priest Thor's
challenge to Christ to settle their conflict by means of single combat; the response of the Prince of Peace is not recorded.

In his Norse form the thunderer was often denoted Oku-Thorr, the prefix
of which Snorri suggests is derived from *aka*—that is, "to drive." Thor is thus
designated the charioteer god, and his association with a sky-cruising wheeled
vehicle might be compared to representations of the sun-god in many cultures. Thor's travel in his chariot specifically associates the deity with thunder, however, and poetic accounts of Thor's arrival often take up the theme of
the tumultuous tempest that surrounds him as he journeys. This relationship
seems to have been a commonplace in the far north, so much so that a number of Lappish loanwords for thunder seem to have been derived from the Old
Norse *reith*, which denotes both wheeled transport and thunder. Furthermore,
Thor's symbol and weapon—his hammer—is both etymologically and symbolically linked to lightning. The fiery red of his beard has been linked both
to lightning and to the red sky that can foretell a storm at sea. Thor was also
the protector of the gods, and his method of dispatching their enemies was
awesome and straightforward, as well befits a lightning god; indeed, the image
of his hammer flashing through the sky not only serves to explain the origin
of thunderbolts but also provides a mythic parallel to their destructive power.
Thor was therefore at one time both protector and destroyer.

The Great Goddess

The goddess archetype is one of our oldest, having very likely taken form in
the Paleolithic in the context of earth as a fertile mother. What we know of
this ancient and perhaps supreme goddess comes to us primarily by way of
Upper Paleolithic (30,000–7,000 BCE) and early Neolithic figurines, cave
paintings, and statuary. Stylized and literal depictions of female genitalia are
commonplace in this material, as are depictions of childbirth. The caves
where so many of the paintings and figurines in question have been found are
themselves appropriate symbols of the mother's womb, to which shamans and
others perhaps retreated for some sort of physical or spiritual renewal. We also
find indications of an early female power in the later myths of such deities as
the Native American Spider Woman, the Indian Devi in her many forms,
and the Celtic great goddess. It seems likely that the early earth-mother goddess relinquished much of her power with the arrival into Southern Europe,
Iran, and India of patriarchal Aryan warrior cultures in the Bronze Age. A
metaphor for this development is contained in the Vedic Indian myth of
Indra's defeat of the dragon-like Vrtra and his frightening mother Danu, as
well as in the Mesopotamian tale of the god Marduk's defeat of the chaotic
mother-monster Tiamat. We also find clear indications of the new order in

the better known Greek and Norse mythologies, where gods like Zeus and Odin, if sometimes pestered or challenged by goddesses, are nevertheless clearly dominant. Moreover, the ascent in Norse mythology of the Aesir war-gods over the Vanir fertility gods serves to underscore a concurrent patriarchal ascent. It thus seems fair to say that the early emergence, and later diminishing of the goddess in her many cultural representations, reflects the early power of women and their later subjection by men.

Celtic Mother Goddesses

DANU AND DON

The insular Celtic great goddess has already been mentioned. With apparent connections to the ancient Vedic Danu, the Irish Danu (sometimes Anu, Ana, or Dana), who in Wales is Don, is the mother of all. Danu is the matriarch of the mysterious Tuatha De Danann or children of Don. Little is known of the particular aspects of this goddess. The Welsh Don is married to Beli, god of death, son of Manogan. Her brother is Math, the god of wealth, and her father was the patriarch Mathonwy. The connection with the Vedic Danu or "Heavenly Waters" is indicated by the association of Danu/Don with the northern English river Don and with the continental Danube. The fact that the Irish Danu's husband was perhaps Bile, the god of death, indicates her association with the generative process of which an integral aspect is death. As the apparent mother of the great god the Dagda she somewhat resembles the ancient Greek goddess Rhae, the mother of Zeus, who, like the still earlier Gaia, is earth itself. In this connection it is notable that there are mountains in Kerry County, Ireland, called the "Paps of Anu." This name suggests the generally animistic aspect of Celtic religion, the essence of animism being the understanding that all aspects of the world are literally alive in some sense— *animated* by the numinous. The cult of the mother-goddess was apparently always important among continental Celts and the tradition of the mother remained strong among the insular Celts as well.

The Tripartite Goddess

The tradition of the tripartite deity is common among both the continental and insular Celts. There is strong archeological evidence in various parts of Britain of a tripartite Romano-Celtic mother-goddess, or *Deas Matres*. These female figures, like many goddess replicas in Rome, are depicted as nursing mothers or as bearers of the fruits of the earth. The *Deae Matres* are clearly related as well to the single nursing figures or *Deae Nutrices* also found in figurines in Britain. The stone figures of tripartite goddesses in Britain are almost always associated with tripartite figures of hooded dwarflike figures or *genii cucullati*, presumed to be representative of fertility. The frequent presence of tripartite deities and of the number three in general in Celtic mythology seems to suggest a stong sense of the sacred and magical character of that number.

BRANWEN, RHIANNON, EPONA

In addition to Danu/Don, we find described in the Second Branch of the Welsh *Mabinogi* Branwen, who, along with Rhiannon and Aranrhod, is called "one of the three great ancestresses of Britain." It was Branwen, daughter of Lyr, who was mistreated by her Irish husband King Matholwch, causing her brother Bran to invade Ireland. But Branwen and the Irish eponyms Eiru, Fodla, and Banbha are seemingly more mortal than immortal. All of these heroines die. They live on as goddesses to the extent that they stand symbolically for the Celtic lands from which they spring. Rhiannon, too, is somehow both goddess and human. In her goddess form she is associated with nature, sexuality, and fertility. Riding across Wales on her white horse, she is reminiscent of an older continental Celtic mare-goddess called Epona, the only Gaulish goddess to have been worshiped in Rome. Epona was a horse-goddess and according to some she was concerned with the soul's journey after death. Like the Greek Artemis, she is also associated with the woods.

MACHA, MORRIGAN

Another Irish goddess of importance is Macha, mentioned earlier, who in her human form as Nemed's wife is killed in battle. Macha is essentially interchangeable with Morrigan or Morrigu, who, like Pallas Athena, was a great warrior. Morrigan helped the Tuatha De Danann in the Battles of Magh Tuireadh.

MEDB AND FERTILITY KINGSHIP

Still another form of the great battle-goddess was Queen Medb (Medbh, Maeve) of Connaught, wife of many kings, with whom in some stories sexual union was a ritual prerequisite to kingship. The idea of the sexual union of the king with the goddess, who literally represented the kingdom, is an important indication of and aspect of the Celtic concept of the sacred kingship. We saw this earlier in connection with the god Lugh as a sacred solar king in union with Ireland personified as "Sovranty."

This concept of sexual union between the king and a goddess, who represents the land itself and the realm, is an ancient one. It is evident in the figure of Sri-Laksmi or "Prosperity" in India and her union with Indra and/or Visnu, and in the Sumerian-Babylonian union of Dumuzi/Tammuz and the goddess Inanna/Ishtar. It is worth noting, given the character of Queen Medb, that the goddess, who is literally "Sovereignty," often takes the form of a prostitute or of a hag who becomes beautiful only when joined with the king.

Germanic Mother Goddesses

NERTHUS

The Northern European invaders of the British Isles brought with them an ancient mother-goddess tradition. As we have seen, the Roman historian

Tacitus reported the existence of an earth-mother called Nerthus, a mysterious goddess associated specifically with fertility who, like the Greek Artemis, was never supposed to be seen in her nakedness by human eyes. In fact, it seems very likely that the chief deity among the early Germanic peoples was none other than the great earth-mother—the great goddess known in almost every civilization throughout the world—echoes of whom in her various manifestations make up the bulk of the later Norse goddesses. Frigg, Freya, Sif, Idun, and even the primordial Jorth are simply aspects of the same great goddess. As war-gods replaced nature goddesses as chief among the pantheon, the great goddess seems to have been split up into lesser component parts.

The deification of Mother Earth always dies hard, however, and we know that well into the Christian Anglo-Saxon period charms invoking her were widespread. More evidence of the survival in Britain of an earth-goddess also exists. First, the fact that the Angles were named by Tacitus as one of the seven tribes that worshiped Nerthus—though hardly conclusive on its own—suggests that Nerthus might have traveled to England during the Anglo-Saxon migration. Second—and far more conclusive—is the fact that dozens of fertility figures representing the fecund attributes of the earth-goddess are strewn throughout Britain and Ireland. Known in English as Sheela-na-gigs, these fertility idols usually have wildly exaggerated labia that they are holding open for examination and perhaps copulation. The sexual organs of these figures recall the monstrously enlarged erect phalli associated with male fertility gods (and notably with Freyr), and indeed, in at least one English example the Sheela-na-gig is accompanied by a half-human follower with his penis engorged. Figures very similar to Sheela-na-gigs survive from Stone Age times; what is most significant and perhaps surprising is that a number of Anglo-Saxon and even Norman churches are decorated with such idols.

FRIGG

More important than Nerthus to the literary record was the maternal Frigg, a later version of the Germanic Frija. Frigg was the daughter of Fjorgyn, the goddess of earth, who is very likely a version of the old Nerthus. Like other ancient fertility goddesses—the Ugaritic goddess Astarte and the Greek Aphrodite, for instance—Frigg is associated with what can be assumed to be the phallic fish. The word *Friday* comes from Frigg and, very likely, the tradition of eating fish on that day, a tradition later assimilated by Christians. Included by Snorri in the Aesir, Frigg was the great-god Odin's wife, and she shared her consort's knowledge of the future. Frigg is associated with weaving, and this aspect emphasizes both her role as mother-goddess and her abilities as a seeress: she who weaves is one who knows the art of the Norns. Frigg was the mother of the dying god Baldr, and this connection of great mother and dying god is noteworthy given the context of Christian conversion. Frigg is honored as queen of heaven in spite of the trickster-god Loki's malicious accusation of her infidelity to her husband. It seems likely that any implication of promiscuity on the part of this goddess suggests a connection with fertility.

FREYA

Not surprisingly, Frigg-Frija is sometimes confused with Freya, the much better known great warrior-goddess of the Norse. As we have seen, Freya was the most important fertility goddess of the Vanir, the ancient race of nature deities who eventually joined with the ruling Aesir. It has been noted that Frigg and Freya are two faces of the same goddess, and that this two-part deity reflects the combination of the lover and the mother facets of the great goddess. Like the Greek Demeter and the Egyptian Isis, Freya spent much time searching for and weeping for a lost loved one—in this case her husband Od. It is said that she rode through the forests on a wild boar—like her brother, the main fertility god Freyr—or in a chariot pulled by huge cats. She could be called upon for help in affairs of the heart, and she taught some of the Aesir the forbidden magic of *seidr*.

Freya is clearly a love goddess, and as in the case of Frigg, Loki accused her of sexual promiscuity; in this instance the accusation is justified, of course, and again, the overt sexuality of this goddess emphasizes her association to fertility. The myth of the Necklace of the Brisings is just one example of Freya's promiscuous behavior; moreover, the Aesir's willingness to bargain her—as well as the sun and the moon—away in the myth of Asgard's Wall underscores her association with the summer solstice, and thus with spring, with planting, and with vegetative fecundity. Like the lord of Valhalla himself, Freya took a share of the battle dead, and thus, as ever, is burgeoning life linked to the rot of death. Further, also like Odin—her most apt pupil in the forbidden arts—Freya has connections with the world of the dead and with runic knowledge, and is, therefore, thought by many to have connections with shamanic traditions.

The Dying God

It has become commonplace among comparatists to associate the theme of the lost loved one in the great-goddess myths with that of the dying god, the god becoming the planted seed in the fertility cycle. Sir James Frazer, in his classic *The Golden Bough*, is particularly responsible for the fertility connection—one that has been questioned by more recent scholars on the grounds of sketchy evidence. It should be noted, however, that there appears to have been a tradition in the Middle East, the southern Mediterranean, and the Fertile Crescent of dying fertility gods. The Phrygian Attis and the Greek Adonis and Orpheus die violently and then revive in one way or another—usually as vegetation; their deaths are often celebrated in the fall, their revivals in the spring. There is a disputed tradition that the ancient Sumerian and Babylonian shepherd-god Dumuzi/Tammuz, the sometime consort of

Inanna/Ishtar, was killed and sent to the underworld and then allowed to return for part of the year to bring fertility to the earth. There are Canaanite stories of the god Baal, who dies and is brought back by his sister Anat to ensure the return of vegetation in the spring. In Egypt, the grain-god Osiris is murdered and dismembered by his brother and revived by his sister-wife Isis.

The Christian figure Jesus likewise dies, although he would "let this cup pass him by" if his Father would allow it; he goes meekly to his death in the end, however, and is sacrificed upon the Cross. After his death he is mourned by the Virgin Mary, who for the comparatist is a mother-goddess figure. Jesus returns from his three-day sojourn in the land of the damned transformed by his sacrifice, and through his transformation he offers the hope of redemption to his followers. In the Northern European traditions we find contrasting versions of the dying god, some of which seem to adhere to the fertility pattern described above and some of which seem to draw upon shamanistic rituals concerned with the acquisition of forbidden knowledge. In Norse mythology the death of Baldr participates in the former tradition, while Odin's sacrifice of himself to himself is indicative of the latter. Both of these myths were known in Britain, and that of Baldr clearly seems to have been influenced by the ancient Middle Eastern mythic tradition of death and rebirth introduced into Northern Europe in the form of the Christian Jesus. Both of these Germanic traditions were potent in their own right, however, and as Christianity influenced them, so they influenced Christianity. Long after the conversion of the Anglo-Saxons to Christianity was complete, for example, some significant overtly Christian images of Christ and the Cross displayed a distinctly Germanic mythic flavor.

Germanic Christ Figures

An important dying-god myth brought to the British Isles by the Northern Europeans was that of Baldr. Two somewhat conflicting versions of Baldr exist, however. Both emerge in the early thirteenth century. The Baldr described by Saxo Grammaticus is based on Danish sources and is more like a warlike human than a god. Snorri Sturlusson's *Prose Edda* Baldr, based on Icelandic sources, is a suffering god who seems likely to have been influenced by the story of Jesus's death. The more popular version in the British Isles was that of Snorri. Baldr has many traits that invite his comparison to Christ: he is beautiful, the fairest of the gods, and his shining face mirrors the spotless goodness of his heart. He is generous and loving, and he is the favored son of the all-father and the queen of heaven. His death causes all creation to mourn, but he emerges triumphant from the depths of the underworld to rule mankind in a new golden age.

The Death of Baldr

When Baldr the Beautiful, son of the high god Odin, had dreams foreshadowing his destruction, the gods intervened to save him. His mother, Frigg, convinced everything on earth to swear not to harm her son. Only one small plant, the mistletoe, was overlooked. Believing Baldr was now immune to any threat, the gods enjoyed throwing things at him for fun. But the trickster Loki, in female disguise, learned from Frigg of the neglected mistletoe. He plucked it out of the earth and convinced the blind god Hod (Hodr) to throw the plant at his brother Baldr. Loki guided the god's hand, and the mistletoe struck its victim in the heart, causing instant death.

The gods were bitterly sad at the loss of so wonderful a companion, and Odin realized that Baldr's death foreshadowed the death of all the gods. Frigg called on a volunteer to travel to Hel to bring her son back. Another of her sons, Hermod, agreed to go. He rode to Hel, found Baldr seated in a place of honor, and learned that the god could return to earth only if all things, living and dead, would weep for him. When Odin learned the news of his son, he called all things to weep. And all things did weep—all but a giantess, the disguised Loki, in fact, who snarled, "Let Hel keep her own." And so Baldr was to remain in the land of the dead until the world would revive after its destruction.

The Germanic Vison of the Warrior Christ and the Anglo-Saxon The Dream of the Rood

Baldr would return in glory after Ragnarok, and in this he resembles the Christ described in *The Dream of the Rood*. This is an Anglo-Saxon poem of perhaps the ninth century; it is preserved in only one manuscript, the tenth-century *Vercelli Book*, so-called because it resides in the cathedral library at Vercelli, Italy. No one can be sure how this early Medieval English book found its way to an Italian church. A popular theory, however, holds that the manuscript was in the company of its owner, a pilgrim on the way to Rome (Vercelli lies on the pilgrimage route), when the owner died, and thus the book remained in Vercelli. Whatever the reason for its location, it is only by the greatest of happy chances that this manuscript survives at all. This book contains a number of significant Old English texts, but *The Dream of the Rood* is the most important to us for two reasons: first, it describes a vision of Christ that has the scent of Germanic paganism about it; second, portions of this poem are inscribed upon the face of the Ruthwell Cross, a large, standing stone cross in Dumfries, Scotland. The importance in Anglo-Saxon England of crosses such as that at Ruthwell will be discussed at some length in our examination of the Cult of the Cross in the section on the World Tree in chapter 3. Suffice it for now to note that the Ruthwell Cross is of particular interest to us because it combines a number of different cultural traditions: Christian imagery is surrounded by a Germanic runic inscription and Celtic interlace patterns. Most spectacularly, the runic inscription itself comprises a passage that describes the crucifixion of Christ in language almost identical to that in *The Dream of the Rood*.

The "rood" of the title of the poem is the Cross upon which Christ was crucified, and the dream is that of an unnamed narrator to whom the rood appears in a vision in the middle of the night. The dream vision is a common medieval literary motif (*Piers Ploughman* is perhaps the best-known English example of the genre), and it allows the author to employ the fantastic imagery and intuitive metaphors of dreams to allegorical advantage. *The Dream of the Rood* contains a number of elements of interest to us. First, the Christ of this poem seems more of a traditional Germanic mythic hero than the Christ of the Garden of Gethsemane. Second, unlike almost any other account of the crucifixion, here the Cross itself serves as the narrator of the main action; this personification of an inanimate object is known as *prosopopoiea*, and this act of the Rood telling its own story participates in a long Anglo-Saxon tradition of talking objects, most notably in riddles. Here the self-consciousness of the Cross allows for a graphic, first-person account of the crucifixion that makes the tremendous suffering of Christ seem real and all the more moving.

The Dream

Long ago a man dreamed that he saw a fearsome sight: before him stood aloft a mighty Cross, a rood, around which clustered all the men of this world and all the angels of heaven. This Cross shifted in appearance: At once gilded, bright and beautiful, adorned with gemstones, and then battered, bloody, and wounded, punctured with shafts, with blood streaming down the right side. And so the Rood was at once glorious and splendid and terrible and pitiable. The dreamer watched the Cross for some time, and eventually it spoke to him. It told him that once, long ago, men had attacked it at its home on the edge of the forest, and ripped it violently from its root; they dragged it to a hill and fashioned it into a cross, a gallows upon which the men might hang a criminal.

But it was no felon who was brought before the Cross; No! It was the savior of mankind, and though the Rood wished to fell its enemies, and trembled to embrace the Son of God, it dared not defy the will of God, and so it stood stock-still. Then the young hero stripped himself (Jesus Christ, God Almighty) and eagerly mounted the Cross, as he had it in his mind to redeem mankind. Up then was reared the Rood, and on it Christ the Lord. God and Tree were wounded together: nails were driven through the flesh of each, and their blood mingled. The men mocked them both together, and blood gushed from the side of the man as he sent forth His spirit. Then a shadow went forth, and all creation wept at the death of the King. Christ died on the Cross, and the Rood witnessed it all. Then followers came and took down the Savior's body, and placed it, cooling, in a tomb; they sang a song of mourning. The Rood was left alone, until it was felled and cast into a deep pit, where it remained until followers of Christ found it, and adorned the Cross of their Lord with gold and silver.

The Cross related this all to the dreamer so that he might impart the horror of the suffering of Christ—as well as the joy of his resurrection and of mankind's redemption—to all men. All should honor the Son of God now, in life, so that in death they need not fear his judgment. The dreamer found joy then in his contemplation of the Rood, and each day following his vision he looked forward to gazing upon it again once this life was finished. As his life neared its close and his friends all left this world, the dreamer thought of the bliss of the life to come, and thanked Almighty God for winning the great victory that gained for men an eternal home in heaven. The dreamer's joy then was like unto that of the angels of the Lord when

Christ—surrounded by the mighty host of souls He had freed from the torments of Hell—returned to the city of God crowned with victory and glory.

SCHOLARS HAVE LONG noted that universal mourning is common both to the Norse myth of "The Death of Baldr" and to the Anglo-Saxon poem *The Dream of the Rood*. The weeping of all creation for the gentle Jesus is not unlike the account of the Aesir's attempt to weep the equally gentle Baldr out of the land of Hel. For the Christian Anglo-Saxons, of course, Jesus on the Cross was to replace all of the dying gods of the past, and especially all of those who remained popular in the early Middle Ages in Britain and elsewhere; it is therefore not a little ironic that this dying god comprises several aspects of his predecessors. A further mythic parallel is to be found in the fact that the Christ—"the young hero"—of this poem is eager to mount his gallows to redeem mankind, just as Odin climbs upon Yggdrasill of his own volition, and with no reservations. The militaristic vision of Christ Triumphant also echoes the martial spirit of Germanic mythology. And as Odin on the tree sought the mysterious wisdom of the runes, so the Rood of Jesus reveals its mystical vision—including knowledge of heaven and hell and the joys of Christian resurrection—to the dreamer of *The Dream of the Rood*.

Odin Hangs Himself upon the World Tree Yggdrasill

In Norse mythology Odin and the other gods die at the world's end, but we are also told that they will return in a new world. Further, we are told in *The Havamal* of something like a ritual and sacrificial—although not permanent or irreversible—death of Odin when, as a god more concerned with forbidden wisdom than with battle, he undergoes a process of self-sacrifice, allowing himself to be hanged on the world tree Yggdrasill for nine days and nights. *Yggdrasill* means literally "Ygg's horse," and we know Ygg to be Odin. Thus Yggdrasill is more than the world tree; it is the "horse" Odin rides to death and back: it is his gallows, and by extension it represents the place of sacrificial execution for those dedicated to the god of the hanged. Christ sacrificed himself upon the Cross to transcend the mystery of his duality and to emerge fully divine, and thus to redeem mankind; Odin sacrificed himself upon his gallows to transcend the boundaries of traditional wisdom and ordinary experience and to emerge initiated in a rite that promised knowledge of the very secrets of life and death. These goals are quite distinct, and yet they both are concerned with the nature of mortality and with mystical transcendence.

The temptation is to compare Odin on the tree, pierced by his own spear, with Christ on the Cross, wounded by his enemies. But Odin's goal is not resurrection but rather an understanding of the runic secrets contained in the well guarded by the head of the wise Mimir at the end of one of the roots of Yggdrasill. Moreover, this hanging evokes pre-Christian rites of sacrificial hanging and burning associated with Odin/Wodan and earlier Indo-European gods; both Adam of Bremen and Tacitus provide us with records of sacrifice and ritual binding in groves dedicated to the god of the hanged and to the supreme Germanic god. Odin's sacrifice of himself to himself thus prefigures and validates the ritual sacrifice of victims to him by his priests. It is also doubtless a metaphor for the kind of ritual self-sacrifice practiced by shamans, who journey to the world of death to bring back knowledge and cures; indeed, Finnic shamans are known to have spent nine-night ritual vision quests in the branches of birch trees. Further, although the Odin of this myth is nothing like the Christ of the New Testament, Germanic descriptions of the death of Christ sometimes borrow elements of the myth of the Odinic battle hero. Where the traditional image of Christ's death emphasizes his human suffering and acknowledges his very human desire to avoid pain and death if at all possible, the Germanic Christ is a young hero, a warrior anxious to do battle and to die gloriously, like any good follower of the one-eyed god of the hanged.

The Trickster God

The trickster is a commonly expressed archetypal figure. In India he is sometimes embodied in the Krsna who steals the clothes of the Gopis. In Greece he is the often-mischievous Hermes who steals Apollo's cows and, in the form of the ithyphallic *herm*, is associated both with fertility and his ability to penetrate the underworld. In Native America he is the highly sexed Coyote or the creative Raven among countless other figures. In Africa he is, also among many others, Ananse the Spider.

Whatever form he takes—and it is important to remember that the trickster can take any form he pleases, even either gender at will—this figure is at once self-centered, amoral, possessed of seemingly insatiable appetites, and prone to particularly disgusting deeds. He is a grown-up infant who has no qualms about cheating or lying or stealing. Yet he is clearly the mythic ancestor of the shaman, who can travel between the world of humans and that of the spirits below. And, above all, he is creative—sometimes maliciously so, but always creative. In some stories he even assists the creator-god. As an amoral figure who speaks more to our animal than our spiritual nature, the trickster perhaps reflects, as Carl Jung suggests, "an earlier rudimentary stage of consciousness."

Germanic Tricksters

LOKI AS TRICKSTER

Loki is the foremost trickster figure of the Norse myths, although Odin certainly displays some of the elements of the trickster from time to time. Although Loki is more than simply a trickster, it is those very elements of chaotic mayhem archetypically linked to the trickster that render Loki indispensable to the fulfillment of the preordained fate of the Norse gods. In order to set the stage for the cataclysmic climax of Ragnarok, it is necessary to flesh out the conflicting and conflating mythic facets of Loki's complex character. In simplest terms, we could fairly say that myths involving Loki contain four main themes, although some contain contrasting themes simultaneously. In some myths Loki appears as a merry prankster, a figure of mischief and practical jokes; in some—such as his journey to Utgard with Thor—he is a favored boon-companion to Thor or to Odin. In many he gets the gods into trouble, then—usually under threat of pain—saves them by means of his wits. In the later, darker myths, Loki's evil side becomes more fully realized and his relationship with the gods grows ugly. That his role among the gods should take such a turn should come as no surprise, considering his demonic offspring, and indeed even his most harmless pranks usually seem driven by a malicious undercurrent.

Loki as Merry Prankster: The Shearing of Sif

The sly one smiled as he glided across the room to Sif's bed; her hair rippled across her pillow like a field of wheat swaying in the wind. Quickly the trickster took out his blade, and just as swiftly had he harvested her sheaf of dancing gold. As he made his way from her chamber he laughed low and long, but quietly. In the morning Thor awoke to his wife's screams and sobs, and saw before him the stubble that remained of her glorious mane. It didn't take long to determine the culprit—who else would have dared—and soon Loki writhed in the clutches of the angry thunderer. The prankster seemed far less merry now, and he only escaped with his skin when he promised to enlist the help of the dwarfs in replacing all Sif had lost, strand for strand and gold for gold.

In the caverns of Svartalfheim Loki found the dark elves he sought, the sons of the dwarf Ivaldi, and there he asked the favor of new hair for Sif; he offered little but the gratitude of the gods, but he convinced the dwarfs that the bargain was in their interest, and they consented. They soon fired up their forge and laid out their tools, and before long their task was completed; the hair they produced was so fine, however, that much of the metal they were working was left over, and so they forged on, so as not to waste heat and gold. When they were finished they presented Loki with three gifts to gain the friendship of Asgard: new hair for Sif, for Odin the spear Gungnir, and for Freyr *Skidbladnir*. Leaving with more promises on his lips, Loki thought that he might return safely home; but as he neared the edge of Svartalfheim, it occurred to him that he might turn this day to his greater advantage.

Loki therefore soon retraced his steps until he found the abode of Brokk and Eitri, two more brother dwarfs. They lusted after the treasures he carried, and they agreed to his challenge to make three better items: if they were to win, the lot would be theirs, and Loki would give him his head into the bargain. They soon were hard at work, Eitri working the gold and Brokk handling the bellows, with orders not to pause for the slightest moment. Three treasures Eitri forged, and three times Loki, in the form of a fly, bit the nose of Brokk. Twice Brokk ignored his sting, but the third time he faltered, and Eitri's work was almost ruined; almost, but not quite, and that treasure was the hammer Mjollnir, to be the weapon of the god Thor and a scourge to all giants. It was flawed in that the handle was too short (thus far did Loki succeed in distracting Brokk), but it was in every other way perfect. The dwarfs also sent Gullinbursti, the golden boar which was to serve as Freyr's mount, and the arm ring Draupnir for the great god Odin. Brokk then made his way to Asgard with Loki to take the trickster's head.

The sly god made his way back to the abode of the Aesir, then, with his arms full of treasure and a dwarf in tow. He thought to find a reception warmer than his departure had been. The gods were indeed impressed by the treasures with which he presented them: Sif's new golden hair took root at once, and shone and shimmered as ever before; Odin's new spear Gungnir would always find and slay its target; Freyr's new ship *Skidbladnir* was as roomy and as fully equipped as could be, and yet folded up into his pocket. Brokk's treasures were even greater, however, and the Trickster would rue that: Draupnir dropped eight like rings from itself every ninth night; Gullinbursti was the swiftest and boldest of mounts, and lit his own way through the dark; Mjollnir was the greatest of weapons, and would always return to its thrower, even though its handle be short. This last item swayed the balance, as it guaranteed the protection of the gods from their enemies. At this Loki fled, but Thor brought him cringing back to face his fate. Before Brokk could take Loki's head, however, the trickster noted that the head—and only the head—was part of the bargain; the dwarf might not touch his neck. When the gods agreed to this condition, Brokk thought to pay Loki for his lies and deceptions with needle and thread: he sewed together the lips of the sly god and left Asgard in temper. Loki himself ran and ran, and when he could free his lips, he screamed and sobbed; listening to the laughter of the gods at his humiliation, Loki plotted vengeance, and his mangled lips formed a ghastly shadow of a smile.

SIF IS A FERTILITY figure who had lost almost all significance by the Norse period, but her golden waves of hair surely represent ripe grain, and in this myth it is explicitly described as such: Sif's full head of hair is a field ready to be harvested, Loki is the reaper, and the stubbly pate he leaves in his wake reminds us of the cold, bare fields of late autumn. Thus it is notable that Loki both shears Sif's golden hair in this myth and lays claim, in his "Flything of the Gods," to having bedded her. Here the trickster is yet again associated with fertility and with sexuality, and this association seems an illicit and somewhat violent one. Although Loki acts the prankster in this myth and claims to mean no lasting harm, the laughter of the gods at his discomfiture and his resultant desire for vengeance foreshadow the enmity that is to come.

Into the Frying Pan but out of the Fire:
Loki and Otter's Ransom

Once upon a time Loki went wandering with Odin and Hoenir; it was their custom to do so from time to time. After walking all day the gods found themselves at the foot of a cascading waterfall. At the foot of this waterfall stood a pool, and on the banks of the pool lounged a sleepy otter, its eyes closed to the warmth of the westering sun, its claws firmly set in the salmon it had caught for its dinner. Now Loki thought to show his skill as a hunter: grasping a smooth stone from the near shore of the pool, the trickster launched it across the pool in a neat arc that brought it down right on top of the otter's head. The animal was killed instantly, and Loki quickly ran over to claim both fish and beast, crowing the whole while at his success. The others were nearly as pleased at the prospect of full bellies, and the gods continued on their way.

Just as night was falling the three travelers found themselves within sight of smoke rising from a nearby farm, and thinking to trade some of their bounty of food for a night's lodging, they made their way to the house. The gods were greeted cordially enough, but when their host saw the dinner his guests offered, he overpowered them with the help of his two strapping sons, and soon the three gods lay trussed like hogs on the floor of the farmhouse. It turned out that the owner of this farm—a man named Hreidmar—was the father of three sons, Fafnir, Regin, and Otter. It was the gods' bad luck that the third son lay dead on the kitchen table, and that they—his murderers—had brought him unbeknownst into the house of his father. It seems that this Otter sprang from a family steeped in magic, and that it had been his practice to spend whole days in his guise of fur, playing and fishing like an ordinary otter, and keeping his family well supplied with fresh fish. Now that family demanded vengeance for their loss, and they meant to take it in blood. Odin thought and spoke quickly, however, and he convinced Hreidmar to agree to take wergild in place of the three heads at his feet. Hreidmar's terms were steep, however: Odin and Hoenir would remain as hostages while Loki went to collect enough gold to stuff Otter's skin, and enough again to cover the stuffed skin completely. The gods quickly assented to these terms, and Loki ran off to get the gold.

Now Loki knew that nearby the dwarf Andvari had a forge with a large stock of gold, and he also knew that Andvari was a shape-shifter himself: he haunted the very waters nearby in the form of a pike. The sly god thus hurried off to the home of the god of the sea, from whose wife Ran he borrowed the net with which the goddess captured drowning men. Net in hand the Trickster sped off, and soon enough he had the pike he sought flopping and struggling at his feet. He forced Andvari back into his normal form, and then he threatened the dwarf with pain and death until the poor sobbing wretch had filled all the gold in his forge into two large sacks. Just as he turned to leave, however, Loki caught a glimpse of something bright in the dwarf's hand, and his own eyes glittered; he forced Andvari to open his fist. Curved around one finger was a slender ring, cunningly wrought and twisted as a serpent. The dwarf begged to be allowed this one trifle, but Loki was stern and cruel, and he left Andvari without a single scrap of gold to call his own. As the dwarf escaped the clutches of the god, however, he threw over his shoulder a curse: That ring and all that gold would bring only tragedy and woe to whomever it passed. Loki heard these words, but he didn't tremble; instead the god of mischief smiled at his luck.

Loki returned to Hreidmar's farm none too soon; the gods were stiff, sore, and anxious in their bonds, while the family of the slain Otter was all but out of patience. Loki had his host stuff the skin himself to be sure that there was no trickery, and then the gods—released from their ropes—help to cover every inch of the slain son's pelt. Meanwhile, moreover, Loki secretly had shown to Odin the serpent ring of Andvari, and the all-father took it for himself as a gift; the sly one mentioned no curse. As the gods finished their task, Hreidmar noted that one whisker still poked out from the glittering mound, and he threatened to take his due vengeance if the terms of their agreement were not met to the last wisp of gold. Grumbling, Odin placed his new ring over the offending whisker, and the gods stepped back out into the night. They soon turned, however, and Loki called back over the threshold the curse of the dwarf Andvari; the family of Hreidmar was silent in the face of these terrible words, but the all-father turned a stern gaze upon his treacherous companion. Loki smiled.

THIS MYTH REVOLVES around the concept of ransom paid for blood spilled, and thus is based on the Germanic concept of *wergild*. Wergild—literally "man-money"—is ransom paid for the loss of a kinsman and is meant to take the place of blood vengeance and thereby to help to curb devastating blood feuds between rival clans. This theme is commonly discussed in Anglo-Saxon literature, most notably in *Beowulf*. Cursed gold is a Germanic mythic commonplace, and recurs in *Beowulf* and in *The Nibelungenlied*, to name but two famous examples. The theme of the relationship between all-encompassing greed and such a curse is not uncommon, either; here Loki and Hreidmar both are unrelenting in squeezing the last drop of gold out of their prisoners, and this greed seems to trigger the curse in Loki's case and to reinforce it in Hreidmar's.

The story of Otter's ransom also illustrates several key facets of Loki's character: Here—as in his journey to Utgard with Thor—Loki is a boon companion to the gods, and shares their adventures and misadventures in equal measure. Yet in this myth—as in the story of the loss of Idun's apples—he is also the one who creates trouble for the gods in the first place, even if he doesn't mean to, and even if he does save them in the end. Moreover, Loki's antipathy toward Odin peeks out in this myth; indeed, Loki seems just as ready to put Odin in the way of Andvari's curse as he is to snare Hreidmar. Just as he took Otter and the salmon with one stone, it appears that Loki thought he might have the luck to trap two parties with the same curse of tainted gold. Finally, it should be noted that this myth ties the saga and cycles of the Germanic gods directly to the most famous of the Germanic heroic cycles. Fafnir, Regin, and the cursed ransom of Otter all figure in the heroic saga of Sigurd. The tales of Sigurd certainly were known in Britain; moreover, a scene from this specific myth—conflated with Christian imagery—appears on a cross slab in the churchyard at Maughold on the Isle of Man.

Loki the Gender-Bender: Rebuilding Asgard's Wall

After the war between the Aesir and the Vanir, the wall surrounding Asgard stood in ruins for many generations; the magic of the Vanir had brought it tumbling down, but none of the gods had wanted to expend the time and energy necessary to rebuild it. Still, this chink in the armor of the home of the gods made them all uncomfortable. One day a workman came to the gods and offered to rebuild their wall, taller, thicker, and stronger than before. His price was high, however; he demanded the goddess Freya for his wife, and the sun and the moon in the bargain. At first the gods were insulted, and refused the offer out of hand. But Loki argued that they should trick the builder and get something for nothing: They would agree to all of the mason's terms, but they would give him just six months to complete the work; all agreed that this was impssible, and the gods would end up with part of a wall instead of no wall at all, and for no fee. Odin told the builder these terms, and it was his turn to take umbrage; he knew the wall couldn't be rebuilt by one man in that time. Still, his lust for Freya was such that he agreed, if only the gods would allow him one horse to help him. At first the gods refused this counteroffer, but eventually Loki convinced them to accept the mason's terms; the task, he claimed, was still impossible.

The next day was the first day of winter, and the mason and his horse were up well before dawn. Each day was the same: the builder would haul stone all night with his mighty horse, and all day he would fashion and place pieces. Soon he began to make real progress, and the gods wondered at the wisdom of their bargain. They also began to suspect that only a giant could be as powerful and indefatigable as this mason, but Thor was away, and they had in any case granted the mason safe passage. Still, they began to fret. When three days were left before summer, the builder had all but completed his work and was busy finishing the final gate. Now the time had come for some action on the part of the gods, and they looked to Loki to extricate them from this mess. Odin made things very clear to the trickster: The builder must fail, or Loki must die. The sly one knew what he must do.

That night, as the builder went to gather stone, Loki appeared before his draft horse in the form of a mare. Soon the stallion had been enticed away, and the mason lost a whole night chasing the two horses across field and woods. The next day it was clear to the builder that he had been duped, and that he would not finish on time; in his rage he showed himself to be the stone giant the gods had suspected him to be, and they called on Thor. Thor had little time for niceties like safe passage, and soon Mjollnir's handle jutted out from the dead giant's skull. The gods had their wall back, and they kept Freya and the sun and the moon, to boot. But what of Loki? The trickster was missing for many months, and when he returned, he was leading a beautiful, eight-legged colt behind him. This was his offspring Sleipnir, which he had borne as a mare. It was the price Loki paid to save his skin, and to save the gods from the bargain for which he had argued. He gave the colt to Odin, and declared it to be the finest mount in the world: Sleipnir was swifter than any other horse, more powerful, and braver, and only this horse might take a rider to the very gates of Hel and back.

IN THIS MYTH once again Loki gets the gods into and out of a scrape; in addition, Loki here betrays the classic trickster traits of demonic shape-changing and gender-bending. The gods win their wall through Loki's wiles, and Odin gains Sleipnir, the greatest of horses; but this colt borne by Loki will soon enough bear two riders to Hel and back in the vain attempt of the Aesir to keep Baldr among them, and thus Loki's remark about his offspring's abilities foreshadow this coming fall of the gods. Horses represented power and life in the north, but they often were associated with death, and often were included in burials. Thus even while he is saving the gods from destruction and giving the most valuable of gifts to Odin, the import of Loki's actions belie his supposed friendship.

In other myths we have seen the giants portrayed as the forces of chaos and the natural powers of the icy north, and thus they are represented here, as well; in this myth, moreover, it is Loki's ambiguous position relative to these powers that is of interest to us. Natural forces such as the weather need not be seen as opposed to agriculture, of course—indeed, they are a necessary part of it—but in the short and fragile growing season of the far north often they might well seem to be a volatile ally at best, and indeed an often hostile enemy. In this case the giant mason wants Freya—goddess of fertility and natural fecundity—as well as the sun, which gives life to men, beasts, and crops, and the moon, which regulates tides and planting times. Clearly the giant's sexual lust for Freya is the narrative motive for his bargain (as it was Thrym's motive for stealing Thor's hammer), but the mythic subtext is again that of the forces of nature that seek to destroy civilization and the agricultural life that sustains it. Loki stands between the forces of civilization and those of chaos, and at the end of time, of course, his place will not be with the gods.

The Demon Reveals Himself: The *Flyhting* of Loki

As the events unfold that lead to the death of Baldr, Loki gradually transforms from a trickster—sometimes malevolent, sometimes merely fun-loving—into a demonic force fighting against the gods from within. His active role in the death of Baldr is overtly evil, and his refusal (in the guise of the giantess Thokk) to weep Baldr out of Hel—the lone refusal of all creation—is his refusal to repent or to make recompense for his crime. The gods are certain of his guilt before Loki comes to Aegir's hall to confront and to mock them, but it is here—in the full company of his enemies—that he boasts of his guilt. It is certain at this point that his transformation is as irreversible as Baldr's death, and it is just as certain that the gods will mete out vengeance upon him. Loki will suffer at their hands for as long as Baldr languishes in the court of Hel; that is to say, both will remain in bondage until Ragnarok.

OUR MAIN INTEREST with this episode concerns Loki's admission of guilt, and the transformation that the admission represents. But it is worth noting in passing that the practice of trading insults was a well-known Germanic literary motif, perhaps best exemplified in Anglo-Saxon literature by the verbal duel between Beowulf and Unferth; in Norse mythology it is best represented by this episode and by the exchange between Thor and Harbard the Ferryman. This practice is called *flyhting*, and it involves a competition of sorts in which each participant attempts to insult his opponent the most egregiously, usually by drawing upon embarrassing or taboo acts or failings on the part of that opponent or his or her kin. Therefore we have some reason to believe that Loki's charges are founded upon facts, and to suspect that this factual basis is why the gods are so humiliated by these accusations; indeed, we also can independently verify his charges in several cases, and thus even the uncorroborated charges seem more likely. When he accuses the goddesses of whorishness, the Vanir of incest, and Odin of womanly behavior, Loki is doing far more than simply casting aspersions; he is striking out at the most damning and most secret transgressions of his enemies. Thus this episode serves both to underscore Loki's new, demonic nature and to illustrate the failings and frailties of the gods—metaphorical weaknesses that represent their literal vulnerability in the coming cataclysm of Ragnarok.

ODIN AS TRICKSTER

Perfect as he may be in the role, Loki is not the only trickster in Asgard. Although he favors the ablest combatants and peoples his hall with them, Odin is no straightforward warrior himself; he often prefers to sate his blood lust by stirring up trouble among others rather than seeking it out first-hand, as his more conventional son Thor usually does. Odin is crafty and ambivalent, and is more often able to gain his way through wile than through force. Odin also is a practitioner of the arts of poetry and magic, and a hoarder of arcane and often dangerous wisdom. We already have made mention of the myth of Mimir, and of Odin's resort to necromancy to retain access to Mimir's wisdom. We also have examined Odin's willingness to crucify himself upon the gallows of Yggdrasil in order to gain forbidden knowledge, an act of self-sacrifice with many parallels to that of Christ. Another myth dealing with the same theme explains Odin's famous loss of one eye, and this myth also draws together the elements that associate Mimir, mead, and wisdom.

Fjolnir's Pledge: Odin Barters an Eye

The third root of Yggdrasil leads to Jotunheim, the land of the giants, and at its very foot lies the well of Mimir, which grants great wisdom to all who taste of it. Here Heimdalr, the watchman of the gods, has stored his trumpet Gjallarhorn until the day he must call upon it the blast that announces Ragnarok has come. Every day Mimir drinks the water of this spring from the Gjallarhorn; it is this practice that has lent to him his legendary wisdom. According to the prophecy of the seeress, Odin approached Mimir one day to ask for a taste of the water from his well; to this request Mimir consented, with the condition that Odin leave one eye on deposit at the bottom of the well as a pledge of good faith. This Odin did, and for this sacrifice he gained much wisdom; the more the god tasted of wisdom, however, the more he thirsted for it, and his gain at the well of Mimir left him more desperate for knowledge than ever. Odin's eye is concealed at the base of Mimir's spring, and hence this bargain has been known as "Fjolnir's Pledge"; Fjolnir is one of the many identities of Odin, and it means "the concealer."

ODIN'S SACRIFICE OF an "eye" at the "wellspring" underscores a widespread lexical relationship between the two terms; in Hittite, Armenian, Hebrew, and Arabic the same term may denote both objects, while similar relationships pertain in Persian, Old Iranian, Latvian, and Russian. It has been suggested that the basis for such associations might lie in a widespread conception of mythic fires deep within waters (Grendel's mere might serve as a Germanic example of this genre), or in notions of the power of sight as sparked by fire within the eye. Further, Odin's identity as a monocular war-god is paralleled in Northern European myth by the Celtic Lug, whose own one-eyed battle magic reminds us of the "battle-warp"of his son, Cuchulainn.

Odin also is associated with the forbidden form of sorcery known as *seidr*, a feminine "dirty magic" associated with the Vanir and their fertility cults, and considered unseemly and distasteful by more overtly masculine gods such as Thor. Its practice by a male smacks of effeminacy and sexual perversion, and seems to have been ample cause for summary execution; the violation of this taboo could result in being labeled *ergi*, the worst insult in Old Norse culture. Tacitus informs us that the executions of those accused of the practice of *seidr*—or indeed, that of active male homosexuality, which was seen as related—took the form of ritual drownings and interments in ponds and marshy places, the tannins in which have preserved many of these victims so well that their murders appear fresh to those who find the bodies today. It is noteworthy that these executions take a form quite similar to the ritual drownings of human sacrificial victims rendered unto Freyr at the temple at Uppsala, and this relationship underscores the fact that *seidr* was associated with the fertility gods of the Vanir rather than with the Aesir. Odin was clearly a practitioner of *seidr*, and moreover, as we shall see, he stood accused of gender-bending, as well.

Odin the Necromancer

The thirst for forbidden knowledge Odin first whetted at the well of Mimir became overwhelming upon the arrival of Freya from Vanaheim. Seduced both by her great beauty and by the temptation offered through her secret knowledge, Odin soon became the devoted pupil of Freya in the black arts of *seidr*. Soon the student proved the master, however, as Odin surpassed his teacher, always driven by his lust for more knowledge and more power. It was through these arts that he gained the power to revive Mimir's bodiless head, and it was through this obsession with secrets that he was driven to do so in the first place. Odin's enslavement to this quest even drove him to take the form of a woman as he practiced the wiles of a witch upon the inhabitants of the island of Samsey. Though Odin hoped to keep such transgressions to himself, nothing escaped the watchful eye of Loki, who would one day accuse him of his crimes in the full company of the gods.

THE NORSE ODIN thus represents a combination of some attributes of a classic warrior-god with the androgyny, shape-changing abilities and interest in magic associated with older fertility gods; moreover, his shamanistic folkloric qualities, his interest in converse with the dead, the bloodthirsty cult rituals, and his ambivalent trickster aspect underscore a demonic nature. This nature he comes by honestly both through descent from giants and through close association with the demonic trickster figure Loki.

Odin's Giant Blood

Odin's father was Bor, the son of Buri, who was the first being to emerge from the salty blocks of primordial ice licked by Audumla, the celestial cow; the gods thus trace their descent from Buri, who was called the first man. Bor's wife Bestla, however, who mothered Odin and his brothers Vili and Ve, was the daughter of Bolthor, who was one of the race of Ymir, which is to say that he was a frost giant. Thus the two great races of divine enemies, the gods and the giants, share a common bloodline.

THIS LINE OF DESCENT on Odin's maternal side raises an interesting point that is not directly addressed by the Norse sources: although the gods claim descent from Buri and the frost giants from Ymir, it is clear that—given the small pool of candidates for marriage in the earliest of times—some cross-breeding was inevitable, and indeed is documented in the case of Odin, the father of so many of the gods. That Odin's son Thor manifests so few of the demonic characteristics that might be associated with giants—and that he harbors such a violent animosity toward the entire race—belies this blood kinship, but Odin's eclectic character, in contrast, seems the more closely tied to that of his giant forebears. Indeed, Odin is fully half of the race of Ymir, while Thor might only carry half as much giant blood. This paradox is not limited to Germanic culture; similar cosmologies pitting feuding bands of closely related gods and demigods are common throughout Indo-European mythology, notably in the Indic, Irish, and Roman traditions.

The contrasting elements of Odin's personality reflect a Germanic mythic reality that mirrors an understanding of the world common to many early cultures: from the perspective of frail human beings in harsh environments, the forces of order are constantly at war with those of chaos, and in Norse mythology the gods represent the former while the giants are associated with the latter. Indeed, many of the giants began their mythic incarnations as specific nature deities having to do with places and forces such as mountains, winds, and storms. Thus, although the gods have authority over the wind, the sea, the land, and so on and use this authority largely for the benefit of humans, individual forces are controlled by the giants who are embodiments of those forces, and they strain and chafe under the yoke of order. Like nature itself, they are not necessarily good or evil, but are amoral; from the human perspective, however, these unleashed forces are a source of boundless terror, and the attempts of the gods to rein them in may be associated with the attempt of man to control his environment. Odin's complex and paradoxical character reflects his dual heritage, a heritage which, in turn, reflects the struggle in Germanic culture between these mythic forces. Odin's relationship with and attempts to tap into frightening and forbidden forces thus underscore a society's fear of uncontrollable powers of nature, as well as a desire to exert influence over them.

While it is true that, kinship and similarities aside, Odin often bests giants through his wiles and snares, his moral ambivalence is highlighted by the fact that he sometimes turns these same powers on one of his own; in the following myth, Odin, in one of his classic disguises, deceives and insults his own son, ostensibly for no other reason but that he can. The insult-match engaged in by Odin and Thor in this myth is an example of what is known as *flyhting*. This term comes from the Old English *flitan*, to strive or to dispute, and is commonly defined as a battle of wits involving the exchange of insults, insults which are sometimes based in some part on facts or popularly held beliefs.

The Lay of Harbard: Odin Deceives Thor

One day, on another of his many solitary forays in the wilderness, Thor left behind him the mountains and proceeded across a great plain. Some time before noon, he reached a deep stream with a strong current, far too perilous to ford. The sun shone brightly down upon the water and reflected off of its smooth surface, which seemed to belie the turbulence below. Across the wide channel, Thor could just make out the form of a man napping on the far bank, next to a boat pulled up out of the water. Calling across to him, Thor asked if he were the ferryman and offered to pay him well for the crossing. The ferryman, Harbard (or "Gray-beard"), answered him with insults, and a *flyhting* match ensued. Thor identified himself and his lineage, and interspersed boasts of his victories over the giants with threats of his wrath and the likely fate of Harbard; at the end of each tale of an exploit, Thor challenged Harbard by questioning what he was doing while Thor won such victories. The ferryman, however, remained unimpressed and repaid Thor with stories of his conquests—both in bed and in battle—liberally seasoned with wry comments about Thor's appearance, his character, his wife's virtue, and the like. Noting that Thor's clothes seemed ragged and poor for such a great god, Harbard opined that this appearance was fitting for a god of thralls. Incensed further and further by the ferryman's impertinence, Thor stomped up and down the bank of the river in anger, reiterating threats, until it dawned on him that his wrath would find no purchase here, and his strength availed him not against the rushing stream. Finally defeated, Thor plodded off around home the long way, following Harbard's snickering directions to Asgard. In the heat of his anger, Thor didn't note the fact that Harbard was one of Odin's many names, nor did he pay heed to the clues to his adversary's identity made plain through the exploits he related between his insults.

IT IS QUITE SIGNIFICANT that poor Thor is so thoroughly overmatched in this *flyhting* match; Odin would have had a much worthier opponent in Loki, whose famous *flything* of the gods—in the *Lokasenna*—after the death of Baldr marks his final exit from the company of the Aesir, as well as his unambiguous identity as the champion of the forces of chaos arrayed against Asgard. Indeed, Odin's cozy relationship with the trickster Loki suggests some sympathy of spirit, and in many early myths these two seem on remarkably good terms. They became so intimate, it comes to light, that Odin seems to have sworn blood-brotherhood with Loki, a fact that causes some consternation when Loki raises it in the *Lokasenna*. Odin's trickery in "The Lay of Harbard," his love of deception for the sheer joy of stumping Thor, and his able and witty retorts to threats all bespeak a demonic aspect of his character akin to that of Loki. Further, the fact that some giants display wisdom and wit on a par with Odin's own subtly suggests his kinship to them. Utgar-Loki perhaps provides the best-known example of such a clever giant. Odin's demonic duality and trickster ways stand out in sharp contrast to the consistent character and actions of his son Thor, a much more reliable—although admittedly more plodding and less clever—protector god. This distinction explains in large measure the respective followers of these gods: Thor was popular with farmers, herders, and townsfolk, while Odin attracted the more free-spirited, adventurous, and bloodthirsty.

Celtic Tricksters

THE TUATHA DE DANANN, THE SIDHE, AND FAIRIES AS TRICKSTERS

In Celtic mythology the embattled Tuatha De Danann have trickster qualities, making constant use of their magic to change shapes, to create disorientating mists, and to satisfy their ample appetites for love and success in battle. The term *sidhe* referred originally to mounds or small hills; after their exile to the land beneath the earth the Tuatha De Danann were referred to by this name, as mounds became associated with portals to the nether regions over which they held sway. Over time the term *fairy* or *fay* became more common for these magical, otherworldly creatures.

TRICKSTERS IN *THE TAIN*

Long ago, there was enmity between Ochall Ochne, king of the *sidhe* of Connacht, and Bodb, king of the *sidhe* of Munster. Rucht was the swineherd of Ochall and Friuch held the same post for Bodb, and these two had great affection for one another; both possessed powerful magic and each could change shape at will. These swineherds used to fatten their pigs together, and there were those who resented the amity between the two. The *sidhe* of each country therefore began to boast of the power of their swineherd, and to claim that the other one was not worth an oat. Eventually these words caused a rivalry between the friends, and they took turns cursing each other's pigs; cursed pigs profited no one, however, and soon the swineherds both were released from their jobs. For this each was angry with the other, and both wished to wreak havoc throughout Ireland. To this end they began a great contest of shape-shifting, and they ended this competition by producing the two mighty bulls that were the cause of the entire war of *The Tain*.

First they took the form of two great birds, squawking and fighting the length and breadth of the land; the warfare and bloodshed that was to follow was foreshadowed by their appearance in the shape of men to the people of Munster: The former pig-keepers explained that their ruckus was but a taste of the upheaval to come. Next the pair appeared as battling sea-serpents, then as dueling stags, and then as mighty champions at arms; they struck fear into all hearts as gruesome ghosts, and they then transformed into terrible dragons. Finally each fell from the sky into a waterway as a maggot, and in this manner they were consumed by cows and born again as great bulls. Rucht became Finnbennach, the white bull of Ai, while Friuch was Dubh, the brown bull of Cuailnge; the great war of the Cattle Raid of Cuailnge was fought over which was the mightier, and thus the early whispers of rivalry by jealous voices were echoed later by the trumpets of war.

TRICKSTERS IN *THE MABINOGION*

The Mabinogion of Wales abounds with trickster figures, mortal magician and otherworld fairy alike. Arawn King of Annwn, the lord of the otherworld, overtakes Pwyll Prince of Dyfed in a dishonorable act, and the cost to Pwyll to buy Arawn's friendship and reclaim his own honor is to switch guises with the fairy for a whole year. They live each other's lives and sleep with each other's wives during this period, and none is the wiser of the switch; Pwyll ends his year in exile by slaying Hafgan, Arawn's rival and enemy. This encounter smacks of the formulaic ritual acts that exemplify the trickster in *The Mabinogion*: Arawn has warned Pwyll to strike his foe just once, and no more; this he does, and is victorious. One more blow, however, would have undone the magic, and Pwyll would have lost. Such is the stuff of Welsh tricksters. Rhiannon, that most famous of Welsh fairy figures, appears to Pwyll as he sits upon a fairy mound, and magically eludes pursuers until he thinks to ask her courteously to halt.

The use and understanding of the proper forms of language prove vital throughout this branch of *The Mabinogion*, as Pwyll first loses Rhiannon through careless words and then regains her through the employment of a trick that depends on the victim's thinking that he must say the proper magic words. This trigger phrase springs the trap on the vile Gwawl, who had desired Rhiannon for his own. Gwawl's shame is avenged, however, by the powers of Llwyd, a classic shape-shifter. Llwyd created all manner of mischief in Dyfed, all earmarked by forms of magic indicative of the trickster: a portentous thunderclap, a bewitched mist, and a blinding flash were followed by the mysterious disappearance of the population of Dyfed. Later Llwyd threw in a treacherous enchanted castle for good measure. As a final insult, Llwyd transformed himself and his wife and followers into mice and ravaged the harvest. Llwyd is finally undone by a vow properly formulated, however; upon being exorcised from the land of Dyfed by Manawydan, Rhiannon's second husband, Llwyd acknowledged that had Manawydan not spoken wisely, vengeance would have rained down upon him like that horde of rodents.

MEDIEVAL FAIRIES AS TRICKSTERS

In the medieval tradition the Tuatha De Danann—or *sidhe*—become transformed into what we know as fairies. Indeed, the mighty Celtic god Lugh himself metamorphosed in Christian traditions into Lugh-chromain, "Little Stooping Lugh," or the leprechaun of Irish folklore, an acquisitive little trickster imp if ever there was one. While fairies sometimes appear in folklore and literature as positive, guardian spirits, more often than not they are hazardous and capricious creatures with whom to have dealings. Through fairy rings, wild hunts, charmed objects, food, potions, and the like, fairies often come into contact with mortals at the peril of the poor unsuspecting humans. Generally speaking, fairies are neither evil nor good, except when they have been deemed so through Christian interpretation. It is more fair to note that they do not subscribe to any human code of conduct, and they answer to their own moral code; thus in their dealings with humans they often seem amoral—or morally ambiguous—at best, and downright evil at worst. To the fairy king who captures Lady Heurodis in *Sir Orfeo*—as to the various Puck figures, wild huntsmen, and fairy dancers who inhabit medieval British literature—the feelings and well-being of their human neighbors simply don't count for much. They are, moreover, ideal trickster figures, in that they are often shape-shifters, often display voracious appetites for blood or sex or riches, and are creative in their employment of tricks and traps and carefully worded oaths and vows.

Lesser Gods or Spirits

World mythology contains a variety of deity and spirit motifs in addition to those primary types already discussed. There are figures associated particularly with fate. There are races of ancient giants against whom the ultimately victorious gods must fight. Cyclops and other monsters, centaurs, dwarfs, fairies, and angels all have roles in the world of myth. The mythologies of the British Isles are particularly rich in such figures.

Germanic Demigods and Spirits

In Germanic mythology, two groups of minor figures—the Norns and the Valkyries—are among the most visible female members of the pantheon. Except for occasional bursts of independence by the fertility figure Freya, goddesses act less than they are acted upon in Germanic myth, quite likely as a result of the ascendancy of the warrior cults over those of fertility. Indeed, the connection between the powers of life and death and the Norns, the Valkyries, and Freya might suggest that all of these figures are descendants of the great goddess, who was traditionally associated with these fundamental matters. Hel and giantesses such as Skadi are powerful female figures, but they represent the powers of chaos feared by the gods. The Norns and the Valkyries—although hardly well developed in terms of individual personality—do provide a glimpse of female power and autonomy in the ranks of the Germanic gods themselves, and echoes of these powerful forces can be heard in their distant Anglo-Saxon Christian counterparts.

THE NORNS

The Norns are the Norse goddesses of fate: the three sisters are named Urd, "Fate"; Skuld, "Being"; "Future"; or perhaps "Debt"; and Verdandi, "Present." They guard the well of Urd and decide the destinies of the gods, men, the giants, and all other creatures. It is interesting to note that a being named Skuld is also counted in some lists of the Valkyries. The Norns have an ancient relationship to childbirth—which certainly makes sense, as they determine the fate of every child—and they may in fact have evolved from an early goddess of maternity. Thus the tripartite goddess of the Celts may be thought to have some ancient relationship to the Norns. The myth of the origin of the Norns is obscured by the later records, however, and they are said in *Volsunga Saga* to be related to the races of elves and of dwarfs, as well as to the gods. Some sources suggest that there are different races or sets of Norns, some benevolent, some malevolent. It seems likely that one set of Norns may have multiplied over time. Snorri tells us that the well of Urd lies beneath the second root of Yggdrasill, the world tree, and that each day Urd and her sisters water the lowest branches thereof; that well is also where the gods hold daily assemblies. In the mythic cycle of the gods the Norns appear mainly as types, occasionally making a pronouncement of doom. In some of the sagas, however, they take a more active role resembling that of the Valkyries.

Although the Norns are described as weaving and snipping the destinies of men and of gods—very like the classical Fates—they are also associated with the scoring or carving of wood, as in the cutting of runes or the planks upon which days were counted on Scandinavian farms. Weaving, and the prophetic powers granted to women as a result of this labor, is an association mentioned in the saga of the earls of Orkney; the mother of Jarl Sigurd is said to have woven for him a banner that signified victory to the lord it preceded, but death to the man who carried it. It also has been argued that some scraps of cloth found in Anglo-Saxon cemeteries might be similar talismans of victory. The Norns were known in Britain by the name of Urd, the Old English form of which is *Wyrd*. *Wyrd* is a concept of inexorable fate that was extremely common in Old English literature, and notably in *Beowulf*. Although the metaphorical notion of *wyrd* was quite common, the Norns as a distinct set of beings do not appear in early English literature; the tradition may have lived on in Scots and English folktales, however, a possibility to which the "weird sisters" of *Macbeth* and elsewhere attest.

THE VALKYRIES

In Norse sources the female goddesses and divine spirits were known in general as *disir,* and the Valkyries constitute one branch of this sisterhood, which most likely originated in an Indo-European group of death-goddesses. Warrior-goddess figures such as the Valkyries abound in Indo-European mythology: from India to the lands of the Teutons to the battlegrounds of the ancient Irish, female spirits flitted above and about many an ancient conflict. In Germanic myth, such beings with dominion over the battlefield seem to have been considered demonic in nature; it has been suggested that these figures developed from stories about actual cults of Germanic warrior women. Eventually, in the Norse tradition, the association of these spirits with Odin as his shield-maidens seems to have tempered this conception, and they became known as "Odin's girls," or "wish girls," meaning those who did Odin's bidding. His bidding was to select and to harvest the greatest human warriors for his army of the dead in Valhalla, and this the Norse name *valkyrjar*— roughly "choosers of the dead"—makes clear. The Old English term for these spirits was *waelcyrge*, and those few references to slaughter-choosers that survive in English records seem to indicate that these were perceived to be malevolent, demonic spirits.

The Valkyries served Odin without question, and were zealous in their search for additions to the *einherjar*, the chosen slain. Freya shared some Valkyrie-like attributes—although it sometimes escapes notice, she took her half-share of the battlefield dead, after all, and her feather coat reminds us of the "swan maiden" Valkyries of the saga of Weland, and of German folklore— but she differed from them in at least one fundamental respect: unlike the most of the other goddesses of Asgard, the Valkyries were, by and large, virgins one and all, preferring the "great death" of the battlefield to the *petit mort* of the bed chamber. Each night in Valhalla these shield-maidens turned into barmaids, and the same hands that had singled each man out for slaughter now brought mead to the dead heroes returning from their sport on the battle plain.

At Odin's command, the Valkyries sometimes grant victory to a warrior, and sometimes death; but the first is just a precursor to the second: it is only through glory and victory in battle that a hero might rise to the stature Odin demands in his chosen ones. Thus warriors chosen to fall sometimes rebuke the Valkyries for their faithlessness, but the battle-maidens answer that it was only through their auspices that the warriors succeeded in the first place. The Valkyries are sometimes numbered at nine, sometimes at twelve, and sometimes there seem to be many, many more. It has been suggested that a small number of warrior-goddesses were later supplemented by half-mortal Valkyries who entered Valhalla after lives as mortal shield-maidens. The Valkyries are given suitably gruesome and warlike names in the Norse sources, but these are likely more literary than mythic in origin.

The Valkyries undoubtedly were supernatural spirits, creatures of the otherworld that fit most neatly in a Christian Anglo-Saxon context as demons, handmaids to the Devil himself; indeed, even in material that was not overtly Christian, the Anglo-Saxons seem to have seen only the worst side of these battle-goddesses. In *The Wonders of the East,* for example, they are said to be related to the Gorgons of classical myth, and their gaze is described as steely and deadly. Furthermore, the violent female figures of *Beowulf*—Grendel's mother first and foremost, of course, but let us not forget the evil gaze of Modthrytho, a Gorgon type if ever there was one—are evil monsters who slaughter and invite slaughter.

In a number of narratives of the lives of holy women, however, the old Germanic model of the virgin warrior-goddess is recreated in a new form. As we shall see in our discussions of the hero and of the sagas, the saint's life was a genre through which Anglo-Saxon authors often recast heroic and mythic material. Just as Christ is reinvented into a young Germanic hero in *The*

Dream of the Rood, the Old English poetic versions of the lives of Judith, Juliana, and Elene show us these heroines in the light of the Valkyrie tradition. These holy virgins are steely-eyed themselves, potent battle leaders who single-handedly defeat the agents of Satan in spiritual (and sometimes physical) battle, and who inspire both their followers and the readers of their sagas to carry on the good fight.

THE GIANTS

In Indo-European mythology generally—and in Germanic myth specifically—giants represent the forces arrayed against the powers of the gods; at the same time, however, these rival forces often are much like and indeed often are related to the gods themselves. In this aspect the Germanic giants play a role akin to that of the Irish Fomoire, the Indic Demons, the Iranian Turanians, and the classical Titans. The Old Norse term *jotunn* is cognate with the Old English *eoten,* and both may have come from an Indo-European root term having to do with eating; thus it has been postulated that early forebears of the Germanic peoples may have come into contact with rival tribes to which they attributed cannibalistic behavior. This sense of giants as man-eaters has worked its way into the fabric of Germanic folklore, and indeed, "Jack and the Beanstalk"—perhaps the most notable English tale of giant-slaying to survive into the modern period—is premised upon this aspect of giant behavior.

Giant, rather like *troll,* derives from a catch-all term for monsters and for the rivals of the gods, a word that only later takes on the more specific meaning with which we are familiar; thus in the Norse records we meet a number of different forms of giants and giantesses: some are monstrous and ugly, with numerous heads or limbs; others—while perhaps coarse in manner and mien—are more or less simply huge versions of men; still others—notably among the giantesses—are as beautiful and desirable as the deities themselves. Indeed, some giant-folk (notably Gerd and Skadi) live among the gods as friends and lovers, while some gods (notably Odin) are descended from giants themselves. The Norse giants inhabited Jotunheim, bordering Midgard, the land of humans, on the middle level of the cosmos.

In general, it appears that the giants are described as enemies of the gods in two ways: some, like Thrym and Utgar-Loki, appear to be members of a rival tribe who live in halls like men and gods and array themselves against the gods as a rival army. Others are embodiments of forces of nature, as their categories (frost-, fire-, and rock-giants) make clear. These giants represent the chaos that always lurks at the door of man and that undermines the social structure of the gods by its constant encroachment on men, livestock, and crops. They are ice storms and volcanic eruptions, early frosts and earthquakes: the forces of the natural world that bring blight, death, and destruction to men as readily as the gods bring light, life, and fertility. Perhaps the best examples of giant-kin in early English literature are Grendel and his

Dam, the demons who terrorize the hall of King Hrodgar in *Beowulf*. These two figures—although described in quasi-Christian terms that suggest that they dwell in the darkness of sin outside the light of God—clearly also represent the monstrous forces lurking on the margins of civilization, hating the joy of men, and anxious to extinguish it.

THE DWARFS AND THE ELVES

Little distinction is made in the Norse sources between dark elves and dwarfs, and the names are used almost interchangeably; we are told, however, that the latter inhabited Nidavellir while the former lived in Svartalfheim. In both cases, caves, pits, and mountain hollows are likely places in which to find these creatures. In the Norse sources and throughout the Germanic world these beings are most often considered evil, or at best self-concerned and little interested with the well-being of humans. Dwarfs seem to have evolved in great part from folklore and had little ritual or religious significance. Unlike their Celtic counterparts, the *genii cucullati*—which were associated with fertility, plenty, and the mother goddess—the mythic provenance of these figures seems to have been darker: the Indo-European root of *dwarf* seems to have been something meaning "destruction," "disease," "deception," or "demonic." The dwarfs are master smiths and adept at magic while they are at it, and when forced to labor or to surrender treasure against their will, they are well able to bestow a potent curse for good measure. All the greatest treasures and weapons of the gods, it is only fair to note, were the products of dwarf hands, but always the dwarfs served themselves first: lust, greed, power, and fear—these were the motivations of the dwarfs.

It is clear from the later Norse texts that light elves were friends to god and man, that they inhabited Alfheim—on the upper plane of the cosmos, along with Asgard and Vanaheim—and that they were good, and often mixed with the gods in their halls; but little else about their particulars is known. Unlike those concerning the dwarfs, beliefs about the light elves may have evolved from ritual roots and may have originated in minor figures of veneration, most likely nature spirits. The Anglo-Saxon tradition concerning elves is somewhat different from the Norse and the German, and is noteworthy in that it is one of the few instances in which we see an early English tradition transported into much later German folklore. It is clear that the Anglo-Saxons perceived that elves could be dangerous, as the names of a number of diseases take the term *aelf-* or *ylf-* as part of their name in Old English. Perhaps owing to the Celtic influence in Britain, this dark underside was hidden beneath a beautiful visage, however, as the Anglo-Saxons thought elves to be beautiful, shining creatures, often quite small, and sometimes very well disposed toward humans. A number of Anglo-Saxon names include the word *aelf* as an element, and a common descriptor might be translated "pretty as an elf." This combination of good and evil, beauty and danger, reminds us of later medieval traditions of the fairies, traditions which are clearly Celtic in origin.

THE DIVINE SPIRITS

Vettir is a broad term that encompasses all of the supernatural creatures known to the Norse; these include the gods, elves, dwarfs, giants, and spirits of any kind. The Germanic peoples were somewhat like the Celts in their belief that the landscape was numinous—that is, that it was alive with spirits—and the belief in land and water sprites of various forms and dispositions was widespread. Belief in personal guardian spirits was likewise endemic to the Germanic world. Hamingjar were a kind of personal guardian spirit, and clearly evolved from an understanding of personal fortune and destiny; indeed, the word itself comes from a root meaning "luck." Fylgjur were likewise personal guardians of sorts, and the term derives directly from a verb meaning "to follow, to guide, to accompany." Fylgjur were usually described as spirit beings with the ability to take on multiple forms, but they sometimes were thought to be one's own spirit, which passes on from the body after death. While one's hamingja could be transferred to anyone else after death, one's fylgja was bound within the family circle and might only pass onto a close relative. Both of these concepts of protective spirits seem to be similar to the Christian concept of the guardian angel or the Roman belief in the personal *genii,* and both seem to have developed from an earlier belief that the spirit could take on its own form outside of the body.

THE BEAR'S SON

The folkloric motif of the super-human warrior descended from the union of a great bear and a human woman survives in oral cultures around the globe. Most usually the narrative includes a number of common elements: the bear's son undertakes some quest with a number of companions and spends the night in an abandoned dwelling; during the course of the night one of the companions is wounded or killed by an invading monster—perhaps the owner of the dwelling, perhaps not—and the bear's son stalks this marauder into an underground lair, where he avenges the attack upon his companion. The bear's son himself usually is said to be able to take on the form of his father, and often is impervious to weapons in battle, fighting with the ferocity of a wild beast.

A tale of this type has passed from folkloric to mythic and even epic status in almost every part of the world in which humans come into contact with bears. This is true for a number of reasons. Bears exhibit a number of human-like traits, especially at times a shambling, upright walk. A bear walking upright or standing up to reach might—from a distance in dim light—easily be confused for a man, and large, hairy, gruff men might well remind one of bears. Further, bears manifest a combination of characteristics, including ferocity when cornered and gentleness with their young, which may call to mind the worst and best of humankind.

Bear-hunting families in many regions often traditionally claim descent from the bear; this totemic relationship is thought to have originated in ancient bear cults, which made sacrifice unto their quarry before the hunt in order to appease it, and thought to take on characteristics of the animal through partaking of its flesh or heart. Such rituals evolved from the belief that the bear was a super-human creature with power and prowess only to be overcome if the creature itself willed it; bears often were credited with second-sight, and thus thought to be able to foretell their own doom. Therefore the tremendous courage, terrible ferocity, massive strength, and supernatural intelligence associated with the bear were thought to pass down to those who hunted and were descended from them.

Nowhere is this folkloric cult of the bear more well established than in northwest Europe, where well into the modern period Norwegian and Lappish folktales suggested that young women were stalked and kidnapped by supernatural bears; these bears then mated with their captives, and thereby took their places as patriarchs of leading families of the region. In Old English literature Beowulf certainly manifests some of the elements of the bear's son's folktale, notably in his battle with Grendel and Grendel's mother; further, the Icelandic hero Bodvar Bjarki—who figures prominently in the saga of King Hrolf Kraki—is one of the closest analogues to the character Beowulf, and shares several of his attributes and adventures. Bodvar Bjarki, whose very name means something like "Battle Bear," is explicitly the son of bears and is able to take on the form of the bear in battle, where he is a ferocious and nearly unassailable opponent. Norse Berserkrs, who developed as a warrior cult devoted to Odin, clearly drew upon the potency of the bear's son tradition.

THE DRAUGAR AND HARMFUL SPIRITS

The draugar were the undead of Germanic myth, revenants, or zombies who—unlike mere ghosts—inhabited their bodies after death and in this way walked the earth. The term seems to come from an Indo-European root meaning "harmful spirit," and it has been argued that fire rituals associated with the exorcism of draugar suggest a very ancient origin for this belief. These beings could cause great havoc among the living, and often terrified and even slaughtered both livestock and humans. Draugar might come back to life to avenge some particular wrong, but more often than not the impetus simply seems to have been an evil disposition; those who are unpleasant in life often are more so in death. The bodies of draugar—when exposed in the grave—were usually uncorrupted, although they often blackened and swelled over time. Moving these bodies to a place of disposal often proved difficult because they would become very, very heavy; further, they might well disappear if sought by a party containing a Christian priest. Draugar were exorcised most effectively by decapitating the corpse and placing the head between the buttocks; some sources suggest cremating the remains and scattering the ashes in a safe area—that is, in a place where they will not come into contact with living beings.

The most famous example of a battle with such a revenant is probably

Grettir's fight with Glamr in *Grettissaga*; this story is of particular interest to us because of its connection to Beowulf's battle with Grendel. We will turn to retellings of both episodes in the section on heroic battles with monsters. *Eyrbyggjasaga* contains an episode in which the ashes of a draugar are consumed by a cow, and one of her offspring becomes possessed by the spirit of the undead Thorolf Twist-Foot as a result; this story has obvious resonance with that of the genesis of the two bulls of *The Tain*. The same saga contains a highly engaging account of the exorcism of a number of ghosts through the rather ordinary Norse legal proceeding known as a door-court: each wraith was called to the threshold of the house and charged with trespass and mayhem; testimony was taken and evidence was presented in the normal way, and then sentence was passed. Each spirit in turn was sentenced to banishment, and each in turn stood and left as the order was made. Each parted with a comment that implied that the ghost stayed only as long as it was allowed; cautionary words indeed.

Celtic Demigods and Spirits

THE THREE MOTHERS

In Britain, the mother-goddess is usually rendered in triplicate, as Celtic numerology associated the number three with good luck. Figures of the mother-goddess usually take one of two forms: *Deae Matres*, three goddesses who are often depicted seated and holding or receiving fruits of the field; and *Dea Nutrix*, a seated goddess nursing infants. The first are found in various contexts and were associated with some springs as well as with harvests. The second seem to have been personal protective talismans, perhaps for pregnant women and young mothers; they are most often found in homes or in graves.

GENII CUCULLATI

These hooded dwarfs take their name from the Roman term for a beneficent spirit (*genii*) and the name of the type of Gaulish cape (*cucullus*) they are often depicted as wearing; further, some stone depictions of these dwarfs bear the designation *genii cucullati*. They usually appear in a set of three, and sometimes accompany a mother-goddess figure. The practice of triplicating these figures—and those of the three mothers—is significant, as the number three was considered magical by the Celts and was thought to ward off evil. These dwarfs are common in the north and west of Britain, and they often are grouped around sites that also contain idols of the three mothers. Associated with health and fertility, they sometimes are depicted carrying eggs or offering a gift to the mother-goddess.

SUCELLUS

Like the three mothers, Sucellus was not minor in divine stature, but rather in mythic importance, as not much is known about him; he seems to have been worshiped primarily in Gaul. Sucellus was known in Britain, however, and a ring dedicated to this god was found at York. Sometimes Sucellus is thought to be a manifestation of Dis Pater, and certainly he fulfilled some funereal functions; he also was associated with Silvanus in southern Gaul, however, and hence he also may have been a protector of herds and harvests. He usually is depicted carrying a hammer or mallet, and thus is to be equated with the tradition of the hammer-god. Sucellus is called the "Good Striker"; in this Celtic deity we detect aspects of the ancient hammer-god of Northern Europe that we know most intimately through the form of the Norse Thor.

The Celtic hammerer often appears with a barrel or a drinking horn, perhaps in allusion to his role as a god of wine; moreover, at times he is accompanied by a dog, sometimes three-headed, reminding us of Cerebus, the hound who guards the gates of the classical underworld. Tripling in the Celtic world had an apotropaic function, however, meaning that both the three-headed hound and the hammer of Sucellus might have served to ward off evil. Celtic gods often appeared in pairs, and the consort of Sucellus was Nantosuelta, whose name means "Winding Stream." They were worshiped together in wine-growing regions, where the water-goddess brought moisture and the hammer-god hallowed and fertilized the soil. Sucellus himself had associations with water and was the patron at a number of Gaulish healing springs; his connection with dogs and serpents might suggest powers over both healing and death. Healing, hunting, and death are all associated in Celtic belief, and so it is that the wild hunt can be a bridge to the otherworld in Celtic myth.

SPIRITS IN THE LANDSCAPE

The early Celts held the world to be full of spirits, and every tree, stream, and spring had its particular animus. Therefore, groves and water sources were often believed to be sacred; trees, and especially very old trees, were objects of particular veneration. Through their branches and their roots—systems which mirror each other in aspect—trees both reach up into the heavens and down into the underworld; they therefore provide ideal bridges between the worlds of the gods, the living, and the dead. Water could both bring and destroy life, and so sources of water were held to be holy. Sacrifices were often made into rivers and springs, and often valuable objects were destroyed and cast into their watery embrace; such rituals were common in Britain. Marshes were by their very nature mystical and hazardous, and so might serve as a likely conduit to the otherworld. Bog sacrifices might be particularly opulent, and it is certain that humans were among the offerings to the spirits of some marshes: Lindow Man stands in mute testimony to such practices in Britain. Healing springs especially were venerated, as were the deities associated with them; Sulis, the god of the hot springs at Bath, is probably the most noteworthy of these figures in Britain.

3

SACRED OBJECTS AND PLACES

Mythology, as a religious phenomenon, naturally is permeated by sacred places and objects. Whether Indian or Egyptian, Taoist or Buddhist, Zuni or Zulu, the world for any given mythological tradition is heavily charged with the energy of the numinous. As we follow the deities and the culture heroes and their interactions with the world in which we live, we understand instinctively—archetypally—that a tree is often a world center, that a city can be a human reflection of the home of the gods, that a pool is possibly a gateway to another deeper world, that a garden is a place where humans and immortals sometimes meet, that a rock is probably no mere rock, that mountains can be the breasts of a goddess, that the wind can be her breath. When the hero ventures into the dark wood, we know in the depths of our being that a sacred journey is at hand. Symbols provide the language through which a human being may transcend the individual and participate in the universal. Every people finds such symbols in the landscape that surrounds that people. Like all mythologies, those of the Germanic and Celtic peoples of the British Isles were marked by sacred places and objects steeped in such symbolism.

The World Tree

In many cultures, trees provide a metaphor for the cosmos, reaching as they do at the same time both into the inaccessible heavens and into the unknowable underworld. Trees are mortal and may be felled, but they also may survive for time out of mind and are often venerated for their great age and near immortal status. Thus the tree both exists in this world and seems to transcend it, and therefore may be seen to symbolize the oppositions of life and death and of eternity and transience. Trees are most often associated with life-giving energy, and due to their longevity are quite often thought to be repositories of wisdom: the Egyptian Osiris and the Greek Adonis, as resurrection gods, both are associated with trees, and the Buddha was born again in the wisdom he found under the Bodhi Tree. Sometimes, as in both the Indic and Norse traditions, a tree is thought to represent life and death on a cosmic scale, symbolizing the full manifestation of the universe. In other cultures, trees may be related most closely to personal life, death, and wisdom: In the biblical tradition, for instance, we find the Tree of Life and the Tree of Knowledge, symbols that are reflected and transmuted in the form of the Cross of Christ.

The Norse World Tree: Yggdrasill

Yggdrasill is a mighty ash tree; between the tips of its branches and the ends of its roots it comprises the entire cosmos; it ever has and it ever shall. The most beautiful of trees is ever green, and has three great roots: one reaches down into Asgard, one world on the plane of the gods and light elves; one courses down beyond, to Jotunheim, in the middle plane, that men, giants, dark elves, and dwarfs call home; one spirals far, far below, to Niflheim, on the bottom level, the land of cold and mist, where the dead languish under the dreadful care of Hel, and where the dragon Nidhogg hatefully sups upon the root of the greatest of trees. Thus Yggdrasill connects all three planes of the cosmos—which are stacked one above the other—and the nine worlds of the Norse universe. All life springs from this source, and it sustains its own life, as well; four stags feast upon its tender shoots, and the dew that drips from its branches is the stuff of honey. Its fruit is treasured by pregnant women, as it promises safe delivery. Just so, after Ragnarok, Lif and Lifthrasir will emerge from its bark as if reborn, to renew the race of men.

A well lies beneath each root. The well of Urd in Asgard is at the base of the first root, where the Norns stand watch and sprinkle water and mud from the spring onto the World Ash, thus curing its ills; here also the gods meet in conclave. The spring of Mimir in Jotunheim, home of great wisdom, is the source of the second root. At the bottom of this spring Odin's pawned orb glistens and glitters next to Heimdalr's horn. Into the spring of Hvergelmir in Niflheim, source of eleven great floods, thrusts the third root; here is home to hungry Nidhogg and his host of slithering kin. An eagle sits in the topmost branches, a hawk perched upon his beak; Ratatoskr—old drill-tooth—that incorrigible ne'er do well, is a squirrel who runs along the branches and down the roots, bringing insults from eagle above to dragon below. So he shall continue, until Yggdrasill's branches tremble with the coming of Ragnarok, and the world is ended and begun anew.

The Anglo-Saxon Victory Tree: The Holy Rood

The Germanic conception of the world tree, along with the practice of venerating sacred groves and mighty trees, found a new mode of expression in Anglo-Saxon Christianity. The development of the Cult of the Cross was widespread throughout Christendom, to be sure, but it found particularly fertile soil in Britain, where its expression also was peculiarly Germanic and often martial in some aspects. As was mentioned in connection with *The Dream of the Rood*, the Germanic understanding of Christ as a young hero echoed Anglo-Saxon sensibilities concerning the nature of the Savior, both as God and as man; likewise, Anglo-Saxon perceptions of the Cross often recast it into a battle-standard of Christ Triumphant and of the hope of salvation. In this way the Anglo-Saxons of Britain put a uniquely Germanic spin on a Mediterranean and Neareastern cult of veneration.

Before the fourth century CE, the cross was not widely embraced as a sign of Christianity, symbolizing as it did the gallows of a criminal. This changed after the conversion of the Emperor Constantine; as the story goes, in a dream before a great battle against overwhelming odds, Constantine saw a shining cross in the night sky and heard a voice pronounce, "by this sign ye shall conquer." He hastened to heed these words, and the Roman troops the following day were preceded by banners of the cross; they won a great victory over the host of Huns at the Battle of Milvian Bridge on the Danube, and Constantine ended the persecution of Christians, and converted before he died. It is worth noting that Constantine's mother, Helen, is reputed to have found the True Cross on a pilgrimage to the Holy Land, and that one of the great Anglo-Saxon narrative poems, *Elene*, has to do with this discovery. Whether or not the story of Constantine's vision is apocryphal, it is certain that after his conversion a great deal of prestige accrued to the cross, and it was eventually adopted as the primary Christian symbol.

The Cross became an object of great devotion in the East, and soon various ceremonies, cults, traditions, and relics sprang up as a result of this veneration. This popularity had migrated to Western Europe by the end of the seventh century, and before the middle of that century a number of cross legends are known to have been circulating in Britain. It is during this period that the Cult of the Cross took on a peculiarly British flavor, a flavor that combined subtle hints of Celtic and Germanic pagan traditions along with the predominant eastern Christian taste. In 633 CE Oswald of Northumbria erected a giant wooden cross before the Battle of Heavenfield in a none-too-subtle attempt to co-opt Constantine's strategy for success; he prevailed, and for ages after this date miracles were attributed to fragments of that battle standard. The success of the Cult of the Cross in Anglo-Saxon England was likewise assured.

The most notable and idiosyncratic Anglo-Saxon outgrowth of the Cult of the Cross was the widespread popularity of large, standing stone crosses, which became objects and locations of worship. By the mid-eighth century these icons had become so popular that Boniface complained that they were taking the place of regular churches; perhaps, indeed, the worshipers were hearkening back to the days of sacred groves and trees, and it is certain that the Rood of Christ was often likened to a tree. The poet who wrote *The Dream of the Rood* emphasized the cross's identity as a tree, and also as a battle standard: he even called it "The Victory Tree." Over 1,500 standing stone crosses survive in Britain to this day, and it is reasonable to assume that many more made of wood are lost to us. The most significant of these remaining roods is the Ruthwell Cross.

Standing nearly twenty feet high, the Ruthwell Cross is a striking combination of Celtic artistic traditions (intricate vine patterns known as interlace, interwoven with human and animal figures), biblical scenes, and Germanic runes and warrior conception of Christ, all bound together in an overtly Christian symbol. A number of other British crosses likewise blend cultural and mythic elements, perhaps most notably that at Gosforth. Particularly, the runic inscription running along the east and west faces of the Ruthwell Cross includes a passage from *The Dream of the Rood* describing Christ's mounting of the Rood, and his death thereon; it has been noted that this passage is one that most emphasizes the Christ Militant of Anglo-Saxon belief. It also has been argued that this particular selection resonates with the scene of the death of Baldr. The lone manuscript known to contain *The Dream of the Rood* dates from the ninth century or so, but the Ruthwell Cross itself dates from the height of the Cult of the Cross in Britain—perhaps around the year 700—and therefore some early form of the poem must have, as well. This conception of the Tree of Christ—with all its pagan echoes and warrior ethos—thus predates the beginning of the Viking raids by almost a century, and therefore the Germanic aspects both of the poem and of the Ruthwell Cross are likely to be of mostly pure Anglo-Saxon derivation.

Sanctuaries and Numinous Places

In most mythological traditions there exist hidden places endowed with particularly strong spiritual or magical energy. Often these places are unlikely spots where heroes are born or where heroes and deities meet. The sanctuary at Colonus, where Oedipus talks with Theseus and from which he is taken away by the gods is such a place and so is the stable at Bethlehem where Jesus is said to have been born. Mount Sinai is sacred because Moses received the word of God there. Delphi is a holy place because the ancient oracle resided there. Souls are reborn from the great Erathipa stone in Aboriginal Australia. Jews, Christians, and Muslims find sacred energy in Jerusalem. An important element of Islamic faith is the pilgrimage to the great cube called the Kab'ah at Mecca. Labyrinths are sacred to many peoples. Churches, temples, kivas, and certain grave sites are consciously established holy places—containers of the numinous, where worshipers can ritualize and partake of the power of the "other."

Drunemeton and the Sacred Oak

In about 275 BCE, several Celtic tribes settled in Galatia, in central Anatolia. According to the Greek geographer Strabo, these tribes sent representative druids—religious and civic leaders—to an assembly at a place called Drunemeton, "the sanctuary of oaks." In Romano-Gaul, the oak was sacred to Mars and Jupiter. It was also the tree of the Gaulish god Hesus and of the Germanic Thor. The word *druid* is derived from *dair, doire,* or *duir,* "the oak." The druids were *dairaoi,* or "dwellers in oak." The oak continued to be sacred to the Irish Celts. Ireland has many sacred oak groves. For example, Kildare is derived from *cill-dara,* or "druid's cell" or "Church of the Oak," and Derrynane is *doire-Fhionain,* or "oak grove of Finian." It is said that the oak's acorn represented the male and female principles in union and thus fertility.

Balor's Hill

Another sacred Celtic place in Ireland is Uisneach, or Balor's Hill, sometimes called the "navel" of the country—the center of Ireland, where the great sacred Stone of Divisions, the Aill na Mirenn, marked the meeting of the five ancient provinces. St. Patrick cursed the stones, and Geoffrey of Monmouth claimed that Stonehenge (built, in fact by pre-Celtic peoples) was made by Merlin of stones taken from Uisneach.

Arthurian Sacred Places and Objects

In Britain, many sacred places are associated with the Arthurian legend. Camelot is one such place—the elusive home of the also-sacred Round Table. Tintagel as Arthur's birthplace is important, as is Glastonbury—a place associated with the mythical Avallon, where Arthur was taken after being killed by Mordred. The great king's gravestone can be seen at the Abbey of Glastonbury. Arthur's sword Excalibur has a mysterious and sacred heritage associated with the Lady of the Lake.

Perhaps the most sacred object of all in the Arthurian cycle is the Holy Grail, the cup used by Christ at the Last Supper and brought mysteriously to Britain. The grail becomes the object of the questing knights of the Round Table.

Germanic Sacred Places and Objects

The Germanic invaders of the British Isles seem to have been less concerned with magic and with the aura of particular places in this world than were the Celts. The primary religious places among the non-Christian Northern Europeans were mythological: Yggdrasill or Von, the River of Expectation, formed by the slaver of the great wolf Fenrir. One exception might be burial mounds such as the one at Sutton Hoo in Suffolk, a place associated with King Raedwald, who was converted to Christianity during a visit to the court of King Ethelbert, who himself had been converted by Augustine, the founder of what was to become one of the holiest of British Christian centers, the monastery and cathedral at Canterbury. Of the fifteen burial mounds at Sutton Hoo, the largest, containing an eighty-nine-foot Anglo-Saxon boat, is thought to have been a memorial to Raedwald, who died in about 625 CE. The Sutton Hoo excavations brought to light an amazing collection of valuable objects of primarily "pagan" or non-Christian origin. We know that Raedwald's wife was an adamant follower of the old Germanic religion and that her husband, even after his conversion, placed both Christian and non-Christian objects and altars in his place of worship.

4

HEROES AND HEROINES

As fascinating as the activities of deities and the auras of holy objects and places may be, the myths that have spoken most clearly to the human imagination have been those of heroes. The reason for this attachment has been discussed by thinkers such as Joseph Campbell, Carl Jung, Otto Rank, and Mircea Eliade, all of whom have contributed to the idea of a universal hero pattern behind the many cultural expressions of the archetype—a "hero with a thousand faces"—who represents the human being's journey through life. As the hero searches in remote corners of the world for a golden fleece, a lost loved one, or the kingdom of God, he or she transports us metaphorically into the subconscious world of obstacles that stand in our way on our search for self-identity or full consciousness.

The Monomyth

The archetypal hero pattern, or "monomyth" as Campbell calls it, is made up of a series of familiar elements that we associate with the lives of particular heroes—usually male in the dominant patriarchal cultures—each of whom experiences at least several of these elements.

Typically, the hero is miraculously conceived—often by the joining of mortal woman and divine power. Jesus and Quetzalcoatl are conceived in virgins who have been visited by such power. The Buddha conceives himself by way of a white elephant in his mother's dream. One Native American hero is conceived by a clot of blood, another by a piece of clay. Heroes are often born at the dark time of the year—near the winter solstice—indicating the hope of change in a time of need. The virgin birth signifies the hope for a new beginning—a reestablishment of divine order in the given world. Furthermore, the hero's conception and birth reflect the birth of the hero process within us, the beginning of the process that will take us with the hero on the great quest for identity. Not surprisingly, that identity involves the source of our being; it is for this reason that, in patriarchal cultures, the male hero goes in search of his father.

The hero's quest begins with a call to adventure. Yahweh calls Moses from the Burning Bush, the Holy Grail "calls" the Knights of the Round Table. Often the hero at first refuses the call. "Why me?" is a question asked by such heroes as Jonah, Moses, and Odysseus—even as it is almost automatically asked by us when we face radical change in our own lives. Society itself resists the call in the form of wicked kings or monsters who attempt to stamp out the hero life before it can take form. The Herods of life are always ready to deny or undermine the call.

If the call is accepted, however, the quest involves an initiation—a sword pulled from the rock, a father's shoes found—and confrontation with a host of familiar archetypal figures. Typically we find the *femme fatale* or enchantress, the monster, the demon tempter, and perhaps most important, death itself or a ritual descent to the underworld. Jesus faces the temptations of Satan in the Wilderness, dies on the cross, and descends to Hell to "harrow" it and retrieve Adam and Eve. The Buddha withstands the temptations of Mara the Fiend, including sexual temptation in the form of seductive women. Odysseus must overcome the powers of the enchantresses Circe and Calypso, must defeat the monster Cyclops, and must visit the shades of the underworld before he can achieve the goal that is Penelope and home. As for us, we, too, must face the inner barriers that would prevent us from achieving individuation.

In a sense, the hero's descent is a return to the mother—to the earth represented in his biological birth by the maiden who is often transformed in myth into the goddess. When the hero emerges from the otherworld he is reborn, as it were, like the Egyptian Osiris and the Phrygian Attis, with new powers even over death. He or she represents our new self-identified state. If the hero leaves the world after his adventures, as, for instance, Arthur, Jesus, and Quetzalcoatl do, he is expected to return some day at another time of dark need. Once the hero journey is achieved—in the story and in us—the hero power is always there to be called upon.

In the British Isles of the Celtic and Germanic peoples we find a more than ample expression of the hero myth, sometimes in early "pagan" masks and sometimes in later masks transformed to greater or lesser extent by Christian storytellers.

The Conception, Birth, and Initiation of the Hero

The hero's stature and divine purpose is initially established by his miraculous conception, birth, and initiation. Often the hero is conceived by or watched over by a god or other superhuman creature, and the genesis of the hero almost always has supernatural qualities that mark it as special.

Lugh, Dechtire, and the Birth of Cuchulainn

In Ireland it is sometimes difficult to distinguish heroes from gods. But out of the Ulster or Red Branch Cycle, one great hero emerges in the person of Cuchulainn, the miraculous circumstances of whose birth and initiation place him in the company of the multitude of heroes, including Zoroaster, Jesus, Herakles, Theseus, Maui, and Quetzalcoatl, whose beginnings are extraordinary.

The mother of the hero-to-be was Dechtire, the daughter of the druid Cathbad and the love-god Aonghus. During the wedding feast of Dechtire and the Ulster chieftain Sualtam, the god Lugh took the form of a mayfly and flew into the bride's drink. Dechtire fell into a deep sleep, during which Lugh came to her in a dream and instructed her to leave with him, taking fifty maidens, whom he would disguise as birds. Nine months after the disappearance of the women, a group of hunting warriors followed a flock of birds to the river Boyne, thought to be the home of the gods. There they found a palace, where they were entertained by a handsome man and a beautiful woman surrounded by fifty maidens. During the night the woman gave birth to a boy. Lugh then revealed his own and Dechtire's identity and instructed the hunters to return to Ulster with the mother and child and the maidens. There Sualtam welcomed back Dechtire as his wife and the baby as his son.

The child was first called Setanta. But one day the king, Conchobhar, noticed the boy's prodigious strength and invited him to join him at a feast being given by the smith, Culann. There the smith's huge dog attacked the child, who jammed his ball into the beast's mouth and smashed its head against a rock, killing it instantly. Culann was furious that the child had killed his favorite watchdog, but Setanta promised to find a replacement for the dog and until then to serve in its place as the "Hound of Culann," or Cuchulainn.

The Lineage of Sigurd

The Germanic invaders of the British Isles brought with them the story of the hero Sigurd, the central figure of the late thirteenth-century *Volsunga Saga*, who is also important in the early thirteenth-century Icelandic *Poetic Edda* and is mentioned several times by Snorri in the *Prose Edda*, as well as by Saxo. Sigurd, as several scholars have suggested, is the Arthur of the northern world—perhaps based on a historical figure. He was mythologized in the sagas and was of German rather than Scandinavian origin. As Siegfried, he was a hero of the late twelfth- or early thirteenth-century German epic *The Nibelungenlied* and figured also in much earlier tales.

There are several stories of Sigurd/Siegfried's lineage. It was thought by some that he was a descendant of the gods. In *The Nibelungenlied*, he is the son of King Siegmund and Sieglinde. In the *Volsunga Saga*, he is the last of the Volsungs, the son of Sigmund, and was the only one of his family who could remove Odin's sword from Branstock, the oak. His mother was Hiordis. A tradition exists in which Sigurd/Siegfried's mother, threatened, as a result of unfair accusations of infidelity, hid her newborn child in a bottle, which fell into the river and eventually broke on a shore. The child, Sigurd, was rescued by a doe and cared for by her for a year, by which time he had grown to the size of a four-year-old. One day he ran off into the forest, where he was rescued by the smith Mimir, who named and raised him. Before long, the boy performed miraculous deeds, revealing Herculean strength. The importance of superhuman powers and of the smith as a guardian and namer thus figures in the stories of both Cuchulainn and Sigurd.

Uther, Arthur, and the Sword from the Rock

Among the Celtic peoples of Britain, King Arthur is the most famous of heroes; his conception is at least unusual, and his initiation is well within the universal hero pattern. Following ancient tales and Geoffrey of Monmouth's *History of the Kings of Britain*, Thomas Malory, in the fifteenth-century *Le Morte d'Arthur*, has the magician Merlin tell Arthur the strange story of his conception.

According to that story, when Uther Pendragon (Uthr Bendragon) was king of Britain, he was assisted in his wars against the invading Saxons by the aging Duke of Cornwall. But Uther fell madly in love with the duke's beautiful wife Igraine and made his love so evident that the duke became offended and took his wife away to his castle at Tintagel on the Cornish coast. As the castle was impregnable, Merlin agreed to use magic to help Uther obtain Igraine. While the duke was away fighting a battle, the magician used his magic to make Uther look like Igraine's husband—so much so that the would-be lover was able to enter the castle unchallenged and was admitted to Igraine's bed. That night Arthur was conceived and the Duke of Cornwall was killed.

Merlin predicted that Igraine's child would be the greatest of the kings of Britain. Eventually Igraine married Uther and Arthur was born. It is said that elves attended the birth and that they gave the baby the gift of courage and strength as well as intelligence, generosity, and longevity. When Uther asked Igraine who the child's father was, she admitted to having slept with a stranger who resembled her husband. Delighted by her honesty, Uther revealed that he was that stranger. For his own protection, the baby Arthur was given to Merlin, who gave him to Sir Ector to be raised.

When Uther Pendragon died, the British kingdom was threatened by dissent and disagreement. Realizing the danger, Merlin had the Archbishop of Canterbury call together the nobles of the kingdom to decide who would be king. A stone with a sword in it suddenly appeared in a churchyard. These words were written on the stone: "Whoever pulls out this sword is the lawfully born king of Britain." At Christmas time and again at New Year's, various nobles attempted without success to remove the sword. At that time, Arthur arrived at the stone with Sir Ector and his foster brother Sir Kay, whom he served as squire. Sir Kay asked Arthur to return to their camp to fetch a new sword for him. Arthur returned without having found one, but he noticed the sword in the stone, and while everyone was off at a tournament, he easily removed the sword from the stone and took it to Kay. Recognizing the sword, Kay decided to claim it and the throne. Sir Ector demanded to see for himself that his son could remove the sword from the stone. But when Kay replaced the sword in the stone he could not remove it. Moved by his father's questioning, he revealed that Arthur had given him the sword. When Arthur once again removed it from the rock, Sir Ector and Sir Kay knelt before him as their king. After much resistance, the nobles accepted Arthur as their king, too, and Merlin revealed the details of his parentage.

Heroic Journeys and Quests

At the center of most hero myths is the quest. Through the quest adventure, the hero proves his worth and "makes a name" for himself. The Celtic heroes of the Arthurian tradition in the British Isles are especially known for their quests, the most famous of which—involving such well-known heroic names as Gawain, Galahad, and Percival, and such hallowed places as the Chapel Perilous and castle of the fisher-king—are concerned with the mysterious Holy Grail. These quests will be discussed in detail later in connection with the Welsh sagas. But Germanic heroes are questors as well, and after the conversion to Christianity spiritual heroes such as saints had their own quests.

The Heroes of the Round Table and
the Search for the Holy Grail

The most famous quest in British mythology is undoubtedly that of the Holy Grail; although this myth reached its most well-known and highly refined form in medieval Christian literature, it is of very ancient origin, and the Christian elements seem to have been added as the tradition evolved. The totemic grail itself is most often represented as a chalice, but it sometimes takes other forms, and in its earliest manifestations may have involved a phallic spear dripping life-giving blood into a vaginal cup; these symbols betray the grail's roots in pre-Christian fertility rites. In its medieval form the legendary history of the grail identifies this object as the cup used by Christ and his disciples at the Last Supper, and subsequently employed by Joseph of Arimathea to catch the blood of Jesus as it flowed from his body on the Cross; in this rendering the spear of the ancient fertility rite becomes that of Longinus, and it thus is linked with the sacrificial death that promises new life. Further, the dual function of the cup—to drink wine and to catch blood—clearly links the grail to the miracle of transubstantiation, central to the ritual of the Mass, which echoes and celebrates Christ's words at the Last Supper: "Take this cup and drink, for this is my blood."

According to the medieval tradition of the grail, Joseph of Arimathea took the cup with him to England. After this point several accounts diverge, but the central point is that this life-giving and spiritually redeeming object could be sought successfully only by the pure of heart. The theme of the guileless innocent who may seek the grail successfully is developed in the story of Percival, the English name for this hero, who is first described in French literature as Perceval; he is known as Peredur in his first British form in *The Mabinogion*, and Parzival in the German tale. Percival's quest is sometimes shrouded in the trappings of the legend of the fisher-king. This legend combines the Christian identification of the grail with earlier notions of fertility rites. According to this tradition, the fisher-king is the keeper of the grail and the spear of Longinus, and is dreadfully wounded by that spear, and his potency and the fertility of his kingdom have likewise withered. He awaits the searcher who is pure enough to gain the grail and therefore to take the place of the fisher-king as keeper of the grail; the bleeding-king may then die, and the fertility of his land will be assured. The fertility symbolism of this myth is obvious, and recalls ancient ritual corn-kings who were sacrificed to ensure a good harvest. In the German version Parzival first fails in this quest because his courtesy outweighs his compassion, and he neglects to ask the king the cause for his ailment; this question would have cured him. Later Parzival makes amends. In the most fully realized Medieval English version of the story, that of Malory, Galahad is the last descendant of Joseph of Arimathea, and the only knight pure enough to gain the grail and to heal the fisher-king, and thus to renew the fertility of his kingdom.

Sir Gawain's Quest for the Green Chapel

Sir Gawain's search for the Green Knight and his chapel is discussed at length in the conclusion; one aspect of that quest seems particularly worthy of comment at this point, however. It long has been noted that Gawain's search and the ritual decapitations associated with it are related to ancient fertility rites. Moreover, the themes of vegetable growth and the cycle of the seasons that frame this search call to mind the cycles of life and maturity of man. In this light Gawain's journey is that to manhood, and in his antagonist the Green Knight we find a father figure, a patriarchal shaman who presides over the ritual circumcision—represented here by decapitation—of the boy on the threshold of manhood.

Thor's Quest to Regain his Hammer

Thor is a god rather than a hero, but he is the most heroic of the gods, and at the same time the most human of the Norse pantheon. His attempt to regain his stolen hammer certainly manifests the archetype of the heroic quest. This myth is dealt with thoroughly elsewhere, but it bears mention that Thor's hammer—that emblem which embodies his power and a large part of his identity—is clearly representative of his phallus, his mature and potent manhood. Here again, then, like Sir Gawain, we have a heroic figure who is (re)claiming his virility and dominance through the ritual quest.

Saint Helen Seeks the True Cross

The Roman emperor Constantine is said to have converted to Christianity after his mystical vision of the Cross the night before the Battle of Milvian Bridge, and subsequent traditions linked him and his family with that symbol ever after. The most famous of these traditions is the "Invention of the Cross"—that is, the quest of Helen, the mother of Constantine, for the remains of the True Cross. There are many renderings of this story, including an Old English poem entitled *Elene*, the Anglo-Saxon version of Helen's name. The most direct source for this poem is the Latin *Acta Quiriaci*, the acts of the Bishop Cyriacus; *Elene* follows this source very closely, except for the addition of a passage at the end of the poem. This closing section is unique to this version of the story of St. Helen, and includes a description of doomsday and judgment; we will discuss it in detail during our examination of the archetype of the apocalypse. It is important to our understanding of the hero's quest, however, because this Anglo-Saxon saint's life helps to make clear that Helen's pursuit of the Cross is more than the story of the adventurous journey and discovery of a single individual; it is a metaphor for the quest of every soul for salvation.

> After Constantine's victory over the Huns on the banks of the Danube, he returned home and called together all of his wisest counselors to determine the nature of the sign that had granted to him victory. At first no one could answer him, but eventually some Christians came forward and told him the nature of the glorious Cross. Constantine then submitted to baptism, and requested that his mother, Elene, seek out the remains of the True Cross wherever they might be secreted. She was by no means reluctant to do so, and soon she and a great army had arrived in Jerusalem. Here Elene gathered together all of the Jews of the city and commanded them to bring to her their most learned men so that they might answer her questions. The Jews sent to her a thousand wise men, who gradually were winnowed down; one among this select group was named Judas, and he knew from his father and grandfather that Christ was indeed the Lord, and that he had been executed by the temple priests. Judas, however, was obdurate in sin, and counseled that the wise men must by no means submit to Elene's demands, for if they did the old laws would be tumbled down and replaced by the new. When Elene threatened this group with death by burning, however, they gave over Judas and told the queen that he knew the answer to her questions.

Judas was defiant in the face of Elene's threats, but after she confined him in a cell with no food or water for seven days and nights he saw the error of his ways; he led Elene to the place of Christ's torment, and although he did not know the exact resting place of the cross, his prayers for guidance were soon answered by a plume of smoke marking the location. Judas, now fully converted and eager to unearth the Holy Rood, fell at once to digging and soon had uncovered three crosses. He determined which was the True Cross by hoisting it over the corpse of a recently deceased man; while the other two crosses had no effect upon it, the True Cross brought the man back to life. Elene built a temple upon the spot where the True Cross was found, and encased the Rood itself in gold and gems. Judas received the blessing of baptism, and took the new name "Cyriacus"; he later became the bishop of Jerusalem. Cyriacus then aided Elene in her quest for the nails that had pierced Christ's flesh; these she had made into a bridle bit for her son, so that he might lead his forces to victory and the greater glory of god.

The Hero's Descent into the Otherworld

A particularly important aspect of the hero journey and quest is the descent—to the underworld or to some form of the land of the dead. The purpose for the descent can be the retrieval of a loved one or simply information about destiny. In some cases the journey can be a confrontation with the power of death itself. In the British Isles the hero descent is amply present in both the pre-Christian and Christian stories.

Grettir's Descent into the Water-Troll's Cave

Grettissaga was written in Iceland in the first third of the fourteenth century, and survives in four manuscripts from a hundred or so years later. It has been called the last great Icelandic saga, and it concerns the adventures of a man of that island who lived a short time after the conversion of Iceland to Christianity, which is to say in the early part of the eleventh century. Thus this late medieval text is concerned with events from a period roughly contemporary with the composition of the Beowulf manuscript. This relationship is significant because it is clear that both texts draw upon some common folkloric and mythic elements; the most obvious resemblance between the two concerns the two journeys to the underworld and the two battles with monsters recounted below. Beowulf survives in just one somewhat damaged manuscript that might be dated to around the year 1000; it originally was an oral poem, however, and although estimates of its date of composition vary widely, it might be fair to say that this eleventh-century manuscript is based on an oral tradition from two hundred years or so previous, and that the oral poem contains some historical elements dating from another three hundred years before that. Both Grettir's descent into the cave and Beowulf's journey into the mere may have been derived from an ancient Germanic folktale of a hero's battle with two waterfall trolls.

Grettir spent the night at a homestead that was rumored to be haunted by a troll. That night he lay awake in the hall, and around midnight he heard the sound of approaching footsteps. It was not long before the visitor showed herself: a large she-troll entered, carrying a trough and a cleaver. She immediately attacked Grettir, and the battle was fierce; eventually she managed to drag him outside, although he took the doorframe with him. Finally she wrestled him onto a precipice overlooking a waterfall, and it was clear that she meant to take him to her home through the swirling waters below. They clung so tightly to each other that he could hardly breathe—let alone fight—but just as they reached the edge of the cliff he managed to swing her out far enough so that he might draw his short sword; he gave a quick slash with it, and hacked her right arm off at the shoulder. Screaming with pain and rage, the monster released Grettir and flung herself down into the churning waters. She disappeared under the waterfall, and she did not resurface.

The next day Grettir returned to the cliff with a priest. Grettir pegged one end of the rope into the ground in a place overlooking the waterfall, and he tied the other end to a large stone; this he cast down into the pool below. Grettir then dove into the water, swam to the bottom to avoid the worst of the force of the cataract, and reemerged on the inside of the waterfall, in the space between the rushing water and the cliff face. Here he found a ledge, and, above it, a great cave. Within the cave was a giant troll, and soon enough the two were locked in mortal struggle. Grettir managed to slash a gaping wound in the giant's belly, and the entrails poured out of the monster. The priest, meanwhile, saw the blood bubbling out from the waterfall, and thought Grettir dead. He left for home, leaving the rope in place. Grettir battled on with the troll, and he managed to kill the beast at the last. After collecting treasure and the bones of two victims of the trolls, Grettir dove back into the pool and managed to reach the rope, but the priest had left and so no one was there to pull him up; Grettir had to climb up unassisted, carrying his trophies with him.

Beowulf's Journey into Grendel's Mere

The death of Grendel was a cause for much rejoicing in Heorot, and after Beowulf had mounted the troll's arm above the door, Hrodgar and his Danes followed the trail of gore from their hall to the bank of the pool in which the monster had lived. The water there was bloody and disturbed, and the Danes exulted in the death of their foe; then they returned home again to feast and celebrate well into the night. Their joy was short-lived. That very night Grendel's mother came to call, and she wrought fearful vengeance for the death of her son: she snatched the most beloved of Hrodgar's old retainers from his place among the sleeping benches, and quickly made her escape. Beowulf had slept elsewhere that night, but in the morning he undertook to track and kill the hateful intruder.

Following the path back to Grendel's mere, the Danes and Geats together formed a more doleful parade than they had the day before. Beowulf took his leave at the edge of the water and dove in; he swam down and down, fighting off sea-monsters. His descent took most of the day until, near the bottom, he was snatched and dragged into a cave by the water-hag herself. Her lair kept out the water, and so Beowulf was able to engage in battle with his foe. His sword failed him, however, and he was forced to wrestle the monster. The water-troll now pinned him down and tried to bring her own blade against him, but his mail coat protected the hero. Finally, Beowulf saw near at hand an ancient blade, booty brought to the lair by the sea-witch or her son; he grasped it firmly and brought it against the neck of the ogre-woman. Her neck was cloven—flesh and bones—and life fled from her body. Beowulf then sought the corpse of her son, and he took his head as a battle trophy. Meanwhile, the blood of the hag bubbled up to the surface, and all thought Beowulf lost; the Danes returned home mournfully, while the Geats remained and grieved for their lost leader. Soon their sorrow turned to joy, however, as Beowulf emerged from the loathsome waters with his trophy, the head of his foe Grendel. The Geats returned then to Heorot, and the leader of the Geats proudly displayed the head of the enemy of the Danish folk.

Bran's Voyage to the Land of the Immortals

Bran the son of Febal was visited in his dreams by a vision of a beautiful woman; her visage haunted him day and night, and finally he determined to seek her. He and his foster brothers and their crew therefore set out to find the island from whence she came. They had many adventures on their voyage—including meeting the sea-god Manannan—and they visited a number of magical islands. Finally they came on the Island of the Women, and here they stayed for a long, long time. Eventually Bran's crew grew restless, however, and they determined to depart. Now they were warned that for any man among them to set foot on the shore of Ireland ever again was for that man to sign his own death warrant. They had, in fact, so-journed in this land of immortals for many centuries, and although time had stood still while they remained, to journey home would be to bring age and death crashing down upon them. The men determined to sail for home anyway. In the sight of Ireland one of the crew leapt overboard and swam ashore, and his shipmates watched in horror as he crumbled to dust. Bran himself committed his story to strips of wood carved in Ogam script; these he cast overboard before leading his men on their journey into oblivion.

Pwyll's Journey to the Otherworld

Pwyll's pact with Arawn, the king of Annwn, and his journey to the underworld ruled by his acquaintance are discussed in our treatment of *The Mabinogion*. Suffice it at this point to note that Pwyll gains power and prestige through his relationship with Arawn, a relationship that is cemented by Pwyll's acts of heroism and faithfulness while in the otherworld, and that is denoted by Pwyll's designation as "Head of Annwn."

Sir Orfeo Seeks his Wife in the Land of Fairy

Sir Orfeo is the subject of a good deal of comment in the conclusion to this book. The Orpheus myth generally, however, is a classic example of the hero's descent into the underworld. Orpheus, of course, undertakes this journey to regain his love lost to death, and ultimately bespeaks the human desire to combat and to overcome death. This tradition is traceable in the Western tradition all the way back to Gilgamesh and perhaps beyond; human desire for immortality, however, is always ultimately frustrated. Orpheus and many others fail at the last in their attempts to conquer death. Sir Orfeo himself, however, reaches the land of Fairy and escapes unscathed with his beloved Queen Heurodis. Through this success Orfeo seems to win a respite from the inevitable, and in that aspect differs from the ultimate source of this particular myth.

Christ's Journey to the Underworld: The Harrowing of Hell

After Christ's death on the Cross, he descended to Hell, where he spent the three days prior to his Resurrection. Christ's death was the key to his rebirth, and thus to his immortality. Having conquered death he became once more fully divine, and through his victory offered the hope of similar everlasting life through him to all of his followers. Christ did not return from his sojourn in Hell alone, however; with him were freed Adam and Eve, the Prophets, and all the righteous who had died before Christ came to redeem their sins. Christ ripped open the gates of Hell in order to leave with these good souls, and hence this act is called "The Harrowing of Hell," meaning the opening of Hell; a harrow is a blade used by farmers to rip open the soil. This conception of Christ's violent overthrow of Satan's dominion of the dead was very popular in the Middle Ages, and perhaps nowhere more so than in Anglo-Saxon England, where the Germanic recasting of Christ as a warrior-hero imbued it with the tint of martial victory, and that liberally combined elements of Christ Triumphant with those of Christ Militant.

Heroic Battles with Monsters

A traditional test of the hero on his quest is the battle with seemingly overpowering monsters such as dragons and cyclops. The Northern European invaders brought a great variety of hero-monster stories to the British Isles; traditional Northern European monsters such as trolls and dragons were particularly well represented in early British literary material. Further, under Christian influence the monster in various guises became an image of Satan and the victim of heroes such as the English patron Saint George. Accounts of the lives, miracles, and martyrdoms of saints became a popular narrative form in the Middle Ages, and—not surprisingly—usually manifested important elements of the monomyth of the hero. Moreover, all saints' lives ultimately were modeled on the life of Christ, and thus the heroic battle with monsters took on added levels of symbolic significance as the battle between good and evil, God and Satan, virtue and sin, and Church and anti-Christ.

Grettir's Fight with Glamr

The Norse Grettir displays some of Beowulf's heroic and personal characteristics, but these similarities served each of these heroes differently. Both die at the end of their sagas, but while Beowulf's death may be attributable in some part to his heroic overconfidence and honor, pride is not considered a mortal sin in this poem, and Beowulf is considered a great hero and a good king throughout his tale. Grettir's fortunes change after his battle with Glamr, however, and he suffers outlawry and solitude as a result of his uncompromising pride and actions. Perhaps newly Christian Iceland in the early tenth century could not abide the same fierce and independent heroic spirit in a live troublemaker like Grettir that a more solidly Christian Anglo-Saxon England could celebrate in a safely dead and legendary heroic pagan forebear of the sixth century or so.

A farmer named Thorhall had a hard time keeping shepherds, for his farm in Shadow Valley was haunted by some troll or spirit or another. Finally he managed to contract a man named Glamr to work for him. Glamr was a huge and imposing chap, with the hair and eyes of a wolf, and the disposition to match: he was thoroughly unpleasant and made no attempt to get along with others. He was not a practicing Christian, and he both mocked and lamented the traditions of the Church that caused him the slightest inconvenience. For all that Glamr was a good shepherd, and Thorhall lost no sheep during the period of his employment. For this reason the farmer was willing to put up with his hired hand's eccentricities, and ordered that he be left to his own devices.

One Christmas eve morning Glamr was up early and demanding his breakfast, heedless of the fact that the good Christians of the household were used to fasting on that day. Thorhall's wife fed Glamr as he requested, but she warned him that nothing good would come of it; his response was a derisive laugh. No one ever saw Glamr alive again. That evening he didn't come home at his usual time, nor did he arrive at Church before Mass was over. No one was willing to search for the unpleasant fellow until daylight, so it was nearly noon the next day before they found him; Glamr was dead, his skin had taken on a blue-black hue, and he had swollen up to the size of an ox. Several attempts to bring the corpse back to the church proved unsuccessful, as his body had become so unaccountably heavy, and when they brought along a priest to hallow a burial in the wilds, they couldn't find the body. The next time they searched—without the priest—they found him again, and unable to haul the corpse an inch further they gave up and raised a cairn of stones over it; then they returned home.

It soon became apparent that this grave could not contain Glamr; animals and shepherds were killed or were frightened off, and soon Thorhall's farm was on the brink of ruin. His servants were gone, his stock scattered or slaughtered, and—to add insult to injury—Glamr made a practice of returning to the farmhouse each night, mounting the gables and riding the house like a fierce gale. A light now burned all night in that hall, and the rafters and beams seemed ready to tumble down. Thorhall was at his wits end; he stayed with friends for a while, but when he returned Glamr's hauntings were worse than before, and Thorhall's poor daughter took ill and died from the strain. Thorhall thought he might have to abandon his farm forever.

At this time Grettir heard about the goings on at Thorhall's farm from his uncle Jokul, for indeed, people in those parts were talking of little else. Grettir was much thought of for his exploits, and it seemed to him that a trip to Thorhall's would be just the kind of adventure he relished; his uncle thought it would be the worse for him, but Grettir would heed no warning, and soon made his way to the farmer's house. Here he found that the story had not been exaggerated, and that all was in a shambles; the house seemed about to fall in upon itself, and it certainly was not the most hospitable of dwellings. The farmer was fair in his warnings to Grettir, and tried to convince him to leave; he was especially concerned for Grettir's horse, as Glamr seldom allowed one to escape alive. His words were for naught, however, for Grettir was determined to stay; and the truth be told, the farmer was happy to have such a bold man sleeping under his roof.

The first night passed, and the dawn came with no visit from the monster; the farmer was optimistic. Another night followed like the first, and still the revenant had not mounted the farmhouse roof; Thorhall was overjoyed. When they went out to feed Grettir's horse, however, they found it had been slaughtered. The farmer warned Grettir to leave immediately, if he valued his life, but the hero responded that he felt the life of his horse had at the least paid for a glimpse of the zombie; they both were convinced that he would have his chance that very night. So it came to pass: Thorhall closed himself up in his separate room, and Grettir made himself as comfortable as he might upon the benches in the hall.

At about the third hour of the night Grettir heard a huge racket outside; he heard the crash and rattle of a large creature climbing upon the roof, and soon the rafters and gable shook and swayed so violently that it seemed the whole roof must soon collapse. This went on for a long time, and then the creature seemed to shamble back down off of the roof. Footsteps sounded as the zombie shuffled around to the makeshift door crudely fixed upon its post; the undead night-walker thrust this out of his way, and ducked low to enter the hall. When he stood to his full height inside, his monstrous head grazed the gables. Seeing a figure wrapped in furs upon a bench, Glamr lunged forward; not a word was spoken, but a mortal battle soon commenced. The enemies grappled, crashing around the hall, upending and destroying what little remained whole within the house. Soon the monster began to move toward the door, dragging his foe behind him; Grettir thought himself overmatched as it was, and did not desire to battle Glamr in the wide open field. Glamr was the stronger, however, and toward the threshold they inched; a large rock stood somewhat submerged just in the entryway, and as Grettir felt he could not hold on for much longer, he braced his feet against this stone and thrust himself with all his might against his opponent. The monster was utterly unprepared for this, and the two grapplers crashed through the doorway, the man landing on top of the monster. Glamr's shoulders were so broad that as he fell backward he pulled the doorframe and a part of the roof down with him.

Now Grettir saw the only sight that would ever terrify him: in the cloud-broken moonlight he saw Glamr's demon eyes glowing and glowering; for the rest of his life he saw those eyes staring at him in the dark, and for that reason he was afraid to go abroad alone at night ever after. Now his strength failed him, and the monster pronounced a curse upon him; his luck would turn from that fateful day, his powers would stagnate, and he would be hounded by Glamr's gaze unto death. As the demon finished, Grettir felt his strength surge back; he drew his short sword and hacked the head from the night-walker. This head he placed between the monster's buttocks. Then he and Thorhall burned the body, and buried the ashes far from the habitations of animals and men. Thus Grettir vanquished Glamr the revenant.

Beowulf's Fight with Grendel

Lo! In days of old, Hrodgar, king of the Danes, caused a great mead-hall to be built; it was broad and high, and this greatest of halls he named Heorot. In Heorot,

Hrodgar kept a large and loyal retinue, feasting them on beer and meat and distributing to each man his share of treasure. All were happy there, and the hall was the heart of the community of warriors of the Danes, whose joyful strains wafted away each night from Heorot clear down to the marshy fens and watery borderlands, where a dark creature walked alone. This solitary figure was named Grendel, and he was a demon of the race of Cain. He wandered each night alone and miserable, and the sounds of joy from Heorot filled him with loathing and rage. One night he came to the hall while all within were sleeping, and the fury of his attack was such that there was much weeping the morning after his coming; thus did the joyful song of Heorot turn into a mournful dirge. Nor did Grendel stay away long; he returned the very next night, and soon this nightly slaughter brought an end to the community that had flourished in the mead-hall; all joy was fled, and many was the man who now made his bed elsewhere. For twelve long winters events continued in this wise, until Hrodgar despaired of ever regaining the Heorot and warrior brotherhood of old.

Across the sea in the land of the Geats, Beowulf the young hero heard of Hrodgar's plight, and determined to leave the court of his king and uncle Hygelac in order to cleanse the great hall of the Danish king of this monster; he hoped to win fame and renown in the attempt. In a party of fifteen Beowulf crossed the salt byway to the land of the Danes, and soon was well received in Hrodgar's hall. The Danish king knew his visitor of old, and knew his lineage; his heart was glad to have such a hero as his champion. After feasting Hrodgar and his retinue went to their beds, a safe distance from Heorot; Beowulf and his host, however, took their rest among the benches, and soon all but the leader were fast asleep. Removing his weapons and armor, the hero vowed to destroy his foe with his bare hands.

The watchful one had not long to wait. The hateful visitor soon arrived, and entered the hall as he had so many times before. He reached out for the warrior slumbering on the bench nearest to him, and soon had rent the flesh and bones, slurped the blood and bile, and eaten his victim whole, hands and feet. He turned next to the hero who awaited him, and the demon gripped this man as he had his first. But this man gripped him back, and it was clear to the monster as soon as they were grappled that he had never before encountered such strength; then the evil one wished he were far away in his foul and lonely home in the fens. There followed a terrific tumult and violent struggle; the opponents crashed about the hall, one desperate to depart, the other grim in his grip, both anxious to snuff the life from the other. Finally the troll escaped from the clutches of his nemesis, but at what cost? For he left his arm and shoulder behind him, still firm in the grasp of his foe. Then he who had so joyfully slaughtered many knew the despair of the victim of violence, as he made his way back to the depths of his dank home, mortally wounded. Beowulf exulted in his victory, and next day mounted his trophy over the door of Heorot in token of his glory. Soon enough he would take the head of his fallen enemy, as well.

Sigurd the Dragon Slayer

After Odin, Loki, and Hoenir had paid Otter's ransom to Hreidmar and his sons with Andvari's tainted gold, the kin of Otter fell out over the division of this wergild. Regin and Fafnir—Hreidmar's two remaining sons—wished to have their shares immediately. Their father refused them, however, and as a result Fafnir killed his father in his sleep and made off into the barren wilds with his ill-gotten gains; there he transformed himself into a great venomous serpent, and he spent his life brooding over his cursed treasure and laying waste to the countryside all around. Regin, meanwhile, left penniless, went to the court of King Hjalprek, where he served as smith. After the birth of Sigurd, Regin served as his foster father, raising the boy in his household and teaching him the pastimes of nobility and the mystery of runes. As Sigurd began to grow to manhood, his foster-father attempted to incite in him the pride and heroic spirit necessary to confront Fafnir; eventually Sigurd agreed to do so, on the condition that Regin forge for him a magnificent sword. Regin created two lesser blades that Sigurd shattered upon the anvil, but the third time Sigurd bade him use the two pieces of Sigmund's broken blade, which Sigurd had obtained from his mother as his inheritance. This blade was named Gram, and when Regin had refashioned it, it cut easily through the anvil. Sigurd now agreed to face Fafnir, once he had avenged his own father's death.

Once Sigurd had accomplished this vengeance he returned to Regin and prepared to make good on his oath. They traveled together to the heath upon which Fafnir lived, and searched until they found the track leading from the lair of the worm to his watering hole; Regin advised Sigurd to dig a trench across this track, to lie in wait within the trench until Fafnir crossed over it, and then to thrust his sword into the serpent's heart. Sigurd asked what would happen to him if he were submerged in the dragon's blood, but Regin merely derided him for his cowardice and made off in haste. Sigurd dug a trench as he had been told, but before he had finished an old gray-beard appeared before him and noted that he should dig a series of drainage trenches so that he would not come to harm from the worm's blood. This old wanderer then vanished; it was not the first time the young hero had been helped by the all-seeing one.

Having completed his task, Sigurd hid himself at the bottom of the central trench; he had not long to wait. Soon the earth trembled with the approach of the dragon, and poison spewed all around; but Sigurd was safe in his hiding place. Just as the belly of the beast passed over him, Sigurd thrust the sword with all his might through the heart of the evil one, and thus the serpent received its death blow. Fafnir asked who had slain him and why, but at first Sigurd refused to reveal his identity; finally, however, stung by the taunts of the dying beast, Sigurd foolishly revealed his name, and so the dragon was able to pass the curse of the gold along to his killer. Sigurd did not fear death, however, and so determined to take the gold anyway, and be rich until the day marked out for his fall. After Sigurd had interrogated Fafnir concerning his wisdom about the gods, the dragon died.

With his vile kin safely put to rest, Regin soon appeared on the scene and demanded his share of the wergild of his brother Otter, denied to him for so long: Sigurd might keep all the hoard, but Regin asked of the warrior the trifle of Fafnir's roasted heart. This request Sigurd granted, and then Regin drank of the serpent's blood and fell into a deep sleep. While Regin slumbered, Sigurd roasted the dragon's heart for him. Burning his finger by accident, however, Sigurd thrust his digit into his mouth. Upon tasting the blood of the worm, Sigurd suddenly found himself able to understand the speech of birds and learned from those around him of Regin's plotted treachery against him. Determining now to send one brother upon the heels of the other, Sigurd drew Gram once more and took his false-hearted foster-father's head. Then he ate some of the heart of Fafnir and packed the rest away. Finally Sigurd made his way to the lair of the dragon, packed up all of the treasure he found there, and left to seek the shield-maiden Brynhild.

Beowulf's Battle with the Dragon

After his return from the land of the Danes, Beowulf served his lord Hygelac loyally until that great man fell, and eventually Beowulf succeeded him upon the throne of the Geats. King Beowulf then ruled over a prosperous land for some fifty winters. Meanwhile, in a burial mound stuffed with ancient treasures, a dragon slumbered atop a shining heap of gold. Sorrowful hands of old had raised this mound over the accumulated treasure of a vanished race; he who left it there alone remained of all his kith and kin, and before he joined them in death's long sleep, he entrusted all the wealth of his people into a lonely low hill by the sea. The evil worm sought out all such troves, and for three hundred long years the dragon—greedy and jealous of pride—had called this barrow home. The worm was well pleased with every sparkling gem, every fragment of red gold glistening in the light of his fiery serpent breath.

While he lay undisturbed this fire-drake troubled Beowulf not, but at the end of the king's days an evil mischance brought the hoary hero against his final foe, the dreadful dragon. It seems that some man or other—the banished retainer of a lord—stumbled upon the mighty chamber of the cairn as he roamed the wastes in mournful exile. Although terrified of the wrath of the worm, the intruder thought to buy back his lord's favor with burnished gold: he took a cunningly wrought cup and made his escape undetected. Soon enough the dragon woke, and mighty was his wrath: that very night he began his rampage, and he burned many buildings to the ground. The very hall of the Geats was consumed by fire, and Beowulf learned to his sorrow of the devastation wrought by the worm; and although the serpent sought the safety of his barrow, Beowulf was bound to destroy the dragon.

Knowing full well that his wooden shield must yield before this fiery foe, Beowulf commanded one wrought of iron. Soon he sought the lair of the serpent in the company of twelve men: eleven loyal retainers and the miscreant who had carried off the cup from the barrow; this last served as guide to the others, although he relished not the role. Soon enough they found their way to the barrow by the sea, and Beowulf bade farewell to his trusted retainers; although he could not battle the worm unarmed—as he had Grendel—he thought the glory would be greater should he best the beast single-handed. Soon he engaged his enemy, and the conflict was terrible; Beowulf was bold and brave in the attack, but soon he began to fall back from first onslaught of his foe. The fire was fierce, and the ancient iron at his side failed the aged warrior for the first time.

Beowulf's band soon fled into the forest—all but Wicglaf, his loyal follower and kinsman, who determined to fight by his lord's side; he helped to deflect the fury of the second assault of the serpent. When his wooden buckler was destroyed by the flames, Wicglaf sought the shelter of his lord's shield, and side by side the two continued the fight. Then the dragon charged a third time; he fought through their defenses and gripped the hoary hero by the neck with his cruel and venomous fangs. Beowulf's life began to ebb away as blood and poison surged in waves. Now Wicglaf came to his lord's aid: while the dragon tore at Beowulf with his teeth, he failed to notice the young hero who closed on him from beneath; Wicglaf thrust his sword into the serpent's lower reaches. As the drake howled in pain and fury, his fire dimmed as his life-blood poured out. Beowulf, doomed but not yet dead, saw his chance: He pulled forth a short sax from his side and severed the serpent's skin from neck to middle. The two men were victorious. The victory was not without cost, however, and after Wicglaf had shown his lord the treasures he had won, the bold gray-beard king took leave of this world. Wicglaf chastised the more cowardly retainers with harsh words. Then they gathered up the dragon's hoard. Beowulf was soon consigned to the funeral pyre by his mournful nation, and his ashes found rest in a mighty barrow on a headland, surrounded by the gold—ill-got by the greedy dragon—gained through his glory.

Judith Decapitates Holofernes

The story of the Hebrew Judith's heroic struggle against the evil Assyrian Holofernes belongs to the apocryphal tradition, was included in the Vulgate Bible of Jerome, and certainly was deemed canonical by the Anglo-Saxons. Judith is clearly meant to be a Christian hero, and Holofernes is most certainly cast in the light of a demonic monster. The most common reading of this battle between the chaste and pure Judith and the sinful and debauched villain who wishes to defile her is that the former represents good, the Church, and chastity, while the latter symbolizes evil, Satan, and licentiousness. In the Anglo-Saxon version of the poem, moreover, we might glimpse a Christian shadow of the Germanic Valkyrie virgin battle-goddess. Further, this text comes to us in the *Beowulf* manuscript of ca. 1000 CE, and it has been argued persuasively that its retelling was influenced by the age of the Danish raids upon England. In this light, Judith represents a strong female figure who—through her own martial courage and fortitude—is providing an example for her erstwhile wavering warriors. Thus Judith's speech to the Bethulian host—which previously had trembled before the Assyrian army, but which inspired by Judith's actions routs it—may be interpreted as a call to English valor and honor in the face of Danish invasion. In this example, then, we find a rendering of an archetype of the hero that embodies converging mythic and political understandings of the function of heroism.

Holofernes, lord of Assyria, had laid siege to the city of Bethulia, and had completely cowed the army of the Hebrews. He and his men feasted and drank in their tents, and committed all manner of foul sin. There was one woman from the Hebrews who was more beautiful, pure, and desirable than any other, and Judith was her name. This woman came into the Assyrian camp to visit Holofernes, who intended to put her to unspeakable purposes. Bold in the face of danger and death, the woman stood by while the Assyrians drank themselves into a stupor. Finally they put their drunken king to bed and left Judith in his company to sate his baser desires. Though this was his intent, Holofernes was to find his evening's sport far less to his liking. The lecherous sot was too drunk to move and soon had lost consciousness entirely; he would soon enough wake in Hell. Steeling herself for what was necessary, the courageous virgin crossed to the bed and pulled Holofernes's great sword from its scabbard; heavy and unwieldy in her hands, it yet served her purpose: pulling the hair of the beast toward her, she managed to tug his head into a favorable position. She struck with the sword and buried the blade halfway through his neck; still unconscious, the sinful one still lived, though his blood spurted up through the gaping wound. Struggling to free the blade, the Handmaid of the Lord wrenched the sword from the sinner's neck and brought it down again, hard. Holofernes fled screaming into the pit of Hell as his head spun off of the bed and crashed onto the floor.

Judith lifted her grisly trophy from the floor and handed it to her maid, who placed it in a bag, then the two Hebrew women fled silently from the Assyrian camp. Back in the city, the heroine and her maid were met with wild acclaim; gathering the people around her, she urged the warriors to go forth boldly to cast down the Assyrian host. She proclaimed that God's hand had guided her victory over the monstrous Holofernes, and that his bloody head signified the doom of the army he had led. Now the Hebrews gathered in their might and brought forth a mighty troop against the invaders. The Assyrians were muddled and confused by wine and terror, and the Hebrews struck down many. The generals gathered around their master's tent, imagining him still in the embrace of the lovely virgin, rather than locked in the rigid grip of death. They coughed and made noise, hoping to waken their departed lord, but fearing to disturb his privacy. Finally, one among them grew desperate and bold enough to enter the tent, and he found the maimed and bloody corpse of his king. He grew grim and grieved at the sight, for he knew that this death of his chieftain betokened the larger death of the host. He called out the horrible news to his fellows, who flung down arms and fled. The Hebrews pursued the remnants of the Assyrian army, wretched in retreat. Few of those who had left Assyria found their way home again. Thus the Bethulians gained a great victory owing to the bold acts and wise words of the virtuous Judith; her warriors returned to the city with great gifts for her: the helmet and mailcoat and sword of Holofernes—all gory and bloody—and all of his vast wealth. The finest of maids raised her eyes to heaven and gave thanks and glory unto the Lord.

Miles Christi: *The Hero-Saint Does Battle for Christ*

The theme of the saint as a soldier of Christ is a common one in the medieval tradition, and such soldiers—as it may be expected—often do battle with devils and demons as well as with their human collaborators. The Anglo-Saxon tradition embraced the concept of the Warrior-Christ, as we have noted at some length. It is to be expected that this tradition also produced stories of saints that likewise were bellicose. Saint's lives often passed from Latin and from continental European sources to vernacular (meaning local languages other than Latin) and to British versions; further, some British saints were the subjects of native tales of spiritual warfare. *Juliana* is an example of an Old English poem of a saint based on a very popular Latin original, while Guthlac was a homegrown English saint whose life was recorded both in poetry and in prose. Both saints did battle with demons in the course of their careers as soldiers of Christ.

Saint Juliana: *Shield-Maiden of the Lord*

Saint Juliana was a virgin who was martyred for her faith in the first decade of the fourth century; Juliana was the daughter of a wealthy and influential family in the city of Nicomedia. Although her father was a pagan, Juliana was a devout Christian and had in fact dedicated herself to a life of virginity to glorify her god. When her father betrothed her to Eleusius, a pagan governor, her vow of chastity forced her to refuse the match. The evil pagans both were enraged, and subjected Juliana to many cruel punishments and torments in their attempt to break her will; Juliana was resolute in her faith and her courage, however, and showed no fear. During her confinement in prison, a demon appeared to her in the form of an angel, and this evil spirit attempted to cause her to fall into mortal sin by giving her false advice: he claimed that the Almighty had taken pity on her torments, and wished for her to end her suffering by making some token sacrifice to the pagan idols of her persecutors. Seeing through the evil one's ruse, Juliana seized the demon and forced him to confess to his sins, his mission, and his techniques before casting him head-long back into the pit from whence he had crawled. Every word she forced from the devil was a torment to him, as was the iron grip with which she held him. After her victory over the demon Juliana endured more tortures and fi-nally was executed, but her faith protected her from pain, and the multitudes that witnessed her martyrdom were converted to the faith.

The story of Juliana's life was retold many times, but the first version recorded in a vernacular language was the Old English poem written in the early ninth century by an author named Cynewulf. This we surmise because at the end of *Juliana*—as well as three other poems—the name "Cynewulf" is spelled out in Anglo-Saxon runes. Each rune in this alphabet had a name as well as its value as a letter, and so the clever poet wove his name into the poem by substituting the appropriate rune for a word or concept related to the theme of the line at hand. It is notable that runes also had pagan and mystical connotations, as we discuss in our examination of Odin's sacrifice of himself to himself on Yggdrasill. In this case Cynewulf chose to add a personal reflec-tion on judgment and penitence at the end of a retelling of a classic Latin saint's life, and in so doing he used the peculiarly Germanic runic tradition, a tradition that allusively hearkens back to the pagan past.

Saint Guthlac, Local Hero: Man-at-arms to Man of the Cloth

Guthlac was a member of the Mercian aristocracy and was born in the late seventh century. From an early age he showed capacity for military leader-ship, but by the time he was twenty-four he had given up his arms to carry the Cross into battle for Christ. He entered the monastery at Repton for two years, and then lived a solitary and ascetic life on the Crowland fens in Lin-colnshire. Such a life of voluntary privation was thought to purify the soul and bring one closer to god, and clearly in origin it was modeled on the prac-tices of the Desert Fathers of the ancient church. It is noteworthy, however, that early British asceticism such as Guthlac's seems more directly derived from Irish monastic practices, which added a component of grouped solitude and Celtic mysticism all their own. After fifteen years of this harsh life Guth-lac died peacefully, still a relatively young man. A year later his body was dis-interred and found uncorrupted, and Guthlac was declared a saint. The re-maining versions of Guthlac's life are rich in militaristic imagery, and in them Guthlac is said to carry the emblem of Christ into battle against the devils. Several incidents are related of his struggles with these evil spirits, and per-haps most telling is the description of how Crowland blossoms and grows green with Guthlac's final escape from and victory over his foes. Such regeneration of nature with the release from bondage of a representative of Christ necessarily reminds us of the archetype of the dying god. Further, all saints' lives are fundamentally recastings of the story of Christ, and thus lead us to the topic of the apotheosis of the hero.

The Rebirth, Return, and Apotheosis of the Hero

The hero's life begins miraculously, turns into a quest, and ends with some sort of a remarkable return. The return can take many forms. Osiris is reconstructed and revived by his sister-wife Isis. Jesus comes back from death. J.R.R. Tolkien's fictional hero Frodo returns a changed creature from his ring quest, bearing the burden of a new wisdom. Theseus and Herakles and Aeneas experience the underworld and return to perform great deeds. Some heroes promise to return at some future time of need; Jesus and Quetzalcoatl are of this category. In the British Isles two hero returns stand out: that of King Arthur and that of the dying god Baldr, who in this context of mortality, functions more as a hero than as a god.

The Once and Future King

In 1113, some French clergy visited Bodmin near Dartmoor in Cornwall in search of Arthurian sites. There they learned of the Cornish-Breton tradition that, as prophesied by the magician Merlin, King Arthur, who some said had been killed by his son or nephew Mordred (Modred) in battle, was in fact alive. It was believed that he had been wounded and taken away to be cured by certain fairy queens—some say by his sister Morgan Le Fay—to the mysterious island of Avallon (Avalon), called the Isle of Apples by Geoffrey of Monmouth and the Isle of Women in older Celtic tradition, from which place he will one day return to save Britain. In Sicily a story developed of Arthur's remaining forever young because he was fed from the Holy Grail. In many places Arthur was associated with the strange figure of the fisher-king, whose wounds are somehow tied to the physical and spiritual fertility of the land. In the early thirteenth century, Gervase of Tilbury supports this association by asserting that Arthur's wounds reopened each year. These and many other stories are part of the popular belief in and de facto apotheosis, or deification, of the "once and future king."

The Return of Baldr

Certain similarities exist between the myths of Arthur and those of the Norse Baldr, suggesting a possible single source for both stories. As Arthur was slain by his son or nephew, Baldr was killed by his brother, and as the wounded Arthur was cared for by women, Baldr was sometimes associated with the supernatural warrior-women called the Valkyries. Like Arthur, he partook of magical food. Furthermore, his death, like Arthur's wound and promise of return, can be tied to the idea of fertility.

Scholars have long sought Baldr's origins in the fertility gods of the Middle East—gods such as Attis, Baal, Adonis, and Osiris, who died and returned with the plants of the spring. Arthur's origins, too, could be there. Baldr's particular plant—the one Snorri tells us killed him—was the mistletoe, which attaches itself to the sacred oak, a tree sacred also to the Celts from ancient times. Finally, Baldr is a dying hero who returns. After the end of the world in Ragnarok, Baldr, with several sons of the old destroyed gods, will return from the underworld to reign over the world.

5

CREATION AND APOCALYPSE

If myths are cultural dreams, they can obviously reveal a great deal about the cultures that dream them. Probably the most telling myths are those of creation and those of the end of the world, whether through a flood leading to a second creation or through an apparently final cataclysmic event. A creation myth is a given culture's record of what Mircea Eliade calls the "breakthrough of the sacred into time." It is the defining story, the story of a people's being brought into existence, the story in which divine power gives a society particular significance in a universe that is otherwise seemingly irrational, arbitrary, and devoid of order. As such, creation myths play an important role in the re-creation of order when things have fallen apart. A new creation typically follows a flood or an apocalypse. In many cultures, creation myths are a necessary part of curing rituals.

There are, of course, many types of creation myths. Some peoples of central Asia and North America favor myths in which an animal in ancient myth time dives into the primal depths and brings up the beginnings of earth. Other North Americans—especially the indigenous peoples of the Southwest—believe that they emerged from a series of earlier worlds beneath the present world. In China and many other places a primal egg is the source of creation, and in Australia the world was dreamed into existence. By far, the most popular form of creation is the *ex nihilo* (from nothing) model in which a creator god thinks, speaks, excretes, or crafts the world. Frequently, as in the traditions of India, Greece, and the Old Testament, there is a war between powers of good and evil or primitive and less primitive forces in Heaven.

As for the flood myth that typically follows the creation in Sumerian, Hebrew, Egyptian, and so many other cultures, the point seems to be that a cleansing is called for so that creation itself can be cured and reestablished. The apocalyptic death of the universe by fire is also a cleansing, and so we have the concept, for instance, of a ritual baptism by fire as well as by water. Yet apocalyptic or end-of-the-world myths are the ultimate nightmare. As chaos gives birth to cosmos in creation, cosmos gives birth to chaos in the apocalypse.

The creation stories of the British Isles contain many of the creation motifs found in the rest of the world, but they reflect at least three very different visions of the human and divine roles in the universe.

Creation in the British Isles

The ancient stories of the Norse and Celtic creations in Ireland and Britain obviously come into conflict with the Judeo-Christian stories of Genesis. The Irish monks who recorded the ancient Celtic myths and the Norse writers such as Saxo and Snorri all worked from a Christian perspective, so that the purity of the original "pagan" myths is perhaps lost to us. Still, the difference between the myths of the three traditions is clear enough. Genesis and the Judeo-Christian apocryphal tradition tell the story of God's *ex nihilo* creative act followed by a war in Heaven between the forces of the all-powerful patriarch and the upstart angels of Satan and a subsequent fall of humanity followed by a great flood. The Germanic stories of creation also involve a war between two divine forces, and there is a flood, but the details of the creation bear little resemblance to Genesis. In Ireland there is the tradition of the emergence of Ireland after the Great Flood—the one described in the Old Testament—but the details of the creation of Ireland have nothing in common with the Judeo-Christian tradition.

The Prose Edda Creation

Basing his *Prose Edda* story primarily on the late tenth-century eddaic poem, the *Volupsa*, Snorri Sturlusson tells of a strange creation derived from both fire and ice. In this myth, creation occurred between two entities that were already in existence—Muspell in the south and Niflheim in the north. Muspell was a place of fire where Black Surt with his flaming sword waited for his chance to destroy the world that would be created. Niflheim was a place of ice and snow, at the center of which was Hvergelmir, the spring from which the Elivagar, the eleven rivers, flowed. Between these two places was Ginnungagap, the great void into which the rivers poured, creating a desolate iciness in the north, which stood in contrast to equally desolate volcanic-like moltenness in the south. But in the middle of Ginnungagap, at the meeting of the two conflicting climates, was a mild area where melting ice became the evil frost-giant Ymir. From under the left armpit of the sweating giant came a man and a woman. His legs came together to give birth to a family of frost-giants. From the melting ice of the center a cow called Audumla was born, and Ymir drank the four rivers of milk that poured from her. Audumla licked the ice for three days until a man named Buri appeared. Buri's son Bor married Bestla, the daughter of the frost-giant Bolthor, and Bestla gave birth to the gods Odin, Vili, and Ve. As the de facto mother of the gods, Adumla seems to have roots in the Egyptian cow mother-goddess Hathor.

As they hated Ymir and the savage frost-giants, the three sons of Bor killed Ymir. The great giant's spilled blood became a flood that drowned all of the frost giants with the exception of one Bergelmir and his wife, who escaped in a vessel made of a hollowed tree trunk. Then the three gods used Ymir's body to create the world; his flesh became earth, his bones became mountains and stones, his blood served well to make the lakes that dotted the world and the seas that surrounded it, and his skull was used for the sky. A dwarf stood at each of the four corners of the sky. The dwarfs were named East, West, North, and South. The gods made the sun and moon and stars from the sparks of Muspell. To the giants they assigned a place called Jotunheim. The brothers then created a protected and fertile area called Midgard from Ymir's eyebrows, and they created a man from a fallen ash tree and a woman from a fallen elm. Odin gave them life, Vili gave them intelligence and emotions, and Ve gave them senses. Ask was the man and Embla was the woman. These were the parents of the human race.

The similarity of elements of the Norse flood to those of the Sumerians, the Hebrews, and others suggests a common Indo-European source, as does the familiar story of a dead primal god's body becoming an animistic world.

The story continues. Odin took Night, the daughter of the giant Narvi, and placed her in a chariot in which to ride across the sky at set intervals. Night had married several times and had given birth to Earth by Annar and Day by Delling. Odin placed the shining Day in another chariot in which to cross the sky.

A man named Mundilfari had two children, a beautiful daughter whom he called Sun and a handsome son he named Moon. Odin did not appreciate this arrogance so he caused the two children to guide the chariots of the actual sun and moon. The gods allowed two wolves, Skoll and Hati, to chase Sun and Moon to keep them moving.

Out of the maggots that had come from Ymir's rotting flesh the gods made dwarfs. These beings were presided over by Modsognir and his assistant, Durin.

As for the sons of Bor, they formed a family of gods and goddesses called the Aesir, led by the father-god Odin. They built a wondrous home over Midgard and called it Asgard. The two zones were linked by the rainbow-bridge Bifrost.

Over all of the parts of the universe rose the world tree Yggdrasil, the three roots of which reached to Asgard, Midgard, and the old hot Niflheim, which became a kind of hell under the world.

The upper world contained not only Asgard but also Vanaheim, the home of the ancient fertility gods or Vanir, who at first went to war with the Aesir and then agreed to a truce and union with them.

Cesair and the Creation of Ireland

Little is known of early Celtic-British creation myths. We have discussed above the invasions of Ireland and the creation of the Irish nation as described in the Leabhar Gabhala or Book of Invasions. These stories would seem to be a mixture of history, legend, and mythology, and by the time they were written down they were somewhat Christianized. We are told, for instance, that it was the granddaughter of Noah, Cesair (Cessair), who first came to Ireland. As her father, Bith, had not been invited onto the ark, his daughter suggested that he build an idol, and the idol suggested that they build an ark like Noah's. Cesair and her father did as the idol advised and arrived in Ireland after seven years in the ark. Cesair married Fintan, who had avoided death in the Great Flood by turning himself into a salmon. Although a magician herself, Cesair was unable to preserve her life or those of her followers, all of whom, with the exception of Fintan, died before the later invasions of Ireland.

Amairgen and the Singing of Ireland

Still another tradition mentioned earlier in connection with the Milesian poet Amairgen is perhaps of more importance as an Irish creation myth. Amairgen, whose Welsh counterpart is Taliesen, follows in the tradition of his Indo-European ancestor, Krsna of the Indian Bagavadgita, who embodies all aspects of the universe. As he sets foot on the land that will be Celtic Ireland, Amairgen, in a sense, sings it into reexistence and further develops the ideal of the prophetic, all-encompassing divine poet-hero who will find later expression in poets like Walt Whitman; Amairgen incants a new world into being.

Apocalypse and Armageddon

Apocalypse comes from the Greek term for "revelation," and has come to mean a revelation or a vision of the end of time; as is befitting for a vision, accounts of the apocalypse often are particularly rich in metaphor and symbolic creatures, events, and symbols of all kinds. Further, *apocalypse* now has a sense that is more or less synonymous with Armageddon, a Hebrew name for an ancient battlefield. Hence *apocalypse* carries its current connotation of violent and cataclysmic destruction, sometimes including a notion of a great cosmic battle between forces of good and evil, order and chaos. Battle or no, the apocalypse often results in the violent destruction of the current physical world, and may include a raising of the dead and a last judgment of the souls of all humanity.

The study of the end of the universe as we know it is properly called eschatology, from the Greek word for "last" or "last things." The study of the apocalypse is therefore a specific subsection of eschatology, the study of the end of things generally. The apocalypse represents a cleansing, and thus is intimately related to the archetype of the Great Flood; to utilize a Christian metaphor, the former is the baptism by fire that is prefigured by the latter, a baptism by water. The cleansing of the apocalypse is generally followed by a rebirth, a renewing of life in a new form or context. In some traditions this new order is that of a higher, spiritual plane, and thus the apocalypse represents a cosmic housecleaning that puts an end to the world we know; in other traditions—notably in Indian myth—the apocalypse is simply one aspect of an endless cycle of renewal, a destructive force of regeneration that kickstarts another cycle of life. As we shall see, British traditions often comprise a combination of these different visions of the end of the world.

Apocalypse in the British Isles

Traditional Germanic visions of the apocalypse involve a final battle between the forces of the gods—who stand on the side of civilization, order, and right—and the demonic forces of the giants, Loki, and their allies, who represent the forces of nature, chaos, and evil. Although the cycle of life is renewed through the appearance of Lif and Lifthrasir from their safe haven in Yggdrasill, and order is reestablished with the resurrection of Baldr, there is good reason to believe that these are later emendations resulting from contact with Christianity. Hence the original Germanic vision of the end of time may well have resulted in a final and irreversible reassertion of chaos over order, a somewhat dismal conception that nonetheless resonates metaphorically with the model of the end of the universe postulated by modern physicists. The Christian vision of the apocalypse embraced by the Anglo-Saxons is somewhat more hopeful, if fearsome in its description of the Last Judgment. Such visions combine a number of mythic traditions under an ostensibly Christian rubric, but in any case they also bring an equally final end to Creation. Pre-Christian Celtic visions of the apocalypse are more amorphous and difficult to define, but given the themes of fertility, resurrection, and the cycle of life that dominate Celtic religious rituals and mythic beliefs, it is reasonable to guess that their visions of the Apocalypse were similarly cyclical. We are on firmer ground when we assert that Old Irish Christian manifestations of the judgment-day theme influenced that of their British neighbors.

The Norse Ragnarok

At last the doom of the gods will fall upon them; Gullinkambi, the golden cock of Asgard, will waken Odin's hosts. His cousins in Hel and Jotunheim will crow likewise. The strife of man against man and brother against brother will increase and not abate. The Great Winter will fall, three years long, and the snows will bury life, the winds will quench it, and the sun will give no respite. The wolf Skoll will swallow the sun, and Hati will devour the moon; their gore will splatter earth and heavens. The stars will flicker and die. The earth will shake and quake, and all Yggdrasill will tremble. The old bonds will be no more. Loki the Trickster and Fenrir the Wolf will burst free, and the seas will overlap their shores with a violent tide as Jormungand—the great Midgard Serpent—makes his way to shore. Naglfar—the ghastly ship made of the nails of dead men—will sail to battle. Loki will captain the ship of the dead from Hel, and Hrim will command a bursting load of giants. Fenrir's wide jaws will scrape both heaven and earth, and Jormungand will spew venom and poison throughout creation. Surt will lead the fire demons of Muspell across Bifrost the Rainbow Bridge, and it will shatter and fall beneath them; fire will encompass them, and Surt's sword will take the place of the sun. The enemies of the gods will gather on the plain of Vigrid, and they will be terrible to behold.

The gods will be no less prepared. Heimdalr will call a blast on his mighty Gjallarhorn, and the gods will rush to assemble. Odin will leap upon Sleipnir and hasten to consult Mimir, while the Aesir and the Einherjar arm themselves; they will don helm and mailcoat, and grasp sword, shield, and spear. Eight hundred strong will march shoulder-to-shoulder through each of Valhalla's five hundred and forty doors; they will be led to Vigrid by Odin, resplendent in golden helm and shining mail. He will grip Gungnir grimly. Odin will greet Fenrir with cold cheer, and Thor beside him will look to settle his old score with Jormungand. The Serpent will prove a match for the Thunderer; Odin may expect to have no help from that quarter. Freyr will grapple with Surt, and well might he rue the day he pledged his mighty blade to Skirnir. After a great struggle, Freyr falls to the fiery sword of Surt. Tyr and Garm the Hound each will prove the death of the other, and Loki and Heimdalr likewise will even ancient enmity. Thor will best Jormungand in the end, but will live to step back only nine paces before he succumbs to the poison the Serpent spewed upon him. Fenrir will swallow the One-eyed God at the last, but his victory will be cut short by Vidar, who will avenge his father and vanquish the wolf by stepping on its lower jaw and stretching the other up until he rips it asunder. Vidar's shoe that day will take all of time to cobble; it will be made of all of the scraps of leather ever snipped off of shoe leather and cast away, and it will prove too thick and tough even for the fangs of Fenrir. Then Surt will cast his fire through the three levels and nine worlds of creation, and all will die: men and gods, dwarfs and elves, birds and beasts, all manner of creatures and monsters. The sun will be extinguished, the stars drowned, and the earth will sink beneath the waves.

The earth will rise from the deeps again one day, green and blossoming, and crops will flourish where none were planted. A new sun will take the place of her mother, and a number of gods will return to the ancient ruins of Asgard, led now by Baldr. Lif and Lifthrasir will survive to renew the race of men; they will have hidden themselves securely in Yggdrasill's embrace, and the fire of Surt will not scorch them; they will survive on the morning dew, and keep watch through the branches above them for the new sun rising. And thus, through its death, the world will be born again.

The Anglo-Saxon Fire of Judgment

On the Day of Judgment, Christ will return in wrath; the earth will tremble, the mountains will fall, the sun and moon will lose their luster, and the stars will twinkle no more. All the acts and sins of each man and woman will be made manifest for all to see at that dreadful conclave, and woe to him who makes not amends in this life. Then a great fire will surge forth, and all the world, sky and seas, will be consumed. The earth will be no more. All of the souls of those dead and living at the call of the Doomsday trumpet will gather before the Seat of Judgment. Many will tremble then who did not repent when they could. Then all of mankind will walk through the Fire of Judgment, and its flames will scathe each according to the nature of that soul. Then all humanity will be divided into three groups. To the righteous—whose souls are like unto refined gold—the fires will be as a warming to burnish them to greater brightness. They need not fear the wrath of their Lord, and the fire will not harm them. To those who have sinned but are not damned—whose souls are like unto silver mixed with lead—the fires will be as a smelting furnace, and the sins will be burned out until their souls are completely cleansed of impurities. Their pain may be great, but it will be of short duration. To the damned, however, the obdurate sinners who heard but ignored the Word of the Lord, and who reveled in sinfulness—whose souls are like unto base metal—the flames will be punishing, and a taste of the painful eternity to come: they will boil and burn for all time, and they will earn no respite. They have earned the enmity of the Lord, and like lead in the furnace they will be consumed by the fires on Judgment Day. For the first two groups it will be different, however, and after their smelting they will emerge from the furnace purged of all sin and wickedness, and their faces will shine like those of the angels.

THERE ARE MANY doomsday visions in Anglo-Saxon literature, and the elements of this one have been drawn from a number of Old English poetic sources including *Phoenix*, *Christ III*, and *Judgment Day I & II*; the most direct source of the smelting metaphor, however, comes from the judgment-day fragment appended to the Old English poem *Elene*. One of the most intriguing analogues to this Anglo-Saxon judgment-day tradition is a Bavarian poem known as *Muspilli*; this poem draws upon the ancient Germanic vision of fiery apocalypse described in the Norse tradition of Ragnarok above (remember that Surt and his fire demons are of Muspell), and in fact may have been based on an Anglo-Saxon original. *Muspilli* is clearly a Christian poem, but alludes directly to the earlier, pre-Christian conception of the end of time. A representative Old Irish analogue to this tradition is interesting in that it takes the form of a *lorica*—the Latin term for "breastplate"—or protective prayer, and thus may have descended from a traditional supplication for protection against the forces of darkness. Perhaps the most interesting element of some Anglo-Saxon visions of the apocalypse is the metallurgical smelting metaphor; this image of the soul as metal to be purified and refashioned in the crucible of the furnace is common throughout many Old English texts, and has roots in a number of biblical passages, and indeed beyond. Throughout the world and the ages many metalworking cultures have embraced such imagery, and it is in fact the ancient ancestor to the belief in alchemy, the mythical transmutation of lead into gold.

6

THE SAGAS

Generally speaking, the Old Norse term *saga* refers to Icelandic prose literary works of the thirteenth and fourteenth centuries; the Old Norse plural form is *sogur*. Many such sagas give us information about the Norse gods, but most of those with which we immediately are interested may be grouped either as "historical sagas" or as "heroic sagas." The former category includes, among others, the *Heimskringla*—a titanic account of the kings of Norway from mythical times until 1177—and the famous *Islendinga sogur*—the "sagas of the Icelanders." The latter includes the *fornaldar sogur*—the "legendary heroic sagas"—as well as heroic narratives from the Icelandic sagas and others. Historical sagas thus deal with accounts of the kings of Norway, the earls of Orkney, and the like, as well as with the early history of the settlement of Iceland and points west by the Norse; these sagas are most notable for their concise and matter-of-fact style, for their attention to realistic detail, and for their appearance of historical veracity. Heroic sagas sometimes include complex

genealogies, as well as mythical and folkloric elements and material from ancient heroic traditions.

It is dangerous, however, to accept any saga as an unimpeachable historical source without corroborating evidence, and likewise, the mythic and legendary material of the sagas is sometimes more fourteenth-century Icelandic
than pre-Christian Germanic. It would be naïve, therefore, to assume that
these medieval Christian literary traditions represent an unassailable link in
an unbroken chain stretching from pre-historical oral traditions to the
threshold of the modern literary period. It also would be overcautious, however, to reject out of hand the relationship between the earlier oral traditions
and the later written sagas; there is doubtless some relationship between the
oral and written traditions, and furthermore, often the trappings of saga may
shroud some useful kernel of mythic or historical origin.

While sagas may be unreliable historical witnesses, therefore, examining
comparatively some narrative elements of the saga genre may be helpful in
determining the mythic function of a number of British heroic tales and
pseudo-historical records. Here we are using the term *saga* to refer to medieval
literary works that represent some sort of link to an earlier oral culture and are
similar to the Icelandic sagas in some significant ways. Most, for example, include some aspects of saga style, many use legendary historic or mythical material as a saga might, and several contain sagalike elements of realistic description. Most crucially, each episode recounted here illustrates narrative
material or archetypal elements of mythic provenance, often associated with
aspects of the hero. Thus, although not all of these works are sagas in the
technical sense, all are reminiscent of sagas in some respects, and so we use
the term for the sake of convenience. We begin this section with Norse accounts of historical personages and events in Britain; we then move on to
Norse heroic narratives that echo heroic elements in English myth and literary history. Next we examine Anglo-Saxon versions of history that draw upon
heroic traditions, and Old English heroic tales that illustrate Germanic historical sensibilities. We conclude our discussion of the sagas of Britain by describing the Irish and Welsh mythic, historical, and heroic cycles that embody narrative elements of the saga.

Sagas of Norse Britain

The Norse were an important force and presence in Britain from the eighth
through the eleventh centuries, and these islands were important stepping
stones in the Viking expansion to the west; thus it is not at all surprising that
several Norse sagas touch upon British topics. *Orkneyingasaga*, the saga of the
earls of Orkney, is the only example that focuses primarily on the Isles of
Britain, but there are notable mentions made in a number of other sagas. We
have chosen to recount three episodes with British settings from three different historical sagas, as well as three heroic passages that illustrate the close
kinship between Norse and English mythic and literary traditions. In 1066,

Harald Hardradi quite possibly could have become the king of England instead of William of Normandy, and so it seems fitting to begin with the
episode from his saga that details the fall of Hardradi's army at the Battle of
Stamford Bridge. Harald lost his life in that battle, and thus he gained his famous "seven feet of English ground" in place of the whole realm he had coveted. In Egil Skallgrimson we find one of the most famous and irascible of saga
heroes, and we include his famous sojourn in York to illustrate the importance
of the north of England in the Scandinavian world of the time. In the saga of
Saint Magnus from *Orkneyingasaga* we find a saga hero cast in the mold of ha-
giography, and this combination reminds us of Anglo-Saxon conceptions of
warrior-saints. In the sagas of Bodvar Bjarki and Grettir the Strong there are
clear echoes of mythic and narrative traditions manifested in the Old English
Beowulf, while in the saga of Volundr we find a Norse reflection of an ancient
Germanic god the Anglo-Saxons knew as Weland. Finally, it is worth men-
tioning that while we do not mean to give short shrift to the Norse mythological sagas, we will not discuss these in this section, as we already have dealt
at length with the cycle of the Norse gods.

Norse Sagas of the History of Britain

KING HARALD HARDRADI WINS SEVEN FEET
OF ENGLISH GROUND

Harold Godwinsson ascended to the throne of England in early 1066, succeeding the reign of Edward the Confessor. Harold's claim to the throne was
contested both by William the Bastard, Duke of Normandy, and by Harald
Sigurdsson—called *Hardradi*, meaning "hard counsel" or "fierce governing,"
sometimes rendered "ruthless"—king of Norway. Harold of England had also
alienated his own brother, Tostig, a marauder of the first degree; their sibling
rivalry comes into the story at Stamford Bridge. On 20 September 1066,
Harald of Norway landed in the north of England with close to 10,000 men
and routed an English army on his way to York. Harold of England surprised
his rival at Stamford Bridge just five days later, however, and the Norwegian
king was killed and his army destroyed in detail. William of Normandy
landed in the south of England just three days later, and Harold Godwinsson had to march down to meet him; the English army was massively defeated at the Battle of Hastings on 14 October, Harold was killed, and
William became king of England. It has long been noted that the double
forced march of the English army—200 miles north from London to Stamford, then all the way down to Hastings—played a key role in the Norman
victory at Hastings. It is entirely possible, then, that—had William landed
the sooner—Harald Hardradi might have been king of England. The passage
below begins with the incognito approach of the Norwegian lines by King
Harold Godwinsson; Snorri's account ignores the facts that the Norwegians
were surprised and that one-third of their forces were miles away guarding
their 300 ships.

Twenty horsemen from the English approached the Norwegians, and asked to parley; this request was granted. One among them asked if Earl Tostig were in the company of the invaders; Tostig then identified himself to the speaker. Another rider then offered Tostig Northumbria as a peace-gift between brothers; Tostig, however, asked what Harald of Norway might expect of the exchange. The rider answered that which Harold had promised before: seven feet of English ground, or however much more was required to bury the giant Harald than was needed for ordinary men. Tostig and the Norwegians, incensed by this insult, sent the English away. After the riders had departed, Harald asked Tostig who the well-spoken man among the English who made the offer might be; Tostig replied that it had been his brother King Harold himself. Harald Hardradi was angry, then, since he might have easily murdered his enemy under flag of truce, but Tostig answered that he would rather be killed by his brother than kill Harold through treachery.

The English cavalry now advanced against the Norwegians, but were forced to ride around them rather than through them as a result of the arrow volleys and spears of the infantry. The English now feinted and fell back several times, until the Norwegians broke ranks and pursued them; then the English horsemen turned back upon their enemies and hewed them down outside the safety of the shield-hedge. When Harald of Norway realized what was happening he charged into the fray, and English fell before him right and left; but too soon he had outpaced his troops, and he was fatally felled by an arrow through the throat. Now the Norwegians rallied around Tostig beneath the Norwegian banner, and although his brother offered them terms for peace and life, they chose to die under the standard of Harald Hardradi.

KING HARALD'S SAGA forms part of the *Heimskringla*, Snorri Sturluson's sweeping account of the history of the kings of Norway, an account grounded in the mythic past. It is stereotypically Germanic in its historic sensibility in that it combines verifiable records of historical events with legendary and mythic pre-history. Likewise, the treatment of known historical events the saga does offer usually are more concerned with personalities, character development, and the narrative unity of a dramatic biography than with wide historical scope or the modern concern with the "big picture." Harald's is a story that invites such a "great man" biographical approach, and his saga develops many themes of the hero archetype: from his youth as a fugitive after the death of his half-brother King Olaf the Saint, through his journey to manhood in the households of the Viking King of Russia and in the Varangian Guard of the Byzantine Emperor, to his ascent to maturity and to the Norwegian throne, the life of Harald as described by Snorri is a classic retelling of the development of the hero. It is also a tale well told, full of intrigue and adventure, and Snorri has crafted it to illuminate most clearly his conception of Harald as an archetypal Viking hero and Norse king. In a sense this is fitting because—all narrative and historical liberties aside—it is true that in the course of his life Harald traveled the length and breadth of the Viking world; it is likewise arguable that with his death we may mark the beginning of the end of the age of Scandinavian dominance in European politics.

EGIL SKALLAGRIMSSON PAYS
HIS HEAD-RANSOM AT YORK

Egil Skallagrimsson, like Grettir Asmundarson, is a freewheeling, multifaceted character who defines many aspects of the Viking saga hero at the same
time as he himself eludes easy definition. The stories of Egil and Grettir are
two of the five sagas of Icelanders that approach the truly epic in tone and
scale; thus it is no surprise that these two characters embody archetypes of the
hero even as they seem types of the anti-hero. In other words, Egil is a bastard
of truly heroic proportions, and in his saga we see attributes—even heroic attributes that might be admirable in smaller measure—enlarged to an absurd
extreme, just as old Egil's very skull grew huge and deformed. His head de-
serves a brief comment here: it was by all accounts almost fantastically ugly,
and the physical condition that caused its deformation pained poor Egil
greatly; but it was an ugliness of epic proportions, and it armored his skull
even as it bloated it. The very cause of his pain and his deformity thus turned
many an axe-blade that might have ended the life within a more comely—
though thinner—skull. Egil's head was larger than life, in a way, and it serves
as an emblem for his saga: poet and pirate, farmer and free-booter, murderer
and mystic rune-master, Egil's story is too large for easy definition, and he
stretched the boundaries of behavior even in his own volatile era. Again like
Grettir, it is through this selfsame recalcitrant individuality that the stamp of
the hero shows most clearly through Egil's ugly features.

The story of Egil sweeps through the northern world, from Scandinavia
through the Low Countries and Britain, and across the North Atlantic to
Iceland; it shows a typical Icelandic interest in the history of the Viking Age
and the settlement and concerns of Iceland, but in true saga fashion it elabo-
rates upon the outline of history with the personality and characteristics of a
memorable individual. The episode with which we will concern ourselves occurs in Viking York, the Norse fortified urban center in England since even
before the days of the establishment of the Danelaw in the late ninth century.
This episode helps to illuminate how a saga may bring to life images of historic Viking Britain and its kings. Eirik Bloodax, the son of King Harald
Fairhair of Norway (who unified that kingdom), made his seat at York in the
mid-tenth century. The saga of Egil Skallagrimsson and his sojourn at York—
as fictitious as much of it may be—takes as its starting place the actual relationships among a number of the members of Egil's family and members of the
Norwegian royal court.

Egil is purported to have committed his first murder at the age of six,
and he was still a nasty old killer in his dotage; his grandfather was said to
have been a shape-changer married to the daughter of a Berserkr. Egil himself had a terrible temper and had a short fuse. There is more than a little
flavor of the demonic in Egil, and it is not without reason that this man was
a worshiper of Odin. Such a man makes many enemies; Egil had the misfor-
tune of counting King Eirik Bloodax and his wife Queen Gunnhild among

his. Egil's blood brother Arinbjorn served King Eirik as a retainer, but most favored in that court was a man named Berg-Onund, a relation of Egil's wife, Asgerd, who was able—through the influence of his royal patrons at the law-moot—to deny to Asgerd her inheritance. Egil killed Berg-Onund and his brothers as a result of this dispute, and killed Eirik's son, who had come to warn Berg-Onund of Egil's approach; then Egil added insult to injury by placing a horsehead on a pole on a cliff and dedicating it to the royal couple. These crimes, in conjunction with earlier enmity between the family of Egil and the queen of Norway, effectively passed a death sentence on Egil, should he fall into the power of King Eirik. It was just Egil's luck that he would do so, but with his skill in words he purchased his head from the angry king, if only for a time:

It is said that Gunnhild was skilled in the black arts, and that she cursed Egil so that he could not rest until he was within her power. Soon after their last confrontation, King Eirik was forced to abandon his claims in Norway and seek refuge in England. Here he raided the holdings of King Athelstan until that king granted him the north to hold against the Scots; Eirik then set up his court at York. Meanwhile, Egil stayed at home as long as he could, until he felt so agitated that he felt he must go roving. He determined to seek service with King Athelstan in England, and he outfitted a ship and crew with this purpose in mind. On the way to Athelstan, however, Egil's craft was forced to land not far from York, and although crew and cargo were saved, the ship was totally destroyed. When Egil learned where he was and who ruled there, he made his way quickly to the house of Arinbjorn his blood brother, who stood high in the favor of Eirik. Arinbjorn took Egil to his king immediately, and gave out that Egil had come by choice to cast himself upon the mercy of Eirik; Gunnhild demanded the immediate death of her enemy, but Eirik stayed his hand when Arinbjorn reminded him that to kill a man in cold blood after dark was murder. Eirik gave Arinbjorn Egil's life for the night, but determined to kill him with the dawn.

Egil returned with Arinbjorn to his house, and his blood brother advised the old verse smith to come up with a *drapa* in honor of his enemy the king; this was an elaborate poem of praise with a repeating refrain. Egil tried to do so, but each time a verse came into his head a noisy bird perched by his window chased it right out again. Finally Arinbjorn climbed out by Egil's window, and although he saw no bird, he noticed an old hag scurrying away; it is thought that she was a shape-shifter in the service of the witch Queen Gunnhild. Now undisturbed, Egil spent the rest of the night composing and memorizing his verses; by morning he was able to recite them to Arinbjorn, and they went back to King Eirik. When the king was still unwilling to grant Egil his head, Arinbjorn remarked sadly that he would have to stake his own life with that of his blood brother; further, he reckoned that the two could take many a good man to the grave with them. Gunnhild called him a traitor to choose his friend over his lord, but Eirik wished to placate his loyal servant. At this point Egil stepped forward and recited his lay, and finer verses were never dedicated to any king; they told of his valor and glory and generosity, and it was impossible to hear these words and remain unmoved. Eirik granted Egil his head for his poem, but only so long as he never came into his sight again; he did this mainly for the love of Arinbjorn. Egil thanked the king in verse for the gift of his ugly skull, and the blood brothers quickly departed. Traveling in the company of Arinbjorn's many armed men, the two soon found their way to the court of King Athelstan, who greeted Egil warmly; the verses Egil sang to this king reflected his true hatred for Eirik, and would have cost Egil that which he had ransomed, if only Eirik had heard them.

THE MARTYRDOM AND MIRACLES
OF SAINT MAGNUS OF ORKNEY

In classic saga style, this tale begins with the legendary and mythic past and then moves rapidly into the historical period and the central concerns of the story. In this case the mythic material is concerned with the division of Norway; the myth has it that Nor and Gor, two brothers, divided all Norway between them, Nor getting the mainland and Gor keeping the islands that were separated from the mainland by water deep enough to sail upon with a ship with a fixed rudder. Later Gor's son hauled his father across the neck of a large peninsula in a ship with Gor's hand upon the tiller, and so Gor vastly increased his holdings. The sons of these brothers squabbled among themselves, and Norway was divided and redivided among their many descendants; this explains the division of Norway into provinces. Later in *Orkneyingasaga*, King Magnus Bare-legs uses Gor's boat ruse to trick the king of Scotland out of the Mull of Kintyre, and this saga returns to the theme of partition and intrigue again and again in discussions of the division of the earldom of Orkney. Saint Magnus himself is a victim of his cousin's desire to rule all of Orkney on his own; thus in the story of Magnus we find an account that combines the problems of partition specific to this tale, the heroic sensibilities of the saga genre, and the narrative form of the saint's life. Both of the latter aspects may help to illuminate some facets of the hero archetype.

During their lives, the brothers Erlend and Paul Thorfinnsson shared the title of Earl of Orkney and divided the earldom between them. After their deaths abroad, Hakon Paulsson petitioned the throne in Norway for the earldom of Orkney and was granted it. Soon afterwards, however, Magnus Erlendsson returned from mainland Scotland and petitioned for his share of the title, which he, too, was granted. At first Hakon thought to deny Magnus his birthright by force of arms, but conciliatory voices prevailed, and the cousins shared power and title for a time without incident. Magnus was generally well liked and was thought to be charitable and just and righteously severe upon wrongdoers; he was also said to be holy and to have refrained from staining his marriage bed with sin through plenty of prayer and liberal plunges into icy seawater.

It is said that the virtues and general popularity of Magnus were part of the reason his cousin Hakon came to envy and despise him. One Lent the acrimony between the earls came to a head, and it was only through the intervention of many powerful friends that Magnus and Hakon came to terms. Soon thereafter Hakon asked Magnus to meet him on Egilsay after Easter. Magnus, truthful as he was, and unwilling to see deceit in his kinsman, agreed to the meeting. On the way there, however, a mighty wave thrust out of a calm and glassy sea and slammed into the seat of Earl Magnus; he declared it a portend of his own death and the duplicity of Hakon, but still he refused to turn back. The treachery of Hakon was clear enough when he arrived with eight ships, but still Magnus was unafraid; he went to church to hear mass, and it was at prayers the next morning that Hakon and his henchmen found the blessed earl.

When Hakon came upon his cousin, Magnus offered him three ways to avoid tainting his soul with the mortal sin of breaking his peace-vow, not to mention staining his hands with the blood of his kinsman. The first offer was that Magnus would leave Orkney for a pilgrimage to the Holy Land; the second offer was that Magnus be handed over in bondage to mutual friends in Scotland; the third offer was that Magnus be mutilated, or else blinded and cast into the dungeon. Magnus made it clear that he wanted to save his cousin's soul if he could. The first two offers did not please Hakon, but he considered the third; at this point his men rose in protest against him, however, and said that they wanted no more division of power in Orkney, and thus that one earl or the other must die. Hakon responded that he himself was not willing to make that ultimate sacrifice, and so it would suit him better if his men killed Magnus instead of him. He looked among his minor retainers for one to sully his hands with this foul deed, and when his standard-bearer refused he appointed his cook to the task; the poor man didn't want this honor, but all involved forced him, and Magnus promised him that he would pray to God for the forgiveness of his executioner. After having said his prayers, Magnus directed his killer to strike him full on in the front of the head, as it would not befit a chieftain to be beheaded like a common thief. So Magnus died.

The rocky, mossy site where Magnus died soon became a grassy field, and this miracle is the first attributed to him. Hakon would not allow his men to carry Magnus to church, and so they departed. This situation was mended by Thora, the mother of Magnus, who approached Hakon with such heartfelt sorrow and gentle humility that he was moved to allow her to bury her son in the church. The site of this grave soon was said to emit light and fragrant odors, and miraculous cures were visited upon the infirm who stood vigil there; but this was kept secret during the years of Hakon's rule. Earl Hakon proved himself an able ruler, however, and was well respected for that; he also undertook a pilgrimage to the Holy Land in later years to pay for his sins. But many of those most closely involved in the treacherous death of Magnus were said to have died horrible deaths. Hakon himself died peacefully in his bed, but strife ensued when his earldom was again divided, this time between his sons Harald and Paul; as unlikely as it seems, Paul gained the whole of the earldom when his mother and her sister wove a poisoned tunic for him. Harald donned the tunic unawares, and so he died instead of Paul.

Meanwhile many miracles were performed at the grave of Magnus: blindness, wounds and infirmities, and leprosy all were healed. Still the bishop did not declare the sainthood of Magnus, nor translate his bones to a reliquary; he feared the enmity of Earl Paul. Finally the bishop made a vow to do so if a voyage home from Shetland went well, but he reneged on this vow and was struck blind for his falseness. Crawling to the grave of Magnus, the Bishop wept tears of true contrition, and was healed when he renewed his vow. This time he was as good as his word and soon had disinterred the bones of the saint, which he washed and found to be bright as snow. He tested a finger bone in a sanctified flame, and it took on the hue of burnished gold. These signs were taken as tokens of the holiness of Saint Magnus. Some time later a man dreamt that Saint Magnus appeared unto him and asked to be moved to the church at Kirkwall; at first the man was afraid of the wrath of Earl Paul, but eventually he approached the bishop and the transfer was made. Many, many miracles of healing were performed there, demonic possessions were exorcised, and many who desecrated the shrine or the day of Saint Magnus rued their mistakes. Here ends the account of the miracles of Saint Magnus of Orkney.

Norse Echoes of English Heroic Sagas

BODVAR BJARKI AT THE COURT OF KING HROLF

Bodvar Bjarki is a major character in the saga of King Hrolf Kraki, one of the *fornaldar sogur* of medieval Iceland. In the tale of Bodvar Bjarki we are presented with a classic Norse account of the hero's birth and journey of transformation; this journey is played out in duplicate, moreover, in that Bodvar—having gained heroic stature and courage himself—leads another ordinary man through the same metamorphosis. The episode that we have excerpted here recounts that second transformation, the rebirth into herohood of a worthless, cringing scapegoat in the court of King Hrolf; Bodvar acts as the midwife at the rebirth of the timid wretch Hottr into the brave hero Hjalti. This theme of the voyage from boyhood to manhood under the auspices of a mentor figure is a common archetype, and Bodvar Bjarki plays both roles in Hrolf Kraki's saga. The Hottr episode also contains a classic example of the hero's battle with a monster, a battle with obvious resonance with Beowulf's battle with Grendel; in both cases a hero from outside the royal court has to come to the rescue of the hapless Danes, who are beset by a magical troll that may not be scathed with ordinary weapons.

The saga of Hrolf Kraki as a whole has many obvious parallels with that of *Beowulf*, and it has been suggested that Bodvar and Beowulf may be analogous characters drawn from the same ultimate source. The Hrolf of the Icelandic saga is equivalent to the Hrothulf of *Beowulf*, and both sources agree that this figure is the nephew of Hroar, who is better known to us as the familiar Hrodgar of the Anglo-Saxon epic. It is in any case clear that both tales take as the central driving force of their narratives stories of strife and struggle within the early Danish monarchy, and the central events of both sagas take place in sixth-century Denmark. Both sagas draw on the same oral traditions, both are classically Germanic in that they plant their roots in the misty, mythic-historic past, and both concern themselves with the origin and rise to prominence of the family of Skjold, called Scyld Scefing in *Beowulf*. This mythical character is said by both accounts to be the patriarch of the Danish Royal House, called the Skjoldungs in Old Norse and the Scyldinga in Old English; both words come from the root for "shield," and refer to the king's role as a guardian of his people. The Anglo-Saxon version is the older of the two by at least a few hundred years, and includes an account of the discovery of the foundling Scyld that is remarkably like the story of Moses; the epithet *Scefing* was added to his name because a sheaf of wheat was found with him. Thus in the Old English tradition the mythical father of the Danish kings was linked folklorically with both protection and sustenance. By the period of the great Icelandic sagas in the fourteenth century, the Old Norse tradition had associated the family of the Skjoldungs with a great many important mythical figures from Adam to Odin; the development of such lineages was a trait common to many medieval historians of Germanic dynasties.

Although written well after the conversion to Christianity, the saga of King Hrolf contains several overt references to the pagan past. Most notable among these are the references to Odin and the Berserkrs, those warriors of insane battle-frenzy who may be linked to shape-changing and to Odinic cults. In this saga Odin is cloaked in the meagrest of Christian trappings, and aspects of his divinity shine through. Bodvar and his two brothers are themselves the sons of Bjorn the Bear-Man, and thus the origin of this hero draws upon the Bear's Son folktale. Bodvar's brother Elk-Frodi was an elk from the waist down, and his brother Thorir had a dog's feet. Bodvar himself had the power to take the form of a bear, as his father had before him. Bodvar reached his full maturity and strength by drinking some blood that Elk-Frodi had drawn from his own veins; the concept of capturing some of the strength or characteristics of a beast by drinking its blood or eating its heart also has ancient folkloric origins, in the Germanic world and beyond. In his role as the mentor of Hottr Bodvar reprises this practice, as we shall see in the following selection.

Bodvar Bjarki rode to the hall of King Hrolf and stabled his horse next to the finest of the king; he asked no man's leave. Entering the hall, he found a small group of men, and he seated himself far out on the benches. After he had been there a bit, he noticed a shuffling sound off in a corner, where a man's hand—black and greasy—reached out from within a heap of foul old bones. Curious, Bodvar ambled over to the great pile of bones and called to him who was within. The answer was timid, and the man identified himself as Hottr. Bodvar asked Hottr why he was within the pile of bones and what he might be doing there. Hottr answered that he had made himself a shield-wall with the bones; it seems that some among the retainers of Hrolf took pleasure in pelting the poor man with their gnawed bones, and it is well known that such sport often proves fatal to the unfortunate target. Now Bodvar reached into the grisly wall of rotting gristle and bone and pulled Hottr out. The poor man was upset that his handiwork had been destroyed, and terrified that Bodvar meant to kill him. Bodvar assured him that this was not the case, and commanded the wretch to keep silent; then the hero took the filthy dog by the scruff of the neck and carried him to a nearby stream, where he scrubbed him clean of grime and grease.

Bodvar then returned to his place on the benches, and he seated Hottr beside him; the poor man—although he sensed that Bodvar meant to help him—was terrified, and he shook like a sapling in a high wind, leg and limb. Soon enough the hall began to fill with the champions of Hrolf, and when they noticed Hottr at his new seat on the benches they thought him over-bold for his station; he, meanwhile, would have returned to his stinking fortress had not Bodvar kept a firm grip on him. Now the retainers of Hrolf began their old game again, starting with small bones pelted playfully in the direction of Bodvar and Hottr. Bodvar pretended not to notice the missiles, but Hottr was terrified and could not eat or drink because he was convinced that he would be hit at any moment. Suddenly Hottr warned Bodvar that a large bone was about to hit him; Bodvar bade Hottr to be silent, and caught the knucklebone as it came to him. It was a great hunk of bone, the knuckle and leg all together. Turning toward his assailant, Bodvar sent the missile back the way it had come, and struck dead the man who had thrown it; all of Hrolf's men now became silent with dread.

Word quickly came to Hrolf Kraki that one of his men had been slain by a most imposing stranger; those who bore the tidings wished permission to slay Bodvar in return, but upon hearing the whole tale King Hrolf would have none of it. Long had he spoken against this sport of his champions, as it brought disgrace upon them all. He commanded instead that Bodvar be brought before him. The king asked Bodvar his name, to which the hero responded that the warriors of Hrolf called him "Hottr's Guardian," though his name was Bodvar. The king asked then what Bodvar offered to pay in compensation for the slain man; Bodvar refused any wergild, claiming that the man had brought his injury upon himself. Then the king asked if Bodvar would like to be his champion, and to take the seat of the slain warrior, but Bodvar answered that he and Hottr came as a set, and that they would need to be seated higher on the bench than had sat the riffraff he had killed. The king declined not the offer, although he saw little merit in Hottr. Bodvar then marched well down the benches, choosing a place of honor much higher than he had been offered; jerking three warriors from their seats, Bodvar seated himself and little Hottr. The men of Hrolf's court took great umbrage at this insult, but none dared to avenge it.

Now Yuletide came, and Hrolf's men became gloomy. Bodvar asked Hottr why this might be, and he was answered that for the past two winters a great winged monster had come to call upon Hrolf's hall, that this greatest of trolls had wrought great mischief, and that weapons bit it not. Furthermore, those who had stalked it had never returned. Bodvar retorted that Hrolf's court held fewer men of mettle than he had been led to believe. On Yule eve the king—wishing to protect his men— bade them all to remain safely inside, and to leave the cattle to fend for themselves. All promised to do as he asked, but Bodvar meanwhile stole away into the night, carrying the protesting Hottr over his shoulder. Soon they saw the horrible monster, and Hottr cried out that it would swallow him whole. Bodvar told him to be quiet, casting the sniveler onto the ground, where he remained motionless. Now Bodvar advanced, but by some magic he was unable to draw his sword from its sheath. Using all of his great strength he was able to shift it a bit, and then he grasped the scabbard and pulled it away from the blade. In the nick of time he cast away the scabbard and thrust the sword under the shoulder of the monster so that he pierced its heart. The beast fell down dead. Now Bodvar went over to Hottr and picked him up and carried him over to the slain monster. Forcing Hottr's mouth open, Bodvar caused him to drink two gulps of the troll's blood and to eat a bit of its heart.

The change in Hottr's character was immediate and incredible; he wrestled with Bodvar for a long time, and then he boldly said that he would never fear any man again. These words pleased Bodvar greatly, and together these two propped up the beast so that it appeared to be alive and about to attack. They went back to the hall then, and no one was the wiser concerning their adventure. In the morning the king asked if the beast had ravaged the livestock, and was answered that all were alive and safe in their pens. Curious, Hrolf sent out scouts to search for any sign of the monster; these came back quickly, reporting that it was nearby, enraged and ready to attack. Hrolf told each warrior to look to his courage then, so that they might overcome the dreadful menace. When they gathered before it, however, the king noticed that it seemed to be standing stock-still; he asked if any among them would dare to approach the creature alone and unaided.

Bodvar answered that here was a task to sate the curiosity of the bravest of men, and he suggested that his benchmate Hottr clear himself of the slander of cowardice by undertaking it, especially since no one else seemed too eager to do so. Hottr quickly assented, and the king noticed at once the change in the man's demeanor. Then Hottr demanded the king's sword, Golden-Hilt, and declared that he would carry the blade to victory or to death. Hrolf replied that Golden-Hilt could only be carried by a warrior both skilled and brave; Hottr rejoined that the king would soon see both qualities in him. Hrolf assented, remarking that a change so complete in other facets might well bode that Hottr was now a mighty warrior. Taking the sword, Hottr charged the beast and struck it down with one blow. King Hrolf was not fooled, however; he guessed aloud that Bodvar had killed the beast, and the hero acknowledged that possibility. Hrolf was well pleased then with both champions, declaring that of all of Bodvar's fine qualities, this one was supreme: that he had transformed a cowardly weakling into a fearless and mighty warrior. He renamed Hottr Hjalti, after Golden-Hilt.

GRETTIR THE STRONG IS OUTLAWED

As in the case of Egil Skallagrimsson, in Grettir Asmundarson we find aspects of the archetypal hero, but like the rest of his character these aspects seem to have developed without any sense of proportion or moderation. Grettir is another rugged individualist—to give this aspect of the hero a modern American face—and like many such before him, he made many enemies as a result of his inability to seek middle ground. Like Egil, Grettir killed a man at a tender age, and spent the rest of his life facing larger and more potent foes. Unlike Egil, however—and indeed, rather like the poet, saga writer, and chieftain Snorri Sturluson himself—this intractability came back to haunt Grettir, and he was eventually killed by his enemies. *Grettissaga* shares a number of characteristics with *Beowulf*, as do Grettir and Beowulf themselves; indeed, these two sagas contain several analogous episodes. Moreover, each of these tales delves into folklore and mines nuggets of historical records with which to forge an allusive and wide-ranging saga. Each hero is stoical and uncompromising in the face adversity, and each seeks risks and dangers that allow him to express his heroic nature and to gain thereby glory, the traditional Germanic equivalent of immortality.

Unfortunately for Grettir, he was born into a Christian era that was rapidly divesting itself of its heroic trappings, and so—unlike Beowulf—Grettir progressively alienates himself through his acts. Further, the *Beowulf* poet recorded his version of that saga several hundred years before *Grettissaga* was penned, and the former is much more straightforward and unassuming in its style than the latter; the story of Grettir, on the other hand, written at the end of the period of the great epic sagas, uses its strong, detailed characterization of its hero—in classic saga style—as an exemplum, in this case as an exemplum of the conflict between encroaching centralized authority and classic Germanic heroic individualism. The first chapters of this saga deal with the centralization of Norway that drove many Vikings—including Grettir's forebears, with whom he shares many characteristics—to Iceland. Even Iceland

lost its autonomy eventually, however, and all those independent individual-
ists eventually fell under the power—however watchful—of a king. Grettir,
then, in this context, is a throwback to earlier times and values. He fights and
wins battle after battle, and with each victory he reasserts his heroic nature;
eventually he falls, however, and his fall echoes the fall of that earlier cultural
system. Christ and the king of Norway prove too strong.

In the episode at hand, Grettir has gone to Norway to seek a position in
the service of the new king, to whom he is distantly related. An arrogant act
of courage, however, ends in the unintentional death of a number of important brothers, and Grettir's subsequent inability to suffer any affront to his
honor ends in his expulsion from Norway. His arrival at home brings no joy,
however, when he learns he has been outlawed—for life—there as well, for
the same killing; this episode, then, spells the beginning of the end for Grettir. In the splash of Grettir's plunge into the icy waters of the channel south of
Stad we hear an echo of Beowulf's swimming contest with Breca, fueled by a
similar sense of boastful heroism. In this instance, however, Grettir's heroic
sensibilities backfire.

When King Olaf took complete control of Norway, many were those who thought
to turn old debts of friendship to their advantage; one such was a man named
Thorir, who thought to send his sons to Olaf to enter his service. Another such was
Grettir Asmundarson. The Thorirssons had reached the harbor below Stad a few
days before Grettir, and had taken up residence in a house built for sailors using the
channel; there they spent their time in drinking and feasting. One night the merchant ship upon which Grettir had booked passage found itself facing a severe
storm just south of Stad, and found safe anchorage across the channel from the
Thorirssons. Still, the merchants had no fire, and they loudly complained that they
might well freeze to death unless fire were procured. Suddenly, one of them noticed
fire across the channel, and they bemoaned the fact that they couldn't sail over
there because of the storm. Grettir endured their pathetic whining as long as he
could, and finally he announced that such a feat was no challenge to a real man;
the merchants then asked him whether he thought he was up to the task himself.
He answered that he was, but he thought that little good would come of it, and
they would hardly thank him as they should.

Stripping down to woolen tunic and drawers, then, Grettir dove into the channel and crossed with the aid of a large barrel. Reaching the other side he found himself nearly frozen stiff, and so he burst into the house of the Thorirssons huge and
blue, with clothes and hair stiff with ice and salt. The Thorirssons and their friends
thought him a troll, and attacked him as soon as he entered; many began to hit at
him with flaming brands, and in their drunkenness they soon spread the fire
throughout the house. Grettir, for his part, paid them no heed, and ran out as soon
as he had grabbed the fire he sought. As Grettir reboarded the merchant ship with
his hard-won fire, his hosts greeted him most warmly; soon enough they changed
their tune. In the morning they sailed across the channel to thank their benefactors,
but all they found was ash and bones; calling Grettir a murderer they cast him out,
and he had a devil of a time finding his way to Trondheim to see the king. By the
time that he did, the story had proceeded him, and at his audience with Olaf Grettir
had to defend himself against charges of arson and willful murder. Finally the king

granted Grettir the right to prove his vow of innocence through the ordeal of the red-hot iron, but on the appointed day a young boy—some say a demon in disguise—mocked Grettir in the church, and Grettir struck the boy in that sacred place. After such sacrilege Grettir could not undergo his ordeal, and so he had to leave the court of Olaf and Norway forever, with the vilest of charges over his head; it was his bad luck that these charges would precede him to Iceland.

VOLUNDR THE SMITH

This Norse heroic saga shrouds the myth of an ancient Germanic god, one whom we know to have been worshiped by the early Anglo-Saxons; Weland is mentioned specifically by name in the Old English poems *Deor's Lament* and *Waldere*, and his name crops up in a few other documents, as well. Moreover, weapons of quality were sometimes designated "the work of Weland" by the Anglo-Saxons. Through such references we know the Old Norse Volundr, Nidud, and Bodvild of the present saga to be equivalent to the Anglo-Saxon Weland, Nidhad, and Beadohild. Swan maidens are important to this saga, and such creatures of Germanic folklore and legend usually are associated with the Valkyries, and perhaps with Freya's feather coat. In this saga Volundr fashions himself a similar coat, thereby providing one of several narrative links between his saga and the story of Daedalus, the imprisoned master craftsman who fashions wings for his escape. This similarity was not lost on the Norse, who called the Labyrinth of Daedalus the *Volundarhus*, which we might render, "the house of Weland." Another obvious relationship to ancient mythology is that between the hamstrung Volundr and Vulcan/Hephaistos, the lame smith-god of the classical world. Finally, the ring taken from Volundr and given by Nidud to his daughter Bodvild is classic in its vaginal imagery, as we have seen before; meanwhile, Nidud's seizing of Volundr's sword—ever a phallic image—smacks of an act of violent male dominance, and ultimately taps into a mythic vein of castration anxiety. Likewise, Volundr's attempt to avenge himself upon Nidud through the rape of Bodvild underscores both the sexual imagery and the struggle for male dominance of the two antagonists.

Long ago three swan maidens had doffed their feather garb for a time by the shore of a lake and were spending their time spinning and weaving flax. While these maidens were in their human guise, Volundr and his two brothers came upon them. Seizing the maidens without their cloaks, the brothers took them to wife, and the three couples lived together in love for seven years. At the end of this time the wives grew weary of their mortal lives, and they donned their flying coats and fled while their husbands were hunting. When the brothers returned they were distraught, and two of them went in search of their wives immediately; Volundr, however, remained where he was and plied his craft as smith. His fame as an artisan spread far and wide, and eventually the evil King Nidud sent men to seize him and his treasure. Volundr was out hunting when these men arrived, so they stole one of his most beautiful rings and hid themselves; when Volundr returned, he noticed that a ring was missing, and he was overjoyed with the thought that his wife had returned to him at long last. He began roasting his kill, and fell asleep waiting for his wife to appear. Volundr awoke to discover himself shackled hand and foot by the minions of Nidud, who soon brought him before their king. Nidud took Volundr's sword for his own, and the most precious of Volundr's rings Nidud gave to his own daughter Bodvild. Then, taking the advice of his queen, Nidud had Volundr hamstrung and set ashore on a deserted and lonely island, where only the king visited him.

On this island Volundr was forced to use his hammer and tongs to the profit of his captor, and he spent many, many lonely and toilsome hours brooding over his escape and his vengeance. Finally an opportunity for both arrived. One day the sons of the king came to visit Volundr in secret; showing them his many treasures, Volundr promised to make them rich even beyond the dreams of their greedy and miserly father. They returned the next day to collect the promised riches, and Volundr opened his greatest chest so that they might gaze within; when they had stuck their heads well and truly in the trunk, however, Volundr brought down the lid upon their necks in such a manner as to decapitate them. Their bodies he hid under his floor, but their skulls he lined with silver and cunningly crafted into goblets for their father, King Nidud; their eyes he fashioned into jewels for their mother, the queen; their teeth he formed into brooches for their sister, the princess. Soon thereafter the opportunity arose for Volundr to seal his victory. Bodvild, the daughter of his nemesis, came to the smith in secret and asked him to repair her ring, which she had broken; she begged him to keep silent about her visit. Volundr greeted her kindly, and promised to do as she asked, and more; he was so generous to her that she suspected no treachery when he offered her a drink to refresh herself. Drinking deeply from the cup of the smith, Bodvild soon fell under the spell of Volundr's liquor and thus was powerless to defend herself from the attack that soon came: the lame captive took his vengeance on the father through the defilement of the daughter on the filthy floor of the smithy. Then Volundr donned the feather coat he had fashioned and flew away, never to return; from the safety of the sky he crowed down to Nidud the terms of his vengeance, and the king in his rage and despair was impotent to exact his own.

Sagas of Anglo-Saxon England

The Germanic oral traditions that informed the saga writers of fourteenth-century Iceland clearly were known to and used by Anglo-Saxon authors, perhaps beginning with the earliest written records in Old English, which probably date from the seventh century. Thus the Anglo-Saxons drew upon a much more recent memory of these traditions, and therefore a comparison of the employment of similar oral material by these two literatures is likely to be both interesting and informative. Furthermore, both literatures might be said to have had a similar sense of history. It is fitting, then, that we begin our examination of the Anglo-Saxon saga with two epic accounts of historical confrontations between the Anglo-Saxons and their adversaries, both Norse and Celtic; here history meets heroic sensibility in a manner that echoes later Norse historicity: in *The Battle of Maldon*, for instance, individual personalities bring to vivid life an otherwise spotty historical record of a relatively minor regional clash. *The Battle of Brunanburh*, on the other hand, deals with an event of much more widespread importance, and uses traditional heroic diction with a relish we might almost describe as patriotic fervor. We conclude this section with two examples from *Beowulf* that illustrate that the Anglo-Saxons used quasi-historical legendary material as an inherent part of their epic heroic structure in a way very like that of the Norse sagas, although the Old English material predates the Old Norse by several centuries.

Anglo-Saxon Historical Sagas and Heroism

THE BATTLE OF BRUNANBURH

The Battle of Brunanburh was fought in 937 CE by a combined force from Wessex and Mercia against an alliance of Vikings and Scots; the multi-ethnic nature of this conflict seems particularly appropriate for inclusion in this study. The record of this battle as related here survives in a number of copies of the *Anglo-Saxon Chronicle*, of which there are multiple versions. This chronicle began as a simple list of years with one or two major events recorded for a given entry, more or less as a device to jog the memory of the compiler as to which year was which. Over time the records for each year became more and more elaborate, some of them—like the present example—even employing the metrical patterns and heroic rhetoric associated with Old English poetry. The style of *The Battle of Brunanburh* is sagalike in its sparse use of language combined with ample specific detail. This account is entirely devoid of a sense of the urgency of Christian combat against pagan invaders so obvious in *The Battle of Maldon*, although Athelstan elsewhere is noted to have been a great patron and defender of the Church. Instead, the writer has chosen to focus on a sense of this battle as representative of the final consolidation of England into one kingdom, a consolidation which seems to him to have been the inevitable end result of the conquest of Britain begun by the invading Angles, Saxons, and Jutes. Hence this saga seems to have been meant as a paean of sorts to the scion of Wessex and to the final domination of his house.

At Brunanburh King Athelstan and his brother Edmund—both sons of Edward—won victory and great glory over the hated Vikings and Scots, enemies in league against the West Saxons. From dewy dawn to dying dusk they shattered the shield-wall of their enemies, uprooted the war-hedge, as was fitting of those who bore the blood of their forefathers; land, home, and gold were ever safe in their keeping. The Norse and Scots felt the keen blades of the warriors of Wessex as they stumbled and ran in disarray, their ranks broken in their flight from fierce fury; nor were the men of Mercia less terrible in dealing out death and destruction to the Vikings of Olaf, who left the flood and flow of the salty sea for that of blood weltering from their wounds; five kings and seven earls suffered the wrath of the West Saxons and their Mercian allies that day. Countless were the dead of lesser rank among the Vikings and the Scots.

Olaf, king of Vikings, made his way to his ship with greater haste than he had left it, and with a retinue far diminished; tiny and tattered was the remnant that fled the field that day and boarded their bark for home, dreary and desperate as they departed for Dublin. Little more cause for joy had Constantine as he scurried for the safety of the north; he would brag no more than would Olaf. The Graybeard King of Scots was sheared that day of many a loyal kinsman, and of his own sons, cut down by the fury of the onslaught of the sons of Edward. Likewise did the victorious brothers, prince and king, head for home from the site of the slaughter, but theirs was a different song; glad with glory, they sang their joy as they returned to the land of the West Saxons. They left behind a feast of carrion, the bodies of their enemies exposed for those with the taste for carnage: the raven and the eagle, the hawk and the gray wolf enjoyed the fruit of battle's labor. We know from the records of the ancient ones long past that no greater victory had ever been won on this island, since first the Saxons and Angles journeyed hither from the east, wreaking havoc on the hapless Welsh, winning wealth and land and glory in the creation of kingdoms.

THE BATTLE OF MALDON

The Battle of Maldon occurred in 991 CE at the point on the Blackwater River where a tidal causeway links the mainland with an island. A band of marauding Vikings had made their base on that island, and the local Anglo-Saxon forces—led by Birhtnoth, the earl of Essex—came out to put an end to the ravages of the Northmen. The English refused to pay the tribute demanded by the Norse, and so battle was joined; it is ironic in retrospect that the English crown indeed submitted to this blackmail later in the same year, paying ten thousand pounds in gold and silver—called *Danegeld*, or "Dane-money"—to buy off the great fleets of raiders. The English would pay more as time went on. At Maldon the forces of Essex were successful at first in defending the bridge by single combat, but eventually Birhtnoth allowed the Vikings to cross in force to engage in a full-scale battle, and this decision proved costly; Birhtnoth fell, and after his death a retainer fled on the dead earl's horse, causing a collapse of the English lines when many conscripted soldiers followed their leader—as they thought—in retreat. The Vikings routed the remaining forces of Essex.

The local forces led by the earl were made up of a small body of aristocrats and full-time warriors in the household of the earl, and a large levy of freeman farmers who made up the *fyrd*, a sort of local militia. The household warriors of Birhtnoth would not have had much personal experience of warfare—the victory of the English forces at Brunanburh had bought the kingdom over fifty years of peace—but they would have been steeped in the heroic tradition of their forebears, including the social mores of the Germanic warrior band called the *comitatus* by Tacitus. Simply put, this social code called for generosity on the part of the leader and loyalty unto death on the part of each follower. After the death of Birhtnoth, the voice of the young warrior Aelfwine most clearly illustrates this code in the present poem: "Many is the night we boasted over mead at our prowess in battle; now is the time to match deeds to words. I will not quickly flee the slaughter-bed, to find reproach at home, now that my lord lies dead upon the field." Whether the

recorder of this episode composed this speech in part upon the actual senti-
ments expressed on the day of the Battle of Maldon, or whether he drew
solely upon the heroic poetic traditions of his people, may not be the point; it
is undoubtedly clear that he is transmitting a cultural ideal, although—as this
poem amply illustrates—this is an ideal that was not always brought into
practice. In any case, in the voice of Aelfwine we hear an echo of Wicglaf's
words to Beowulf's wavering thanes in the closing episode of that heroic epic.

The recorder of *The Battle of Maldon* accused Birhtnoth of *ofermod*—
perhaps best rendered "overconfidence"—because the earl allowed the raiders
to cross the causeway as a force, and thus the battle was lost. It is probably
likely that Birhtnoth expected that the Vikings would flee in their ships to
another, unguarded location to continue their raiding if he failed to destroy
them in detail when he had the opportunity; his was therefore a calculated
risk. Moreover, this act of courage and honor—although we might deem it
foolhardy with the benefit of hindsight—was well within the bounds of the
heroic tradition that the writer otherwise embraced; therefore his bitterness
might be attributed to local criticism of the earl in the direct aftermath of the
loss. This poem clearly draws upon oral traditions, but more than that, like a
saga it fleshes out its characters with a wealth of local color and detail; further,
also in a sagalike way, the poet uses a few individual characters, well described, to make larger moral and historical points. This account clearly was
recorded locally a short time after the battle.

In *The Battle of Maldon* a heroic sensibility dooms the protagonists, although they gain glory in death, and the description of them by the poet reminds us of the pagan Germanic concept of the immortality to be gained
through fame and honor and glory; Birhtnoth's fall, indeed, can be likened to
that of Beowulf. Both heroes fall in a battle against monsters; Beowulf's
dragon is replaced here by Vikings described in the terms of vicious marauding animals. Both heroes are old men past their prime who suffer death in a
final conflict and are translated through apotheosis as a result. Beowulf's
apotheosis is traditionally Germanic in the sense that his name and deeds
live on in song; Birhtnoth, on the other hand, is a Christian version of the
warrior-hero, and through his martyrdom at Maldon a cult of Birhtnoth rose
at Ely. The poet self-consciously frames this struggle as that of the *Miles
Christi* Birhtnoth against the pagan Vikings, who are the hounds of hell; this
Christian interpretation of the conflict between English and Danes is notably
absent in *The Battle of Brunanburh*.

> Lord Birhtnoth placed his men in position, riding to and fro and instructing them;
> when all was prepared to his satisfaction, he dismounted and stood with those re-
> tainers he knew to be most steadfast and hardy. Then the messenger of the Vikings
> spoke, his voice ringing out across the water: Tribute he demanded, gold for peace,
> if the earl of the English wished his foes to take to their ships without strife.
> Haughty were the words of the pirate. Birhtnoth responded, the sea-wolves waited
> not long for their answer: Point of spear and edge of sword would he pay, war gear
> to profit not the greedy jaws of the slaughter-beasts in their feast of defenseless En-

glish. Birhtnoth commanded the Viking herald to take back to his people a grimmer message, harsher an answer: A steadfast thane of Aethelred stood with his army, ready to repulse the invaders; Christian soldier should have victory over heathen dog, and it would be too shameful for words should the earl offer tribute to those who had come unbidden so deep into England. Death would he deal before tribute.

Then, as the tide moved out and the causeway was fit to pass, the earl of Aethelred placed loyal Wulfstan in defense, with Aelfere and Maccus at his shoulders. As quickly as war-hungry wolves advanced they found a bitter welcome at the end of a spear, and drank deep the draft of death in the briny waters at Wulfstan's feet. The Vikings might not pass in this way, and when they saw this it came into their minds to trick Birhtnoth, to use his courage against him; they asked for leave to pass the ford unmolested, so that battle might be joined in force. This devious request the earl granted; many men would regret his show of confidence. The earl placed the matter in the hands of the Lord. The Vikings advanced across the receding waters, and then in the slaughter bed soon slept many a Dane and Essex man. Spears flew and blades clashed, and din of battle rang over the water; edge to edge the English held their shields in the war-hedge. Wulfmaer, sister-son to Birhtnoth, fell in the onslaught, and him Eadweard avenged with Norse blood; when chance allowed, loudly thanked the earl his man for the payment of this debt! On all sides battle pressed in, and Birhtnoth steadied his men with words of wisdom and comfort. The brave Graybeard earl then led his men, charged into the fray, brought shield and sword against the heathen; with a Viking spear he was wounded, but he shattered the shaft with a stroke of his shield, and thrust through the throat with his spear the seaman who had harmed him. Thrusting again, he hit in the heart the heathen dog, and the earl laughed and gave thanks to God for granting this gift.

The earl's joy at bloodletting soon slackened, however, as a spear of the seawolves sank in his side; Wulmaer son of Wulfstan, a boy young of winters, withdrew this woe-wielder from the wound. He shot the spear back the way it had come, and struck down the sailor who sent it. Thanks gave Birhtnoth to the Lord then for long life and many joys; he entrusted his soul to his Savior. Then the earl was hacked down by the damned heathens, and Aelfnoth and Wulmaer were laid low beside him, as befits thanes loyal to their leader. Then many fled the fight who found fear on that field; Godric, son of Odda, was first to seek safety, seizing the steed of his stricken sire. Both his brothers he bore with him. This is how Godric thought to repay the earl who had granted him so many fine mounts. Many followed that foul and faithless friend who thought him their lord. It would have been better had more men minded the goodly gifts granted them by Birhtnoth's benevolence. So Offa had harangued them, that boast over beer often is bolder than deed on a dire day.

Those still loyal to the lord laid low surged at the sea-dogs; Aelfwine, warrior young of years, reminded retainers of old oaths. This man of Mercia meant not to fail the fame of his family; death beside his dear lord and kinsman he preferred to dishonor. Full of fury he fought the foe, and he gave heart to his friends. Offa gave thanks to Aelfwine for his wise words and cursed the traitor Godric; Leofsunu likewise for his lost lord vowed vengeance, and dreaded dishonor far more than death. Dunnere the farmer, far from his fields, bolstered his betters with words befitting a warrior; he fought for the *fyrd*. These doomed men deemed death no disaster, now that their noble earl was no more; they fought and they died, pressing on against the pirates. Aescferth son of Ecglaf, a Northumbrian hostage, and Eadweard the Long, and Aetheric, and Offa and Wistan, all fought till they fell. Oswold and

Ealdwald—bold brothers—brought heart to the host, as did Byrhtwold; this hoary old hero sought the sleep of the slaughter-bed beside his battle-chief. Godric son of Aethelgar hewed many a heathen until he fell in front of the *fyrd*; he was not the Godric who flew from the field.

Beowulf *and the Anglo-Saxon Heroic Saga as History*

BEOWULF AND THE HISTORY OF THE SCYLDINGS

The origin of the Danish royal house offered as the opening of *Beowulf* embodies a typical saga interest with genealogy; it also draws upon the mythic archetype of the origin and birth of the hero in its attempt to link the king of Denmark with a quasi-deity from the misty past. This practice is by no means limited to Germanic myth, but it is noteworthy that such attempts abound in the Scandinavian and Anglo-Saxon sources, and that the kings of those nations regularly validated their right to rule through such family trees. *Widsith*, one of the oldest extant Old English poems—dating to perhaps the seventh century—contains little more than lists of ancient kings and peoples, and attempts thereby to link the heritage of the Anglo-Saxons with that of the Romans and the Hebrews. Thus the poet of that work used these links with older nations as a sort of cultural validation, just as kings created legitimate roots in the heroes and gods of old. The *Widsith* poet also celebrated the important function of memory of the court scop, who served as the only historian available in the pagan Germanic world; such a role gave poets the power of posterity, in a sense, but their need to please a royal audience makes them—at best—suspect witnesses.

We touched upon the narrative of the lineage of the Scyldings—that is, the descendants of Scyld Scefing—in our discussion of Hrolf Kraki's saga, so we will avoid repetition and note here only how that information is used in *Beowulf*. The lineage of Hrodgar may be merely of tangential interest to a modern reader, but to an audience steeped in the oral tradition of the north it served as a conduit through which elements of the present story were connected with many other tales. Thus, although the "plot" of the epic—as we tend to think of narrative structure—does not start until the end of this "prologue" of sorts, to the original audience the prologue itself served a vital function: it provided the immediate context for the saga to come, a context that is not intrusive but allusive, and therefore all but invisible to those who don't spot the keys. In other words, the attack of Grendel—which immediately follows this passage—did not happen just anywhere to anyone, but in a place and to a people already familiar to the audience of the poem. Such oral compositions as *Beowulf* originally were by their very nature volatile and allusive, with shifting episodes and elements to suit the needs and emphasis of the moment. Genealogical passages are one of these allusive elements of oral poetry, and a modern audience more comfortable with linear narratives ignores these allusions at its peril.

Lo! Often have we heard of the glory of the Spear-Danes of yore, how those heroes great deeds did. Scyld son of Sceaf took many a mead-hall from the hold of his foes, rose from obscurity—orphaned, a waif on the waves—to be lord of his land, mighty in main. Scyld took tribute from foreigners far over floods. He was a good king! Beow the Dane was his son, granted by God as a pillar for his people when Scyld should leave this life. Beow the boy gained great glory, as is fitting for he who hopes not to fall short of the fame of his father; so should he succeed his sire successfully. On the day of his death the Danes set Scyld adrift—as earlier he had deemed—from shore in a shapely ship. The corpse of the king was covered with treasures, in truth a trove; set high over his head was a standard of gold, which greatly did glitter. So sailed Scyld, so soon as soul had fled, far over the floods that he as foundling had fared. None the poorer was he, in departing his people, than when the princeling first put in to port. To what haven he headed, traveling with treasure, dead on the deck, none could name. Then Beow became king of that country, beloved lord of that land; his son Healfdene inherited his high-seat. A wonderful warrior, Healfdene fathered four offspring, hardy and hale: Heorogar and Hrodgar and Halga were sons of that sire, and his daughter did he dower to Onela the Heatho-Scylfing. Hrodgar gained glory until his war-band was waxing, full of famous fighters; meanwhile he meant a mead-hall to raise up. The greatest of halls, all gilded and glorious, grandly gabled and high, Heorot he named it.

BEOWULF AND THE BATTLE OF FINNSBURH

The story of the tragedy of Hildeburh is included in *Beowulf*, but it also survived for many centuries in a fragmentary form that is now lost. The episode in *Beowulf* is typically Germanic and sagalike in that individual characters are fleshed out to bring to life a historical narrative and to assert moral values. *Beowulf* as a whole and this episode in particular both concern themselves with the social practices of "ring-giving" and "peace-weaving." Ring-giving is the practice through which a lord regularly presents his followers, called thanes, with gifts of treasure, armor, arms, and the like, in return for their steadfast loyalty unto death. One of the primary duties of such a follower—as we saw in *The Battle of Maldon*—is to avenge the death of his lord at any cost.

Peace-weaving is the practice of marrying a daughter of high rank from one tribe to a leader or son of high rank in an enemy tribe; the theory is that the love between these two, and more importantly the relationship of both tribes to the children of this union, will serve to bring the two groups together peacefully, and thus to patch old rents and fissures. Unfortunately, as Hildeburh learns to her great sorrow in the Finnsburh episode, these two practices and the social forces that form them often are at odds, and the intense pressure of the desire for honor and vengeance often overwhelms the greater goal of peace and prosperity for all. Indeed, the very mechanism of ring-giving requires warfare and raiding as a means of the production of treasure for the king to give to his thanes, and thus attempts at peace are perhaps doubly endangered.

The Finnsburh episode is told from an overtly Danish perspective, and thus any historical value must be questioned, even within the narrative framework of the poem. The episode seems to be used in *Beowulf*, however, as a device for foreshadowing the strife between kinsmen that is to come, and as one of several examples that illustrate the fragility of peace-weaving. In both cases Hrodgar's family will suffer—Hrodgar's sons come to be displaced by his kinsman, and his daughter herself will be an unhappy peace-weaver—but he does not hear his doom in the words of the scop, although the audience is meant to. Finally, the Danes of the Finnsburh episode are sometimes equated with the Jutes, and it is perhaps noteworthy that the Hengest of this passage has sometimes been linked to the Horst and Hengest credited with beginning the invasion of Britain by the Angles, Saxons, and Jutes. This Germanic myth of founding is thought to derive ultimately from an Indo-European well-spring, and so may reflect an archetype of origin concerning twins or brothers; the most well-known manifestation of this archetype might well be the story of Romulus and Remus and the founding of Rome.

Hoc, king of the Danes, thought to end the long feud between his people and the Frisians by marrying his daughter Hildeburh to Finn, the king of that nation. All was well for a time. One year, however, Hnaef, son of Hoc, came to Finnsburh to pay a visit to his sister Hildeburh, and the old enmity surged up anew in the hearts of the Frisians; they ambushed the Danes in their guest quarters. Hnaef was among the Danes killed, but a host of the Frisians also met their doom, including the closest kin of Hildeburh; hence this unhappy woman lost brother and son in conflict against one another. Ample was Hildeburh's reason to mourn, and well might she lament the treachery of the Frisians; the Danes were to serve her equally ill, however, in a very short time. It seems that both sides had sustained mighty losses, and a truce was reached before they fought to the very last man. As they all were locked in together by ice for the winter, the Frisians offered to the Danes a hall and high-seat of their own, and an equal share in power, honor, and treasure. Hengest for the Danes and Finn for the Frisians compacted this peace with solemn oaths, although Hengest by necessity now served the slayer of his rightful lord Hnaef. No word nor deed of malice was to be brooked nor provoked on either side, and for Frisians to mock Danes for accepting treasure at the hands of their king's killer was to invite instant death.

Then Finn drew gold from his own hoard, bright gleaming treasure for the pyre of Hnaef; that lordly man was all surrounded by ornaments and armaments, and Hildeburh commanded that her son be placed at his uncle's shoulder. Thus Hnaef and his nephew—kinsmen and enemies both—were consumed together by the flames of the pyre. Well might that lady sing a song of sorrow then; her dirge was accompanied by the dark music of the bursting of bones and the welling of wounds within the flames. Heads exploded and joints popped, and those two warriors sailed from Finnsburh as black ash lifted by smoke. No white ship's sail might so speed away Hengest, however, until the spring thaw. He longed to journey home from exile, but even greater was his desire to avenge his fallen lord, truce or no truce. So when Hunlafing placed a naked blade in his lap as token of his loss and of his duty, Hengest did not hesitate: Finn died then in a bloodbath in his own hall, and the Danes returned to their ships sated with vengeance and with the wealth of Finn's treasury. Hildeburh they took with them, back to her home of old in the land of the Scyldings. Her homecoming was melancholy: through no fault of her own she had lost husband, brother, and son within the space of one winter to the same hateful feud she had been sent to heal.

Sagas of Ireland

The Irish sagas are traditionally divided into three types: the mythological cycle, concerned with the gods and origins; the popular heroic cycles concerned with such figures as Cuchulainn and Fionn Mac Cumhail; and the so-called historical cycle or cycles of the kings, the subject of which is kings and sacred kingship in Ireland.

The Mythological Cycle

The mythological cycle is found primarily in *The Book of Invasions*, transcribed for the most part in *The Book of Leinster* and including the important mythological narratives of *The Battles of Magh Tuireadh*. We have already discussed the "five invasions" of Ireland in connection with the pre-Celtic pantheon of deities in that country. The mythical "history" of Ireland preceding the arrival of the Milesians, or Goidelic Celts, is dominated by the Tuatha De Danann and the stories of their struggles with hostile inhabitants of Ireland.

THE BATTLES OF MAGH TUIREADH

In the first battle of Magh Tuireadh, the Tuatha defeated the ruling inhabitants of Ireland, the Firbolg, and then formed an alliance with the Fomorians. The Tuatha king, Nuada, had lost his arm in battle and was replaced as king by Bres, who was of both Fomorian and Tuatha descent. But after the removal of the oppressive Bres, the Tuatha would eventually be forced to fight the magical single-armed, single-legged Fomorians in the second battle of Magh Tuireadh.

Nuada, whose lost arm had been replaced by the silver one made by the medicine god Dian Cecht and then by one of flesh made by Dian Cecht's son Miach, had once again occupied the Tuatha throne. One day, as he presided over a feast at Tara, the place of his court, there arrived at his gates the warrior Lugh, who through a series of tests, proved himself master of all the arts of war, art, and technology. Lugh was given leadership of the Tuatha, and with the Dagda and Ogma as his primary generals he prepared for the war with the Fomorians.

The Dagda gained strength through sexual relations with Morrigan, one of the three Kali-like goddesses associated with death and destruction in battle. He was sent by Lugh to spy on the Fomorians. After offering and receiving a promise of truce from them, the Dagda was maliciously turned into a comic big-bellied buffoon of a character, consuming an enormous amount of food and making a huge ditch by dragging his gigantic phallic club along the ground. While with the Fomorians, he also slept with the granddaughter of their great mother goddess Domnu.

In the great battle itself, the Fomorian Ruadan, son of Bres and the Dagda's daughter Brigid, was sent to kill the smith-god Goibhniu, but was himself killed, causing Brigid to wail and thus to institute the Irish tradition of keening. Nuada was killed but Lugh killed the gigantic Balor and decapitated him. He spared the Fomorian poet Loch Lethglas in return for a promise that Ireland would never be raided by the Fomorians.

When the battle was won, Lugh, the Dagda, and Ogma chased the enemy into the hinterlands and recovered the Dagda's magic harp, which the Fomorians had stolen. The lowing of the black heifer given to the Dagda as a prize caused all the cows of Ireland to return to grazing. In all of Irish mythology, the state of cattle is a good indication of the state of the nation.

THE DEMISE OF THE OLD GODS

After the invasion and victory of the sons of Mil, however, the Tuatha and the Fomorians seem almost to have merged as a single fairy force, causing mischief and magic from their places under the earth and the waters.

The Heroic Cycles

The so-called heroic sagas, as opposed to the mythological, represent the world of heroes rather than gods, although heroic characters and events seem sometimes to be earthly forms of characters and events in the world of deities. Thus we have the repetition in the heroic sagas of themes such as decapitation, the loss of an arm, sacred cattle, warrior-goddesses associated with kingship and fertility, the slingshot as a powerful weapon, and so forth. And characters such as the warrior-queen Medb and Cuchulainn are clearly linked to mythological figures such as the war-goddesses Morrigan and Macha and the god Lugh. Questions of honor, war, and the heroic code are basic to the heroic sagas and clearly grow out of the mythological stories.

THE ULSTER CYCLE

The greatest heroic cycle of Irish mythology is known as the Ulster or red branch cycle. The sources for this collection of sagas include *The Book of the Dun Cow*, *The Book of Leinster*, and *The Yellow Book of Lecan*. Central to the Ulster cycle is the most famous of the Irish epic narratives, the *Tain Bo Cuailnge* ("The Cattle Raid of Cuailnge"), a tale *The Book of Leinster* tells us was told by the hero Fergus mac Roth (Roith), risen from his grave. Certain characteristics of *The Tain*—the weapons, cattle raiding, chariot warfare, single combat, decapitation, heroic boasting—suggest an Iron Age culture of the first century CE, and even more ancient links to Indo-European roots in India. The story itself dates perhaps to the eighth century, with earlier verse and oral sources. The second of the heroic cycles is the more romantic Fenian or Ossianic cycle, parts of which were perhaps in written form as early as the seventh century, with oral sources dating to as early as the third century, but which comes to us in comprehensive form in the late twelfth-century *Acallam na Senorach* ("The Colloquy of Ancients").

• *Conchobhar and Fergus*: The defining struggle in the Ulster cycle is that between between Ulster and Connaught, the two northern provinces of Ireland. Ulster is led by King Conchobhar Mac Nessa (Conor) from his court at Emain Macha (the "Twins of Macha"), named after a mysterious woman who had given birth to twins under duress at the hands of Ulstermen. In return she had cursed all the Red Branch, the guardians of Ulster, the equivalent of King Arthur's Round Table. Macha foretold that the Ulstermen would lose all energy during a time of greatest danger and that the period of their incapacity would last for the period of a woman's confinement. Only the hero Cuchulainn would be spared, since he was an Ulsterman only by adoption. It was he who would be credited with King Conchobhar's ultimate victory.

Conchobhar was a despot known for duplicity. His mother, Nessa, had agreed to marry Fergus Mac Roth, the then king of Ulster and brother of her late husband, but only on condition that he allow her son to reign as king in Ulster for one year. Being in love, Fergus agreed to the plan, but after the agreed-upon year Conchobhar reneged on his pledge. Fergus was, nevertheless, loyal to the new king until the disaster that befell the Red Branch hero Naoise (Naisii, Noisiu).

• *Deirdre and Naoise*: Conchobhar demands to be allowed to marry Deirdre, known as the most beautiful woman in Ireland—this in spite of a prophecy that she will bring ruin to the kingdom. Deirdre, however, falls in love with Naoise, and the two elope and go into exile. When Conchobhar claims to have forgiven the couple and sends the faithful Fergus to bring them home, Deirdre is suspicious, but Naoise trusts Fergus. During the couple's first night back at court Conchobhar has Naoise killed and soon takes the now even more reluctant Deirdre as his wife. After a year, having tired of his mournful wife, he gives her to Naoise's executioner, causing her to commit suicide. Two intertwining pines grow from the graves of Naoise and "Deirdre of the Sorrows." Enraged by Conchobhar's use of him in this terrible breach of honor, Fergus, with many other outraged Ulstermen, joins the forces of Connaught in the war with Ulster. It is said that with Fergus's help, Medb would have won *The Tain* battle but for Fergus's having to abandon the battle because of a personal pledge to the Ulster hero Cuchulainn. Although he would win the battle in question, Conchobhar would be wounded in the head by a "brain ball" from the slingshot of the hero Conall Cearnach ("Victorious"). The king would remain alive, but in misery until after seven years his temper became so explosive that the ball split and caused his death.

• *Cuchulainn*: If Conchobhar is the Agamemnon of the Irish heroic cycle, Cuchulainn is its Achilles. We have already learned of his unusual conception and birth and of his childhood defeat of Culann's hound. This greatest of Irish heroes was particularly supported and helped in battle by his real father, the god Lugh; some believe that Cuchulainn was an incarnation of Lugh. Cuchulainn's wife was Emer, who in spite of her husband's relationships with other women remained true to him and tried to prevent his tragic end. That end was in part brought about because of Cuchulainn's refusal of the advances of the terrifying Morrigan, the warrior-goddess of death and destruction, the Kali of Irish mythology. In fact, in the struggle that followed his refusal of the goddess, Cuchulainn managed to wound her, a fact for which he would pay at his own death when Morrigan sat on his shoulder as a crow and savored the vision of a beaver drinking his blood.

The great tragedy of Cuchulainn's life, however, was his confrontation with his own son, Conlai, whose mother was Aoife of the Land of the Shadows, a warrior princess of an underworld-like land only reached by Cuchulainn after much hardship and many supernatural deeds. Before leaving his mother's land for Ireland, Conlai had promised neither to identify himself nor to refuse combat with anyone who challenged him. In spite of a warning as to the boy's identity, Cuchulainn carried out his duty to fight anyone who refused to identify himself. The inevitable result was the playing out of the ancient Indo-European drama of the father killing the son, a drama enacted, for instance, by Theseus and his son Hippolytus, who, like Conlai, was the offspring of a hero and a warrior princess. Ultimately, heroes often are at the mercy of impossible choices arranged by the fates or the gods.

• *Queen Medb*: Conchobhar's and Cuchulainn's main rival in the story of *The Tain* was Queen Medb (Maeve), wife of King Ailill of Connaught and the one-time wife of Conchobhar himself. *The Tain* concerns Medb's attempt to capture the Brown Bull of Cualigne. The bull itself is a highly symbolic animal in Irish myth. It stands, as it does in most ancient Indo-European cultures, for power and virility and is associated in Ireland, especially, with sacred kingship. According to *The Book of the Dun Cow*, the election of the Irish king was marked by a ceremony in which a druid ate a bull's flesh and drank its blood and then in a deep sleep dreamed of the future king.

• *The Tain Bo Cuailgne*: The great war of the *Tain* developed out of a "pillow-talk" argument between Medb and Ailill over the relative value of their possessions. Zeus and Hera had such arguments and so did the Indian god Siva and his wife Parvati. When Medb realized that her possessions were inferior to her husband's, owing to his ownership of Finnbennach, the White-horned Bull, she determined to obtain for herself Donn Cuailgne, the great Brown Bull of Cuailgne. This bull could engender fifty calves in a day and could carry fifty boys on its back. It could shelter a hundred warriors with its body. The two bulls had once possessed human form as swineherds—one served the king of Connaught, the other the king of Munster. The two swineherds, once friends, had become jealous of each other and had fought over the relative values of their herds. In these fights they had taken various forms—warriors, ravens, and monsters. Finally they changed themselves into maggots, and one swam into a river in Cuailgne and was swallowed by a cow belonging to the Ulster chieftain Daire. The other swam into a Connaught stream and was consumed by one of Queen Medb's cows. The former swineherds were reborn as the White-horned Bull of Connaught and the Brown Bull of Cuailgne.

Medb asked Daire for the loan of the Brown Bull for a year, and Daire agreed until it was reported to him that the wily queen's ambassadors had boasted that if the loan had been refused she would have taken the bull by force anyway. Daire took back his agreement to the loan, and an enraged

Medb prepared for war with the exiled former Ulster king Fergus as her general. Fergus hated Conchobhar because of the betrayal involving Deirdre and Naoise, but he remained loyal in spirit to his "foster son," the Ulster hero Cuchulainn, and warned him of the impending war.

Medb assumed that because of the enfeebling curse on the Ulstermen, victory for Connaught would be a simple matter. But she had not reckoned on the fact that Cuchulainn was not by birth an Ulsterman. When Medb attacked Ulster, she was confronted by Cuchulainn in his war chariot driven by the faithful Laig (Laeg) and drawn by the greatest of war horses, the Battle Gray. The slingshot of Cuchulainn was a deadly weapon and before long countless Connaught warriors lay dead. Amazed by the prowess of this mere seventeen-year-old, Medb determined to meet him and hoped to bring him over to her side with her charms. After much haggling, Medb and Cuchulainn agreed that from then on Cuchulainn would fight in daily single combat any warrior sent to him. The Connaught army might advance for only as long as it took him to defeat his daily enemy. While Cuchulainn defeated warrior after warrior with ease, allowing Medb's army only marginal advances, the devious queen took advantage of the hero's preoccupation by stealing the Brown Bull while Cuchulainn was occupied with single combat.

Now the gods had been watching Cuchulainn's amazing feats of battle and the war goddess Morrigan, especially, had noticed his prowess. Appearing to the hero in a red dress and riding in a red war chariot, the goddess attempted to seduce him. She thus resembled the great Inanna who practiced her wiles on the hero of the Sumerian-Babylonian epic of Gilgamesh. Claiming that it was she who had made his victories possible, Morrigan demanded repayment in the form of love. When Cuchulainn rashly claimed he needed no woman's help in battle, and reacted disdainfully to the goddess's charms, she became his mortal enemy and made his tragic fate inevitable.

Soon Medb sent the old warrior Loch out to fight with Cuchulainn at what became ever after a famous ford. Loch was assisted by Morrigan in the form of a heifer, an eel, and a wolf, each of which Cuchulainn defeated. But Loch was able to inflict many wounds on his enemy, and the combination of warrior and goddess was about to prevail when Cuchulainn decided, reluctantly, since he considered such tactics dishonorable, to make use of his magical spear, the Gae Bolga, a weapon against which there was no defense. Loch was thus killed. The much-wounded Cuchulainn was given a strong sleeping potion by his true father, the god Lugh, and during three days and nights of sleep was cured by the ministration of the god's powerful medicine.

Sensing impending defeat, Medb now insisted that Fergus himself fight Cuchulainn. A battle with the youth he considered his "foster son" was anathema to the former Ulster king, and he agreed to it only after Medb called him a coward and only without the assistance of his magical invincible sword. As the two friends and great warriors approached each other, they tried to find a way to avoid the fight. Finally they agreed that Cuchulainn should pretend to run from Fergus in fear on the condition that in a similar situation in the future Fergus would run from Cuchulainn. As Cuchulainn ran away after a mock battle, the forces of Medb mocked him.

At this point, Medb decided to put an end to Cuchulainn even if that meant breaking her oath of single combat only. She sent the wizard Calatin with his twenty-seven sons to fight her enemy. It was only with the help of Fiacha, another Ulster exile sent by Fergus to watch the battle, that Cuchulainn was able to destroy the wizard and his children.

With her next ploy, Medb was almost successful. Against Cuchulainn she sent out Ferdia of the impenetrable skin, a childhood friend of the great hero. The two friends had sworn eternal friendship, and it was only the threats to their reputations and honor that led them to fight each other. The two fought for three days, and each night Cuchulainn demonstrated his love by sharing the medicine of Lugh to cure Ferdia's wounds. Finally, the anger of battle prevailed, and Cuchulainn once again made reluctant use of the Gae Bolga, as Karna made use of the magical weapon in the Indian epic the *Mahabharata* and King Arthur made use of Excalibur. As Ferdia died at his feet, Cuchulainn moaned in agony at the loss of his friend.

The battle with Ferdia had left Cuchulainn badly wounded. Unable to continue the war alone, he sent his adopted father Sualtim, who had come to nurse his wounds, to ride to Ulster on the Battle Gray to call on the Ulstermen for help. It was only when Sualtim's severed head—which was cut off by his shield as a result of the abrupt movement of Cuchulainn's horse—continued to cry out the call for help that the Ulstermen arose from their long, curse-induced stupor and sent an army to aid their hero. The speaking severed head is a common motif in Celtic myth.

When the forces of Conchobhar approached those of Medb, Cuchulainn revived, and he joined them. Facing Fergus, he demanded that his old friend fulfill his part of the oath of retreat, and Fergus turned and ran, causing havoc in his own army, which fled in disarray.

The battle was thus won, but the Brown Bull remained in Connaught, and his old hatred of the White-horned Bull revived. A great battle of the bulls resulted, and eventually the Brown Bull defeated his enemy, essentially dismembered him, and with much bellowing, returned to Cuailnge, where soon his heart burst and he died.

As for Cuchulainn, his doom was manipulated by the witch daughters of the enchanter Calatin and by the young kings of Munster and Leinster, whose fathers—as well as the father of the witches—Cuchulainn had slain in battle. And, of course, the offended Morrigan was an interested party in her enemy's destruction. The witches used their magic to lure Cuchulainn out with only the horse the Battle Gray and the charioteer Laig. In spite of terrible omens, Cuchulainn insisted on venturing toward the standing Pillar of Stone. There he met the three witches and was taunted by three bards, who used threats of poetic dishonor to cause the hero to throw his three spears at them. The bards thus were killed, but Lughaid, king of Munster and Erc, king of Leinster, threw the spears back at Cuchulainn, first killing Laig, then the Battle Gray, and then wounding Cuchulainn in his guts. The dying hero struggled to the pillar stone and tied himself to it so that he might die standing. At this moment Morrigan arrived as a crow and sat proudly on the dying man's shoulder, and Lughaid cut off his head. The hero's falling sword severed Lughaid's arm, however, and soon Cuchulainn's friend Conall would sever Lughaid's head to avenge the unfair defeat of the greatest of Irish heroes.

• *The Tain Bo Fraoch*: Another popular cattle raid (*tain*) was the *Tain Bo Fraoch*. Again, Queen Medb and her husband Ailill play an important role. They have a daughter named Findbhair ("Fair Eyebrows") whom the king and queen had offered to the hero Ferdia during the *Tain* war in order to entice him into combat with his friend Cuchulainn. In the *Tain Bo Fraoch*, Findbhair is in love with the hero Fraoch and he with her. Fraoch is a great fiddle player, who impresses even the queen with his skill. He tries to convince Findbhair to elope with him, but although she gives him her thumb ring as a token of love, she insists that he speak with her parents about a marriage. Fraoch refuses to pay the huge price Medb and Ailill demand for their daughter. Believing that her lover will now certainly elope with Findbhair, the parents decide to bring about his death by having him swim in a lake known to contain a terrible monster.

When Fraoch has removed his clothes and entered the water, the king finds his daughter's ring among the belongings of her lover and hurls it into the water in a rage. A salmon—always an important fish in Irish myth and legend—catches it and in turn the fish is caught by Fraoch, who has seen what occurred. The hero hides the salmon on land and when Ailill insists that he swim to the other shore, the monster attacks. Fraoch calls for a sword and Findbhair throws off her clothes and leaps into the water with one. Her furious father throws a spear at her, but Fraoch catches it and kills the monster. Medb and Ailill are impressed and decide to spare the hero. He is bathed in honor by beautiful women. But Findbhair is condemned by her parents for having given away the ring. She would have been put to death but for her lover's having produced the ring from the salmon. He claims to have found it some time before and to have intended to return it to Findbhair. The parents are fooled by this story and they agree to the marriage if Fraoch will use his large cattle herd to help in a theft of the cattle of Cualinge. A later part of the Fraoch story tells how Fraoch, helped by Conall, the avenger of Cuchulainn, saves Findbhair and their three children and their cattle from kidnappers.

THE FENIAN CYCLE

The Fenian, or Ossianic, cycle of Irish heroic sagas is made up of old oral ballads and prose stories that have long been popular in the British Isles but that achieved a comprehensive literary form only in the twelfth-century *Acallam na Senorach*. It is important to note that the Fenian tales have been popular rather than canonical literary texts. Whereas the Ulster cycle was treated as almost sacred aristocratic narrative preserved by the guild of *filid* and probably was written in some form by the seventh century, the Fenian cycle is a much looser collection more subject to the variations of popular transmission and generally not present in the lists of stories the *filid* were required to know. By the time of the *Acallam*, the Christian influence was apparent, as in that work the narrator Cailte, the Fenian poet, or sometimes Oisin, recounts the deeds of his group to Saint Patrick.

• *The Fianna*: The Fenians, or Fianna Eireann, were an association of warriors led by Finn (Fionn) Mac Cumhail and his son Oisin (Ossian) during the reign of Cormac Mac Art in the third century CE. The Fenians were different from the warriors of *The Tain* in that comradeship rather than individualism was what motivated them. They were a band of foot soldiers—even commoners—rather than chariot-riding aristocrats, and this in part explains their continued popularity in Ireland. The stories of the Fenians are more romantic and more nostalgic than are those of the Ulster cycle. The vision associated with the Fenians is one of bygone days of warm manly comradeship in arms and of the kind of love story we find in the romances of the troubadors.

• *Finn*: Finn (the "Fair") himself is very much the hero of myth. His father was Cumhaill, a warrior leader who was killed. Finn was thus abandoned and raised secretly in the wilderness by his mother. As a boy, whose name then was Deimne, he was adopted by a wise druid near the Boyne River, where as we know the Dagda was said to have retired; the Boyne is a river generally associated with the gods. The druid's name was Finn or Finegal. For seven years he had attempted to catch the salmon of wisdom in the river, as it had been foretold that the flesh of that fish would bring great wisdom to a man named Finn. When old Finn finally did catch the salmon he gave it to Deimne to cook, and when the boy burned his hand doing so and put the blistered hand in his mouth, he inadvertently tasted the fish. The horrified druid asked him if Deimne was his only name and the young man revealed that as so many people referred to him as "The Fair One," he had also taken the name Finn. Finegal realized the significance of this and encouraged Finn to eat the salmon. This he did and so became the wisest of all people. Finn went on to assimilate his father's enemies into his own followers and to form and lead the Fianna. The Fianna took vows never to retreat in battle, never to seek familial revenge, never to deny hospitality, and never to require a dowry or to be rude to women. They killed dragons, monsters, and invaders for various Irish kings. They were also huntsmen and poets. Finn had two magical dogs who were, in fact, his sister's children, who had been transformed into canines by magic.

• *Oisin*: Finn fathered a son with the goddess Sadb, daughter of the Dagda's son the Bodb Dearg. When Sadb became a deer, Finn found his son and called him Oisin (the "fawn"). Oisin became the greatest of the Fianna warriors and himself produced a son named Oscar.

• *Diarmaid and Grainne*: The most famous story of the Fenian cycle is that of "The Pursuit of Diarmaid and Grainne." When Finn was an old man he wished to marry the king's daughter Grainne. But the princess fell in love with the young Fianna warrior Diarmaid, whose face was marked by a love spot put there by the love-god Aonghus. Diarmaid refused Grainne's love out of loyalty to Finn. But as a result of the princess's reminder that a member of the Fianna must not offend a woman, he gave in, and the lovers eloped and found shelter in a place called the Wood of the Two Huts. But, in spite of the advice of his son and grandson, who warned him against jealousy and revenge, Finn led the Fianna in pursuit of the lovers and successfully surrounded them. Grainne was able to escape with the help of a mantle of invisibility placed on her by her lover's foster father, Aonghus, and by means of a great leap, Diarmaid, too, was able to escape Finn. Later, Diarmaid and Grainne were hiding in the magic quicken-tree when they were discovered by Finn, who promised his armor to any of the Fianna who could produce Diarmaid's head. It was Aonghus who again came to the rescue. As each warrior climbed the tree to get at Diarmaid, Aonghus gave the warrior the likeness of the hero, and when Diarmaid kicked each successive warrior to the ground the warrior's head was cut off. Soon the ground was littered with the heads of Finn's followers. Then once again the lovers escaped with the help of Aonghus's cloak and Diarmaid's leaping skill.

After many years of wandering, the lovers were received back by the Fianna. But once Finn went hunting with his rival, and when Diarmaid was wounded by a wild boar, Finn refused him water until it was too late. When the Fianna brought Diarmaid's body back to Grainne, the Fianna women keened and Grainne sang a song of despair about her love having been the cause of Diarmaid's fall. Aonghus took the body of his foster son to the home of the gods. Only after much grieving did Grainne agree finally to reconciliation and union with Finn. There are elements of this story that remind us of the story of *Tristan and Isolde*.

• *Oisin's Journey to the Other World:* In the more Ossianic part of the Fenian cycle there is the story of Oisin's going with the mysterious Niamh to the otherworld, where he stays for three hundred years. When he returns in search of his father, Finn is of course long dead and Oisin, who now becomes an old man, tells the story of Finn to St. Patrick. A persistent tradition is that Finn, like King Arthur, will someday return.

The Historical Cycle

The third type of Irish saga is that which has been called the historical cycle or cycle of kings. The subjects of these tales are the ancient High Kings of Ireland—Conn of the Hundred Battles, Cormac Mac Art, Domnall, Eochaid Airemh, Niall of the Nine Hostages, and others, as well as the nature of the Irish kingship itself. These tales are a combination of myth, legend, and history.

TARA

Irish kings held court at Tara, located in County Meath. According to one legend, Tara was cursed by Christian saints of Ireland in 560 CE, so King Domnall moved the court to Dun na nGed on the Boyne. There he created a replica of Tara with four halls representing the four provinces of Leinster,

Munster, Connaught, and Ulster, around a central hall representing the center of Ireland, the place of the High King. This arrangement is based on a center and the four directions and can be found in other Indo-European contexts, perhaps most notably in the Vedic idea of the four directions surrounding a fifth direction, which is where one is—that is, at the center.

EOCHAID AIREMH AND ETAIN

Central to the concept of the High Kingship was the person of the queen. We are told, for instance, that the coronation of the High King Eochaid Airemh was postponed because he lacked a queen. The result of a search for the most beautiful woman in Ireland was his discovery of and marriage with Etain, daughter of Etar, a follower of King Conchobhar. This Etain was, in fact, the daughter of another Etain, a second wife of the god Midir, whose first wife had turned her rival into a fly that fell into the cup of Etar's wife. When Etar's wife drank the fly she became pregnant and eventually gave birth to Etain, who became Eochaid's wife. But Midir the Proud, son of the Dagda, appeared at Tara, won an embrace with Etain in a gambling match with her husband, and then whisked her off to the otherworld. Eochaid was able to win his wife back by distinguishing her from fifty clones created by Midir.

ETAIN OIG AND MESS BUACHALLA

According to one story, Midir appeared again later and claimed that Etain had been pregnant when he took her away and that the Etain Eochaid had chosen from the fifty had in fact been his own daughter. Whether this was the case or not, the daughter's name was Etain Oig. Later she married Cormac of Ulster and became the mother of Mess Buachalla. Cormac ordered that his daughter be killed because he had wanted a son. Mess Buachalla, however, was taken in by the cowherd of the High King Eterscel. Heeding a prophecy that a woman of unknown origins would give birth to a great son. Eterscel determined to marry the beautiful Mess Buachalla, whose origins were unknown. Before the wedding took place, however, Mess Buachalla was impregnated by the bird-god Nemglan, and the result was the great Conaire Mor, whom Eterscel accepted as his son. Echoes of the Krsna and Theseus stories are evident here.

CONAIRE

Among many of the *geis* (*gessa*) or taboos placed upon Conaire by his bird-god father was that he must walk naked to Tara, carrying only his slingshot and a single missle. Only in this way would he become High King. This *geis* Conaire followed, but he broke all the others, and this led to his death, described in the most famous of the Conaire tales, that of "The Destruction of Da Derga's Hostel."

The Destruction of Da Derga's Hostel

Like Cuchulainn, who ignored warnings of his impending death, Conaire seemed almost consciously to place himself in the position of ritual victim. He began the
process by forgiving his plundering foster brothers, the sons of Donn Desa, thus
breaking the bird-god's taboo against plundering. Joined by the one-eyed Ingcel, the
foster brothers headed from Britain to Ireland when Conaire had gone to Munster to
break another taboo by attempting to settle a quarrel between two other foster
brothers. Noticing naked men and bands of warriors around Tara, the king led his
men on a hunt that was also a taboo before the whole party retired to Da Derga's
hostel to rest. As Conaire approached the hostel, he was passed by a black one-
eyed giant who announced that he had been expecting the king. Inside the hostel a
terrible hag appeared and prophesied doom for Conaire. Then Ingcel and the sons
of Donn Desa landed in Ireland, causing the world to shake. In spite of a growing
reluctance on the part of the foster brothers to harm Conaire, Ingcel demanded the
right to plunder in return for the plundering by the brothers in Britain. The druids
accompanying the invaders dried up the water in Ireland so that Conaire, who had
already killed six hundred of his enemy, could not be refreshed, and we are reminded here of the treatment of Diarmaid by Finn. The hero Mac Cecht succeeded
in finding water, but he returned to the hostel only in time to witness the enemy
cutting off the head of Conaire. Mac Cecht fed the water to the head, and in keeping with the tradition of the speaking severed head in Celtic mythology, the head
praised his loyal friend, who then pursued the few remaining invaders.

CONN

Another of the great High Kings is Conn of the Hundred Battles, whose
name is associated eponymously with the northern half of Ireland, the *Leth
Cuinn*, as opposed to the southern half, which is *Leth Moga*, the "Half of
Mug," represented by the kings of Munster. One such king was Mug Nuadat
or Eogan, who fought against Conn and was killed. Conn married the sinful
Becuma, who had been banished from her homeland, the Land of Promise, or
otherworld, to the world of humans. As a result of this inappropriate marriage, the cows of Ireland refused to give milk, symbolizing the pollution of
the sacred kingship, an institution based on the fertile relationship between
the king at the high court of Tara and the female personification of Sovereignty ("Sovranty"). Once, when Conn was lost in a deep mist, he came upon
the god Lugh accompanied by the beautiful Sovranty, who gave the king food
and drink as Lugh called out the names of all the kings who would follow
Conn.

CORMAC MAC ART

A great High King who is said to have ruled from 254 to 277 CE, Cormac Mac
Art (Airt), was the patron of the Fianna, grandson of Conn, son of Art.
Cormac's life contains many elements of the general hero myth of the Indo-
Europeans. Thunder sounded to greet his birth, but his father died, leaving
him to be suckled by wolves. Eventually, accompanied by his wolves, he

found his way to Tara, where, though still a youth, he proved his wisdom and was installed as king in place of the usurper Mac Con. Cormac was a good and righteous king, a fact reflected in the more than normal flow of milk from the cows and the general abundance of nature's gifts during his reign.

A famous tale of Cormac is that of his journey to the Land of Promise in the otherworld. One day, as Cormac stood alone on the ramparts of Tara, there appeared a mysterious warrior who carried a silver branch with golden apples. The branch made a music that lulled to sleep all who heard it. Cormac begged to have the branch, and the warrior gave it to him in return for three wishes. In a year the warrior returned and asked for and was given Cormac's daughter. A month later he came and demanded and was given Cormac's son. Finally, he took Cormac's wife, causing the King to follow the warrior to a place full of marvels, which turned out to be the Land of Promise. There Cormac was greeted by a warrior and a woman and given a bath. A man appeared, cut a pig into four parts, threw the parts into a cauldron, and proclaimed that only truths could cook the pig. Cormac's truth was the fact that he had lost his family. As he was being served food, Cormac mentioned that he always had his followers with him at meals. Fifty warriors arrived and with them came Cormac's wife, son, and daughter. It was then that Cormac noticed the beautiful golden cup belonging to his host, who turned out to be the god Manannan Mac Lir. The cup was the cup of truth. If three lies were told under it, it broke into three parts. If three truths were told, it would regain wholeness. Manannan Mac Lir gave the cup of truth to Cormac and thus provided him with a source of great wisdom. The Hero's journey to the otherworld is a well-known archetype, of course, but the journey in search of a loved one is especially common in Celtic and Celtic-influenced literature.

NIALL

A story that illustrates clearly the connection between the sacred High Kingship and the land as personified by a woman is that of the founder of the Ui Neill dynasty, Niall Noighaillach, said to have been High King from 379 to 405 CE. Niall had been abandoned in the wilds by his wicked stepmother, but like so many heroes in this predicament, was saved and adopted—in this case by a bard and a smith—as we have seen, traditional mythic characters in Ireland, as well as in other Indo-European cultures. The smith foretold that the abandoned child would one day be High King. One day, when Niall and his foster brothers were hunting, they met a hag who promised them much needed water only if they would kiss her. Only Niall reacted properly, giving the ugly old woman an enthusiatic embrace. In an instant the hag became a beautiful woman and announced that she was Sovranty (Sovereignty) and that Niall would be High King. The story, one of many like it in Irish mythology and legend, seems to tell us that the land can become whole and beautiful only when in union with the king. From earliest times, then, as seen here and in the Ulster and Fenian cycles, the Irish sacred kingship has been rooted in a concept of fertility based on union with the land, personified as a goddess, a concept expressed, as noted earlier, in many other Indo-European cultures; an example is the concept of *sakti*, or female creative power associated with Hindu gods. The theme of the magical hag or prostitute is one that survives well into the medieval period and is present in quite a number of British works.

Sagas of Wales: *The Mabinogion*

Welsh mythology as it has come down to us is essentially contained in a collection of eleven medieval tales known in modern times as *The Mabinogion* (*Mabinogi*). The styles of the tales indicate literary sources from the eleventh to the mid-thirteenth centuries. There are, for instance, parts of what seem originally to have been mid-eleventh-century written versions of a few tales in an early thirteenth-century manuscript known as *Peniarth 6*, and, of course, we can assume still earlier oral sources. What we know as *The Mabinogion*, however, is found in two fourteenth-century manuscripts, *The White Book of Rhydderch* and *The Red Book of Hergest*. The collection takes its name from the four tales called "Four Branches" of *The Mabinogion*, which probably found literary form between the mid-eleventh to the early twelfth centuries. Also included in the greater *Mabinogion* are four tales called "Independent Native Tales" by the Lady Charlotte Elizabeth Guest, the first translator of the Welsh stories into English. This group of tales includes the earliest known Welsh Arthurian story, "Culhwch and Olwen." The last part of *The Mabinogion* is made up of three later Arthurian romances.

The term *mabinogi* has been associated with the tradition of the *mabinog*, or young apprentice bard, and with the Irish *mac ind oc*, a name sometimes given to the Dagda's love-god son Aonghus—the "son of the eternal youth." As the "Four Branches" are concerned with the children of Don, who resemble the Irish Tuatha De Danann, this theory seems at least reasonable, especially since the only character to figure in all four tales is Pryderi, who in Wales was always the *mac ind oc*. Finally, the *mabinogi* has been associated with Maponos, the divine-youth god popular in northern Britain and the continent, who is the Arthurian warrior and hunter Mabon in Wales. Thus, the theory goes, *mabinogi* is derived from "Mabonalia." The mother of Maponos was the mother-goddess Matrona; in Wales she became Madron. In some stories we learn that Mabon was stolen from his mother soon after his birth. This theme occurs, as we shall see, in other Welsh tales as well.

The Four Branches of The Mabinogion

The four branches are independent narratives that are, however, related, as certain characters appear in more than one tale. As noted, only Pryderi, whose birth story is the subject of part of the first branch, appears in all four. It has been argued that the four branches originated in a series of tales concerning the birth, quests, and death of the hero Pryderi, but if this is the case other material now submerges all but an outline of that heroic saga.

THE FIRST BRANCH

Pryderi is the son of Pwyll ("Good Judgment"), lord of Dyfed, and Rhiannon. Dyfed is the land of the Cauldron of Plenty, a symbol representing perhaps the Holy Grail, and in this context Pwyll is the Arthurian Pelles, the Guardian of the Grail. He is also known as "head of Annwn."

While hunting in Glyn Cuch, Pwyll insults another hunter, who turns out to be the mysterious King Arawn of the otherworld realm called Annwn (Annwfn). Pwyll's offense is driving away the king's hounds and substituting his own in the pursuit of a stag. To pay for his discourtesy he is made to take Arawn's face and to occupy his throne in Annwn for a year. There he sleeps in Arawn's bed, keeping a promise not to make love with his wife, and he defeats the king's enemy Hafgan, another otherworld king. Pwyll wins the fight with Hafgan only by restraining himself from administering a second blow, which would have restored power to his enemy.

Soon after his return to Dyfed, in southwestern Wales, Pwyll holds a feast at his court, Arbeth. He takes his place on the throne mound, knowing full well that by so doing he will suffer pain or bear witness to something wonderful. A beautiful woman rides by on a white horse. After a fruitless chase of the woman, Pwyll begs her to stop, which she does. The woman reveals herself to be Rhiannon, and she offers herself as Pwyll's wife. Rhiannon is the Welsh form of the goddess Rigantona, herself a figure comparable to Matrona and to the horse-goddess Epona.

At the wedding feast a year later, Pwyll foolishly grants a wish that results in his losing Rhiannon to Gwawl (Light), the son of the goddess Clud. But Pwyll wins his wife back at the wedding feast of Gwawl and Rhiannon. Rhiannon has given him a magic bag, which he tricks Gwawl into entering. Once there Gwawl is badly kicked and beaten by Pwyll's followers, who thus originate the game called "Badger in the Bag."

After three years of marriage, Rhiannon gives birth to Pryderi. The women who are supposed to watch over the mother and child fall asleep, and the baby is mysteriously abducted, reminding us of the story of Mabon's similar abduction. To save themselves the women smear the blood of some killed puppies on Rhiannon so that she is accused of killing her child and is wrongly punished by her husband.

After several years, the child is discovered to be alive and safe in the home of Teyrnon of Gwent and Is-Coed and is returned to his parents. The child has been named Gwri, or "Golden Hair," but Rhiannon, relieved of her worry—her care—renames him Pryderi, or "Care."

It seems that Teyrnon had amputated a giant clawed arm that had reached through a stable window on May Eve to take one of his foals. He had rushed out to give chase to the intruder but had found no one. On his return to the stable he had found a baby, and he and his wife had raised the boy, who turned out to be the lost son of Pwyll and Rhiannon. Pryderi's birth is thus related to horses, and his death is connected to a gift of horses; both situations suggest an almost totemic association between this hero and his mother, who as we have seen is mythically linked to a Celtic tradition of horse-goddesses.

THE SECOND BRANCH

The second branch of *The Mabinogion* concerns the children of Llyr (Irish Lir, perhaps King Lear): The gigantic Bran the Blessed, king of Britain; the gentle Branwen, sometimes thought of as a goddess of love; Manawydan, the sea-god; and their half-brothers, Efnisien, the bringer of strife, and Nisien, the peace-maker. Efnisien is responsible for much of the tragedy in the story of Branwen's marriage to King Matholwch of Ireland. According to some sources, Llyr's first wife was Iweriadd, or "Ireland," and she was the mother of Bran and Branwen. According to others it was his wife Penardun, the daughter of the mother-goddess Don, who was the mother of Bran and Branwen and certainly of Manawydan. She is also the mother of Efnisien and Nisien by a later husband, Eurosswyd.

Matholwch comes to Harlech in Wales to ask for Branwen in marriage. All goes well at the marriage feast in Aberffraw until Efnisien, angry at not being a part of the marriage arrangements, damages Matholwch's horses. To cool the bridegroom's anger, Bran gives his brother-in-law a magic cauldron—perhaps the Cauldron of Plenty—that will bring the wounded back to life but leave them without the power of speech.

During her first year in Ireland, Branwen gives birth to a son who is named Gwern, on whom the "Sovranty" of Ireland is bestowed so as to bring lasting peace between Bran and Matholwch. But the people of Ireland continue to be outraged by the behavior of Efnisien at the marriage feast in Wales, and they demand that Branwen be made to suffer. So it is that for three years she is made to work in the court kitchens and to experience the daily blows of the court butcher. Thus Branwen—like Rhiannon before her—suffers wrongfully at the hands of her husband, reminding us of the folkloric theme of Constance, the good wife tried by adversity.

Branwen teaches a starling to speak, however, and it takes a message to her brother concerning her misery. Bran invades Ireland, his gigantic body forming a bridge between the lands by which his army can pass into Ireland. We are reminded here of the exploits of the monkey-god Hanuman in the Indian epic *The Ramayana*, in which the god-hero Rama invades Ceylon to free his captured wife Sita.

Matholwch sues for peace to save his country, but Efnisien destroys the truce by hurling Gwern into a fire. A terrible battle ensues in which Efnisien sacrifices himself and in so doing destroys the magic cauldron that is constantly causing the resuscitation of the Irish. Bran is wounded by a poison arrow and orders his followers to cut off his head and to return it to Britain. The severed head goes on talking and eating during a long and difficult voyage back to Britain. Once more we find the old Celtic theme of decapitation and the talking severed head, suggesting a belief that the soul resides in the head and lives on after death. Very few people survive the great war, remind-

ing us of the Irish second battle of Magh Tuireadh. Five pregnant women remain alive in Ireland and are the source for that island's future population.
The survivors from Bran's forces include Manawydan, Pryderi, Taliesen and
only four others. Soon after Branwen lands in Britain with these survivors she
dies of a broken heart over the destruction for which she blames herself. She
is buried along the Alaw in Anglesey. The river is renamed Ynys Branwen.

THE THIRD BRANCH

Pryderi has now married Cigva (Cigfa) and succeeded his late father Pwyll as
lord of Dyfed. His mother, Rhiannon, marries the wise and patient Manawydan, a surviving son of Llyr. Manawydan plays the major role in the third
branch. Clearly he is a descendant of an earlier Celtic sea deity and a close
relative of the benevolent Irish sea-god who came from the Isle of Man. As
the Irish Manannan mac Lir, he is associated with rebirth, serving as lord of
the land of eternal youth.

During a feast at Arbeth, the two couples sit on the magic throne mound
and are covered by a mysterious mist following a huge clap of thunder. When
the mist clears they find themselves in a land empty of living things. They
wander about the deserted Dyfed for two years and then go to the land of
Lloegyr (England), where Pryderi and Manawydan work as saddlers, shoemakers, and shieldmakers. The story of a noble who suffers such a fall from
grace with humility and dignity reminds us of the legend of Saint Eustace,
and this theme is a common one in medieval romances.

The four return to Arbeth, and the impulsive Pryderi, disregarding the
advice of Manawydan, allows himself to be enticed by a magic boar into an
enchanted castle containing a fountain in which a golden bowl sits on a mar-
ble slab. This represents perhaps the Cauldron of Plenty and/or the Holy
Grail. When Pryderi tries to grasp the cauldron he loses speech and cannot
release his hands from it. When Rhiannon tries to rescue her son, she, too,
loses speech and ability to release the cup. The two now disappear into a mist.
The author of the enchantment and abduction of the hero and his mother is
Llwyd, a friend of the evil Gwawl, who had once attempted to marry Rhiannon through trickery.

Manawydan, accompanied by Cigva, goes back to shoemaking in England, but eventually returns to Arbeth, where he grows corn. Having discovered an army of mice carrying the corn away, he captures the slowest moving
of the army and is about to hang it as a thief on the throne mound when a
bishop turns up and announces that the mouse is his pregnant wife. He reveals himself as Llwyd. In return for the life of his wife, Llwyd ends forever the
spells suffered by the heroic family of Manawydan.

THE FOURTH BRANCH

The fourth branch of The Mabinogion is dominated by the family of Don, especially Lleu, who resembles the Irish god Lugh. We begin with Math of

Gwynedd, son of Mathonwy. Mathonwy is also the father of Don, the Welsh equivalent of the Irish Danu and the mother-goddess of the House of Don. Math is a god of wealth and is possibly a cognate of the Irish Mathu. He is best known for the story we have already encountered in which it is required that his feet be held in the lap of a virgin when he is not at war. It is the ruse of two of the sons of Don, Gilfaethwy and the magician Gwydion, that deprives him of his footstool. Gwydion also dupes Pryderi in this process and the result is his death in a war against Gwynedd.

Gwydion attempts to substitute his sister Aranrhod for the stolen maiden. But Aranrhod drops a male child as she steps over Math's sword in a test of her virginity. And soon after the birth of her first child, the sea-god Dylan, she drops an object that Gwydion takes and hides in a box, only to discover there later another child, who is actually the incestuous offspring of Aranrhod and Gwydion. Aranrhod is ashamed and refuses to name the child, but Gwydion and the child appear in court as shoemakers, and Aranrhod inadvertently names him by exclaiming over his brightness and skill. Thus he becomes Lleu Llawgyffes. Now the boy's mother swears that he will never bear arms unless she gives them to him, but Gwydion's magic overcomes this oath. Aranrhod also swears that Lleu will never marry into a race "now on earth," so Math and Gwydion create a woman—Blodeuwedd, or "Flower"—named for the blossoms of the oak, the broom, and the meadowsweet; she becomes Lleu's wife.

Blodeuwedd falls in love with Gronw Pebyr of Penllyn, however, and the lovers plot to kill Lleu. Like many *femme fatales* before and after her, Blodeuwedd convinces her husband to reveal his particular weakness and learns that he can never be killed in a house or on horseback or on foot outside. So one day when Lleu is taking a bath outside, he is tricked into standing with one foot on the tub and the other on a goat. In this position he is vulnerable and falls victim to Gronw's spear. He disappears as an eagle but is found by Gwydion, who gives him back his human form. Lleu returns to Gwynedd and kills Gronw. Blodeuwedd is turned into the despised owl.

Four Independent Welsh Sagas

The four independent tales are a combination of folk history and popular themes and lack the narrative depth of the four branches.

MACSEN WLEDIG

Macsen Wledig, sometimes called "The Dream of Macsen," concerns Magnus Maximus, a Spanish Roman who came to Britain in 368 CE and married Helen, or Elen Lwddog. In 383, he proclaimed himself Western Emperor, crossed over into Gaul, and attacked Rome. Defeated by the Eastern Emperor Theodosius, he was put to death in 388. Elen returned to Britain and settled in what would become Wales with her children, whose offspring would be kings. "The Dream of Macsen" tells the story of Macsen's hunt, on which he was joined by thirty-two other kings, reminding us of a similar Irish story, "Bricriu's Feast," in which Conchobar is accompanied by thirty-two heroes to Bricriu's Hall. The number thirty-three is important in Indo-European mythology in general. There are, for instance, thirty-three gods mentioned in the *Vedas*.

LLUDD AND LLEFELYS

The story of Lludd and Llefelys is based on a Welsh translation by Geoffrey of Monmouth in the *Historia Regnum Britanniae* in about 1200 CE. Lludd (Nudd) and Llefelys were sons of the Beli, the husband of Don. With the help of the wise counsel of his brother, King Lludd of Britain puts an end to three plagues that devastated Britain. The first plague was caused by the highly knowledgeable little Coraniaids, the second by the hideous scream of a British dragon fighting a foreign dragon under the very center of Britain on May Eve. It is probably more than coincidental that it was also on May Eve that Teyrnon amputated the mysterious invasive claw in the first branch of *The Mabinogion*. In any case, the dragon scream undermined fertility all over the land. The third plague was brought about by a giant who ate prodigious amounts of food. These plagues bear some resemblance to those that the Fomorians in Ireland levied on the Tuatha De Danann or to the mysterious events that took place in Pryderi's Dyfed. The story is full of the fantasy of fairy tale. Some have suggested that it is a popular account of mythological invasions of Britain.

CULHWCH AND OLWEN

Dating from the mid-eleventh century, the tale of Culhwch (Kulhwch) and Olwen is based on several traditional folktales and is the earliest Arthurian story in Welsh. Culhwch is the son of Cilydd and Goleuddydd, who loses her mind and runs into the woods and gives birth to Culhwch. Realizing she is about to die, she makes her husband promise not to marry again until a two-headed briar grows from her grave. Cilydd respects his wife's wishes and waits the seven years until the briar grows as indicated before he marries again.

The new wife hates Culhwch and puts a curse on him because he refuses to marry her daughter. According to the curse, the youth will never marry unless with Olwen, the daughter of Ysbaddaden Pencawr (Benkawr), a terrifying giant. Olwen resembles Etain in Irish mythology; she is said to be so beautiful that white flowers sprang up in her tracks as she walked.

Culhwch goes to his cousin King Arthur's court to learn the arts of knighthood and to discover the whereabouts of Olwen. Stopped at the king's door he bursts into Arthur's hall on horseback, asks that Arthur perform on him the initiatory rite of the cutting of his hair, and requests that the king obtain Olwen for him. He asks these favors in the name of a host of Welsh heroes. Arthur agrees to help and sends out scouts to find Olwen; when that search fails Culhwch goes with several knights to find Olwen himself.

One day the party comes upon a castle, near which they meet a shepherd named Custennin, who is Ysbaddaden's brother; Custennin's wife is Culhwch's mother's sister. The couple bring Olwen to meet Culhwch, and the hero asks the beautiful maiden to marry him. Olwen, however, will agree to the marriage only if her father consents, as according to a prophecy, he will die when his daughter marries.

Culhwch and his companions enter the castle, where servants hold open the giant's eyes with forks so that he can see his visitors; these monstrous orbs remind us of Balor's evil eye, the lid of which could be lifted only by four strong men. Culhwch asks for Olwen's hand in marriage, and the giant agrees to consider the matter, but as the knights are leaving he hurls a spear at them. Bedwyr catches it and hurls it back, wounding Ysbaddaden in the knee. The same thing happens the next day and the next, causing wounds to the giant's chest and to one of his eyes.

Finally, Ysbaddaden agrees to the marriage if the hero can complete thirteen tasks. The tasks, reminiscent of those of Herakles and of the world of fairy tales, are, in effect, preparations for the marriage feast that the giant hopes to prevent. Culhwch must clear a forest and prepare the land for the growing of food for the wedding feast, he must find linseed for the flax that will be used for his wife's veil, he must find perfect honey for the wedding drink, the magic cup of Llwyr to contain it, and four other magical vessels, including the famous Irish cauldron of Diwrnach for the cooking of the meat. He must even obtain a magical harp and the birds of Rhiannon so that there will be music at the feast. He also must take a tusk from Yskithyrwyn, the head boar, to serve as Ysbaddaden's razor, and procure the Black Witch's blood as lotion for his beard. For the giant's hair management, Culhwch must take scissors and a comb from between the ears of Twrch Trwyth, a king who has been turned into a boar. All of these tasks and some twenty-six additional ones are accomplished with the help of the Arthurian knights, various animals, and even some gods, including Gofannon son of Don, Gwynn son of Nudd (Lludd), and Mabon (Maponos) son of Modron, whom Culhwch rescues from the otherworld, Caer Loyw. Finally Ysbaddaden concedes defeat and is decapitated according to the Celtic practice that we have encountered so often, leaving Culhwch and Olwen free to marry.

THE DREAM OF RHONABWY

Probably dating from the thirteenth century, "The Dream of Rhonabwy" takes place in the context of a rebellion by Iorwerth against his brother Madawc, son of Maredudd. It is Rhonabwy who leads Madawc's troops and who one evening falls asleep on a calf's hide and remains sleeping for three nights. He dreams of King Arthur's game of chess with Owain, who has an army of three hundred ravens, and of the gathering of Arthur's forces for the great Battle of Mount Badon, in which the Celts defeated the invading Anglo-Saxons.

The Later Arthurian Tales

The three late Arthurian tales of *The Mabinogion* are derived from twelfth-century romances of the French poet Chretien de Troyes, whose sources seem to have been earlier Welsh and/or Breton versions. The theme that unites them is that of valid sovereignty and specifically the idea we have found to be so prevalent in Irish mythology that fertility depends on the marriage of the king or hero to a goddess who represents the land in question.

OWEIN OR THE LADY OF THE FOUNTAIN

Owein (Owain), son of Urien, is one of King Arthur's most trusted knights. We remember that in "The Dream of Rhonabwy" he plays a game of chess with the king, a game that, in a sense, can be seen as a preface to the story of his connection with the Lady of the Fountain.

After defeating a black knight, Owein finds himself a prisoner in the Castle of the Fountain, until he is rescued by a ring of invisibility given to him by a beautiful young woman named Luned. Luned instructs him on how to win the love of the Lady of the Fountain, which he succeeds in doing before returning to Arthur's court. There he forgets the lady until she appears and accuses him of being a faithless knight.

Embarrassed and ashamed, Owein escapes to the wilderness where he is saved from death by the ministrations of a noblewoman and her assistants. After killing two monstrous beasts, he saves Luned and twenty-four maidens, whom he finds imprisoned by the Black Giant. He is now worthy of the Lady of the Fountain, whom he marries.

PEREDUR SON OF EFRAWK

The seventh son of Efrawk (Efrawg), Peredur is the Welsh version and apparent source for the hero Percival, or Parzifal. The best-known versions of his story are Chretien's late-twelfth-century *Percival, ou le conte du Graal* and Sir Thomas Malory's fifteenth-century *Morte d'Arthur*, where he is also Percival. *Per* means "bowl" in Brythonic Celtic, and Peredur-Percival-Parzival is always a hero who searches for the bowl that is the Holy Grail. In all of the tales the hero has a rough beginning, living an unmannered, unschooled life in the woods, until he arrives at Arthur's court, behaves in a bumbling sort of way, but is trained as a knight. Perhaps it is Peredur's essential innocence—even naiveté—that makes it possible for him to see the Holy Grail itself. Or perhaps his fortune is guaranteed by the young maiden relative who repeatedly guides him to the right path.

GEREINT AND ENID

The story of Gereint (Geraint) and Enid is a romance about a lover—perhaps based on a king of Dumnonia (the Celtic area of western Britain in early

Anglo-Saxon times)—who has little faith in the constancy of his beloved, Enid, the chieftain's daughter later to be made famous in the Tennyson poem named for her. Because of his doubts, Gereint treats Enid with contempt, but she proves herself in several tests, and eventually the two are reconciled, both drawing upon the Constance theme and once again bringing the hero into proper relationship with the representative of sovereignty.

CONCLUSION

Five Reflections of the Face of the Hero
in the Medieval English Romance—
Trials, Tribulations, and Transformative Quests

Long after the ancient indigenous myths of
gods and cosmos had faded from English
memory, myths of the hero still dominated
British literature; indeed, in many cases
they still do. In the genre of the medieval
romance, however, which ascended to a
height of popularity in Britain in the
fourteenth century, we find a vehicle that is
singularly appropriate for the age-old tales
of journeys, quests, trials, and tribulations—
a vehicle that put new chivalric and adven-
turesome masks on the otherwise familiar
face of the hero of the monomyth. The hero
is, in effect, Everyman, and his trials, tribulations, battles, and journeys of growth and
transformation mirror our own innermost
fears, desires, and needs. There are many
versions of the story of the hero reclothed
in the fashion of the medieval romance,
and the Middle English tradition is particularly rich in these. We have chosen five
such examples with which to conclude
our discussion. These were selected for
their range of quests, journeys, and trials,
and also for their breadth of Celtic and
Germanic mythic elements—elements that

give the face of the hero some particularly British features. These features remind us that the battle for mythic Britain was not after all a struggle between factions of ancient gods and heroes, but rather a war of attrition, a continual reformulation and reassertion of age-old archetypes in the garb most appropriate for the audience who heard their stories.

The Sacrificial Quest: Celtic Fertility Rituals and the Offering of the Corn King in *Sir Gawain and the Green Knight*

Section I

After the fall of Troy, Aeneas and many of his noble brethren settled throughout the far reaches of the western world. Romulus made his way to Rome, where he founded the city that still bears his name; Tirius established the towns of Tuscany, and Langobard great dwellings in Lombardy. Felix Brutus crossed the sea from France to Britain, and founded the host of realms upon that island. There were many kings and kingdoms in that land after the time of mighty Brut, but of all the British kings, Arthur was the noblest. Once upon a Christmastide there was a great banquet at the court of King Arthur; the noblest lords and ladies in the land were in attendance, and many were the tournaments, and jolly that jousting, after which all made their way to the court for caroling. Such feasting lasted fifteen days, with all the food and festivities for which one could ask. Brought together in that court were the noblest knights, the loveliest ladies, and the kindest king in all of Christendom.

On the day after New Year's double portions were served; the king and all his company entered the high hall after chapel, and New Year's gifts were exchanged by all. After washing for dinner they reentered the feast according to rank, as courtesy dictated, and gray-eyed Guinevere, most beautiful woman of all, sat in the center of the high dais. Arthur would not touch food until all were served; furthermore, his youthful exuberance was such that he soon declared that he would not eat until he heard of some mysterious marvel, or until a strange knight might challenge one of his champions to a duel unto death. On the heels of this decision a blast of trumpets announced the serving of the first course of the banquet, and barely had this din passed away before it was replaced by another: murmurs of amazement and alarm. For at this moment into the midst of the company rode a handsome giant of a man on horseback. He wore no armor, but carried a bob of holly in one hand and a great ax in the other; his eyes rolled red in his head and his beard was like a bush, but most marvelous of all, he and his steed were green as green could be.

Arthur most courteously invited the stranger to join the feast, but this great Green Knight answered that he had heard of the renown of Arthur's court, and that he craved a Christmas game. Not wishing to do combat with what he derisively described as the "beardless boys" of Arthur's court, the Green Knight made clear the nature of his challenge: an exchange of blows with the mighty ax held in the stranger's hand. One of Arthur's knights was to give the Green Knight a blow upon his neck with this fearsome weapon, but in a year and a day he who dealt the blow would receive the same in turn. Amazed both by the words and the appearance of this remarkable visitor, the court sat silent. The Green Knight interpreted this silence as cowardice, and questioned the reputation of the Knights of the Round Table. Finally, embarrassed and angered by the Green Knight's mocking tone and thunderous laughter, Arthur rose to answer the challenge himself; he made some terrible feint swings with the giant's ax, but the latter was as unconcerned as if he had been brought a drink of wine.

At this point Sir Gawain intervened, asking for permission to stand in Arthur's stead, as this task seemed too foolish for a king; this request Arthur granted. Gawain, Arthur's sister-son, was one of the youngest and least experienced of the Knights of the Round Table, but was the knight most reknowned for courtesy and honor. The giant Green Man repeated the challenge: Gawain might do his worst with one blow, but if the Green Knight survived, Gawain must seek him out in a year and a day. Gawain struck true, and the Green Knight's head came flying off and rolled through the crowd: the blood spurted bright red upon the verdant body of the man, and sprayed a fountain of crimson as his head bounced at the feet of those watching. Aghast at this grisly sight, the onlookers were further shocked by the Green Knight's reaction to this blow. Springing lightly to its feet, the Green Knight's body calmly trotted over, picked up his head by the hair, and remounted his horse. Holding his head before the court, the Green Knight opened his eyes, glared at Gawain and the rest, and reminded them all of the honorable terms of the challenge: on New Year's next, Gawain was to seek out the Green Knight at the Green Chapel and get his single stroke in return. With these words the Green Knight rode away, leaving the court astounded; soon enough, however, having seen his marvel, Arthur joined Gawain and returned to double portions at the feast.

Section 2

Eager had Arthur been on New Year's to know a novelty, and soon enough—as we have seen—this sire was served surfeit. Glad was Gawain to gain this game, and (do not doubt it) though their destinies seem dreary, men are often merry in their mead. But always the young year yields to time, and never is the same one seen again. Yuletide passed, as seasons do, and soon lean Lent stood in its stead. But time ticks eternally, and green grew the grass and the groves as spring gained the ground. Warm were the winds—and soft—as summer stole in, but the harvest hurried on its heels as grass formerly green grew again gray. Winter ever wends its way once more as the year grows weary, and soon was seen the Michaelmas moon that foretold Gawain's fateful faring.

Gawain determined to depart on the day of All Saints; great was the grieving at his going. Wondrous was the war gear worn by Gawain, and glorious his garb; truth to tell, however, most marvelous of all was his shining shield, sealed with the sign of Solomon. Such is to say that a pentacle was painted on the outer surface; what is more, within was the visage of the Virgin, with which the hero's heart was ever invigorated with valor. With its five fine points the pentacle presents five features in a fivefold manner: the five wits, or senses; the five fingers, or strength; the five wounds of Christ; the five joyful mysteries of the rosary; the five knightly virtues. Fully formed and flawless were each of the five fives found in Gawain: in his corpse, his conduct, and his contemplation.

Gone, then, was Gawain, riding right across the realm into the wastes of Wales; solitary save for his steed, the gallant Gawain had to battle men, monsters, beasts, and the harsh winter elements. On Christmas Eve Gawain knelt down to pray that he might find lodging, not for his own comfort but so that he could hear Mass said on Christmas. Crossing himself three times as he prayed, Gawain looked up to see the mist clearing in front of him, revealing a castle close by. Riding over to this manse, Gawain was soon admitted and treated most favorably; indeed, Gawain's reputation preceeded him, and upon learning his identity all the members of that court were eager to learn the finest points of courtesy from him. Gawain was warmly welcomed and embraced by the Lord of the castle, a large, handsome man with a booming laugh. He also made the acquaintance of the Lady of the castle, whose gray-eyed beauty was all the more apparent through contrast with the ugliness of her companion, a shriveled crone. All the company then went to Mass, after which a feast ensued for three days; the guests began to leave on St. John's Day—the feast of John the Evangelist, on December 27—and Gawain made ready to do the same. At this point Gawain explained his errand to his host, and expressed concern that he had only three days left in which to find the Green Chapel of the Green Knight. At this news the Lord laughed and assured Gawain that he might enjoy three more days of hospitality and leave on New Year's Day; the Green Chapel was hardly two miles distant. Gawain happily assented to the Lord's invitation to remain, and they decided to engage in a Christmas game: the host was to rise early and hunt the next day, while Gawain was to lounge in bed, taking his ease; they vowed to exchange the fruits of their respective day's labors in the evening.

Section 3

On the first day the Lord hunted deer; he was attended by a hundred choice huntsmen, and the blowing of the bugle and the baying of the hounds filled the forest. Meanwhile, back at the castle, the Lady came unbidden into Gawain's chamber, trapping him in his bed and offering him her body; Gawain attempted to hold off her advances without offending her, and in the end he did so, and they exchanged a courteous kiss. The hounds hunted on, meantime, harrying the hart, and the Lord's sport was spectacular: the killing of the quarry, the dressing of that deer, the payment of the dogs' due and the huntsmens' shares encompassed ritual and courtesy no less than that which passed between Gawain and the Lady. Leaving his lover's labor for the day, Gawain dressed, went to Mass, and then to table. The Lord returned and met him, giving Gawain his portions as promised and asking for that which Gawain had gained. A kiss Gawain credited his host, but its source he kept secret. Then they laughed, feasted, and agreed to the same arrangement on the morrow. The second day passed much the same as the first, but this time the Lord bested the bold and bloody boar; likewise, the Lady lay on the more lustily in her game with Gawain, and more ardent were her advances. In the end, twice he tasted the lovely Lady's lips, and these gains gave Gawain to the Lord as they made their exchange, each faithfully forwarding to his friend the fruits of his day's duties. On the third day, however, the Lord fought the fiendish fox, whose wily wit won him some little respite, although in the end the fox's craft failed to fend off the pack, and flayed and furless was his finish. The Lady's line of amorous attack, meanwhile, much like the flight of the fox, was wily and hard to track, and greatly Gawain feared he would fail to fend it off. Soothly, she nearly succeeded in seducing Gawain, who was confused by complex and conflicting courtesies. Finally, however, verily the Virgin vouchsafed him the strength to stave off the Lady. Sorry to be stymied, the Lady quickly queried if Gawain had granted himself to another; he responded that he had not, and she therefore rebuked his rebuff, claiming his crime thus the worse. Thus having taken him to task, she shifted tack, taxing him a token, asking for a trinket that she might take to remember their tryst. This demand Gawain denied, replying that he had none to requite. The Lady therefore determined to grant a gift to Gawain. First she offered a costly gold ring, which Gawain refused as too great a gain; then the Lady granted Gawain her girdle of green and styled silk. At first this favor he refused, but soon its secret she shared: he would not be harmed who wound himself in that smooth silk; she might thus shield him from shedding his blood. With those words Gawain was won. The Lady made concealment a condition, however, and Gawain pledged troth not to surrender this secret. Granting Gawain the third of three kisses she left. The Lord soon returned, gamely gifting his gain unto Gawain, who rapidly repaid his kindness with kisses. The girdle, however, Gawain gave not, serving only silence in its stead, and thus abrogating their agreement. Finishing the feast, Gawain gave a fond farewell to his host, who granted his guest a guide for the morning.

Section 4

Gawain rose before dawn, dressed, and departed; wicked was the weather that dreary day. Well girded with arms and armor, Gawain guarded himself with the green girdle, wrapping that ribbon tightly to his torso. Not gaily did the guide lead Gawain to the Green Chapel, however, but that man gainsaid this goal, and gladly would Gawain this guide have misled; telling terrible tales of the ghastly Green Knight, the man goaded Gawain to forswear this folly and to take another trail. Pleading with Gawain to preserve his own life, the guide pressed him to pass by that perilous place, and for his part the man pledged to perjure himself to his patron, and to tell his Lord that Gawain had gamely gone on to the Green Chapel. Greatly grieved was Gawain by this offer, but courteously concealing his contempt for this contrivance, Gawain gave thanks to the man and asked for the way in words; these directions the guide gave and soon this servant spurred off. Gawain galloped on, running down into the ravine, where he saw no chapel, but only a barrow, like a great green grave, hard by the bank of a splashing stream. Four holes had that hollow hillock: harbingers of hell, he deemed, the doorways to doom. When Gawain had mounted this mound, he heard a hideous sound of stone on steel, like the sharpening of shears; it was the Green Knight honing his hard-edged ax. Upon the first swing of the ax Gawain flinched, for which faintness the Green Knight found fault; then fairly the Green Knight feinted two blows, and soon served the third so as to slightly scratch the skin of Gawain's neck. Great was Gawain's gratification when he gathered that his dread of death had departed; quickly he gained his feet and reminded his rival that his one graze was all that their game granted. The Green Knight then rested his weapon and revealed to Gawain his true identity: he was the Lord who had hosted Gawain, Sir Bertilak of the high desert. The temptations of his wife were well known to him, and he revealed that his three strokes with his ax represented recompense for Gawain: his two passes in play paid Gawain for his honesty the first two nights; similarly, the snick on his skin was for Gawain's faithlessness upon the third evening, when he forfeited his fidelity. But Sir Bertilak avowed that this betrayal was mitigated because Gawain's desire to save his own life was a natural and overwhelming temptation. Gawain quickly cursed himself for his cowardice, and attempted to give the girdle back to Bertilak; his host refused this return, however, and Bertilak bade Gawain to come back to his castle. Declining, Gawain noted that he was not the first knight to be won by the wiles of women, of which wise men ever should be wary. Thanks Gawain graciously gave to the Green Knight for the girdle, saying that he would savor the sash ever as a sign of his shame. Bertilak begged him to return to the castle, confiding that the crone companion to his Lady was Morgan Le Fay. It was Morgan who made the magic whereby Bertilak became the green goblin who manifested such a marvel at the court of King Arthur. She did this to test the tenor of Arthur's troupe, and to terrify and grieve Guinevere. Again Gawain declined, and thus they divided and departed, after exchanging an embrace and a courtly kiss. Soon Sir Gawain came again to the court of King Arthur and told the tale truthfully, wearing the green girdle as a hallmark of humility; however, none of those noble knights deemed this a show of shame. Indeed, each sought solidarity with Sir Gawain by harnessing his own hips with a similar sash.

SIR GAWAIN IS followed by the postscript HONY SOYT QUI MAL PENCE, ("Shame be to the man who has evil in his mind"), the motto of the order of the garter, which was founded by Edward III around 1347. It is thought that a scribe added this postscript to evoke a connection between the tale and said order, but the garters of that order are blue; thus there is no clear connection to be made.

Sir Gawain's quest ostensibly is one of honor, and draws upon the medieval romance convention of the hero's transformative brush with death; archetypally, however, it participates in at least two much older traditions: Gawain's offering of himself to the ax of the Green Knight represents both the mythic hero's coming of age transformation through a symbolic death and the folkloric fertility sacrifice of the sacramental Corn King. The mythic and folkloric significance of the decapitation theme in *Sir Gawain and the Green Knight* is indisputable, and is widely accepted as evidence of Celtic influence; the "beheading contest" in this poem has at least two early Irish analogues, and *Sir Gawain's* debt to these literary cousins has been discussed and accepted for many decades. In the Celtic sources the challenge specifically entails decapitation, however, while the Green Knight of the *Gawain* poem simply suggests an exchange of blows. This point notwithstanding, the beheading contest motif has obviously influenced the Middle English poem. Whether or not beheading is necessary under the terms stated by the Green Knight, Gawain decapitates him, and the rest of the poem directly or indirectly concerns Gawain's need to see this debt repaid and his anxiety concerning the form of such repayment. The poem opens with an act of decapitation actualized, and it closes with a mock decapitation that draws its significance from that earlier beheading. From the moment of the completion of the first act the poem looks forward to the obvious conclusion of that act, and from the vantage of the final act it looks backward to its genesis. The poem begins with Gawain's decapitation of the Green Knight, and it derives its dramatic tension from Gawain's anxiety concerning the decapitation to come.

The decapitation theme is an ancient and transcultural one; the stories of Gilgamesh and Humbaba, Perseus and Medusa, David and Goliath, Judith and Holofernes all draw upon this common theme in their disparate ways. Significant examples of this motif appear in a number of medieval English sources, but in this poem decapitation—comprising the Green Man theme and its relationship to early Celtic fertility rituals—serves as a unifying metaphor that is related to and that explicates issues of sexual and agricultural fertility. Further, this metaphor helps to illustrate the confluence of similar Germanic and Celtic cultural motifs in the culture of medieval Britain.

The theme of the supernatural visitor offering such a challenge recurs a number of times in Old Irish literature; although these contests more explicitly involve beheading than *Gawain* does, it is clear that the general structure is the same, and so it is commonly accepted that the *Gawain* poet self-consciously drew upon this theme. An example of this genre may be found in the Bachlach's Challenge, from the champion's covenant contest in *The Feast of Bricriu*. In this tale three Ulster heroes are vying for the right to claim the hero's portion, and a series of supernatural contests and challengers put them to the test. The salient passage occurs when a giant visitor enters the court and offers them a game similar to that in *Sir Gawain*, although this challenge slightly deviates from that of the Green Knight both in that it specifically involves beheading and in that here the challenger wants to deal the first blow. In both cases, however, a supernatural visitor arrives, issues the challenge, and allows himself to be decapitated, with the understanding and the expectation that he will soon return the favor. But why would a beheading game be such a recurring and important theme?

In Celtic culture, the head was perceived as the source of power and the seat of the soul; a number of sources attest to the head-hunting practices of the Celts, and any number of modern historians would attribute these practices to a belief in the power resident in the head, a desire to control or appropriate that power, and a fear of the danger of the unloosed power of a dead enemy whose head is not safely under one's control. It has been suggested that the twin motives for head-hunting in Celtic culture were desire and fear (familiar terms for those interested in the Freudian association of decapitation and castration): desire to conquer and control the power of an enemy; fear of the danger of that power if it should slip from one's grasp.

Literary evidence suggests that such notions also existed in Germanic culture, but there the concept was more sublimated, and the historical and archaeological records yield less corroborating evidence. In any case, after the Green Knight's decapitation in *Sir Gawain*, we are presented with a vision of a head that can exist independent of its body; such a vision manifests a belief in the wisdom and power of the individual residing in the head, and the ability, through magic, of maintaining the life force after decapitiation. In this example, the power residing in the Green Knight's head even is able to exert power over his decapitated body. After Gawain beheads him, the Green Knight's body adroitly runs over to his head and picks it up; the eyes promptly open, and the head speaks to a terrified audience. The magical properties manifested in the form of the bodiless head of the Green Knight echo ancient Celtic and Germanic practices concerned with accessing and appropriating the wisdom and power of an enemy through his or her decapitated head.

It is telling that, in *Sir Gawain*, the head remains under the control of its own body and doesn't fall into the power of an enemy. More telling still is the fact that most literary examples and ritual practices involved an inversion of the scenario played out in *Gawain*: the point of these is the taking of an enemy's head to appropriate the power residing therein. Myths and stories in both the Germanic and the Celtic literary traditions establish the existence of an abstract belief in this notion of the power of the head. Further, the archeaological record reveals practices such as the ritual decapitation of corpses and the subsequent placement of the head below the body or against the buttocks; such practices seem to indicate concrete rites of exorcism and/or spiritual banishment that suggest that witches and revenants were disposed of in this way. These rituals—common in both the Germanic and the Celtic cultures—suggest that these peoples conceived of the head as quite literally the seat of magical powers, and that each culture prescribed a series of concrete steps that, taken properly, could overcome and dissipate this power. Grettir's decapitation of Glamr in *Grettissaga* has long been noted as an example of a common practice for "laying" a ghost in Germanic practice, and some Celtic burial practices—believed to be associated with witches— likewise emphasize decapitation and suggest similar notions of the magical properties of the head. Unlike their Celtic counterparts, Germanic rituals of human sacrifice did not generally include decapitation per se, although the fact that hanging, strangulation, and throat-cutting often played a role might have some significance. Still, the Germanic custom of laying a ghost clearly has resonance with Celtic analogues.

In both Celtic and Germanic literary sources the head is often construed as the repository of wisdom and power, and is thought able to continue to control and distribute such power even after it has been removed from its body. The story of the demise of Bran and that of the beheading of Olwen's father Ysbaddaden, both from *The Mabinogion*, are illustrative examples of the Celtic tradition, while similar stories in the Germanic tradition include the myth of Mimir, the tale of Grettir's struggle with Glamr in *Grettissaga*, and the saga of Beowulf defeating Grendel's mother and decapitating Grendel's corpse. These narratives, both Celtic and Germanic, may have as their reference points ancient head-hunting practices with which the authors of these stories had no direct knowledge. In any case, they both illuminate clearly the notion in each culture that the head was the seat of and conduit to the soul and mind, and that the preservation of the head might grant access to the power and wisdom of the individual, even after the body was destroyed.

In the Norse sources, decapitation of the undead in the manner described in *Grettissaga* was the prescribed way to ensure that the revenant remained in the grave. In *Beowulf* we see a practice of head-taking that also may suggest both an appropriation of power and a desire to permanently dispatch a supernatural enemy. This tradition for "laying ghosts" seems remarkably similar to that which the Celts employed to ensure the death of executed witches. There are numerous examples of decapitation as a part of complex Celtic burial rituals. Digs at some British sites, moreover, indicate that the ritual removal of the head of the deceased may have had a spiritual and magical significance akin to that which led Grettir to ritually dismember Glamr's corpse. In Dorset, for example, a number of graves have been discovered that might contain the bodies of women accused of witchcraft. The heads of these corpses were removed and placed against their legs, the jawbones were removed, and spindles were placed in the graves. It is simply a theory that the bodies recovered during these digs were those of witches; a number of theories might likewise explain the time, trouble, and grotesqueness associated with these rituals. In any case, however, such decapitation certainly seems associated with the containment of the power and life force the Celts associated with the head, and it seems reasonable to assume that these rituals, like the Germanic one recorded in *Grettissaga*, were intended to permanently sever this power or life force from the body of the victim as surely as the head itself (the symbol of power) was removed from that body.

It is clear that the head was considered the nexus of personal, spiritual, and magical power in both Celtic and Germanic cultures. It would not be much of a leap to acknowledge the association between the head and the phallus, and thus to suggest associations between the physical and spiritual powers residing in the head and the generative power residing in the phallus; indeed, the psychoanalytic associations between decapitation and castration have been commented upon widely, and often in association with cultures that were far less invested than the ancient Celts in the role of head-hunting in establishing male dominance. Fortunately, however, in the case of *Sir Gawain and the Green Knight*, we need not make any such leap blindly, trusting in the universal applicability of psychoanalytic theory. The Celtic tradition of the Green Man from which *Sir Gawain* derives its archetypical pattern overtly equates the head with the phallus, and the decapitation of a sacrificial victim with vegetative fertility and sexual fecundity. Further, the Middle English poem itself relies on metaphors of vegetable growth to unify its two primary acts of decapitation.

The concept of the Green Man is hardly limited to Celtic culture; we can find similar concepts in folklore from around the world, from the sexual agricultural rites of pre-Classical Greece to the sacrifice of the Corn King of the Aztecs. Such figures all share certain fundamental attributes: these figures are associated with vegetation and deities of vegetation; they are involved in fertility rites that exist to ensure vegetative growth and fertility; and they are involved in some form of sacrifice that usually culminates in ritual death, often by beheading. The Green Man of Celtic tradition is associated with the death and rebirth of the year at midwinter, and therefore with the passage of time, the change of seasons, and the resurrection of the slumbering earth after a period of cold, darkness, and death. It can be no accident that *Sir Gawain* is set at midwinter, nor can the familiar form of the Green Man, presenting himself for sacrifical decapitation at just the appropriate time, be merely coincidental.

Sir Gawain is a poem that concerns itself with the cyclical passage of seasonal time, and it is significant that all of the action of the poem takes place at midwinter.

Further, the poet's description of the decapitation itself—with its vivid and graphic images of sharp steel shearing through flesh and bone, and bright red blood spurting onto the verdant green of the Knight's body—seems designed to underscore both the nature of the midwinter sacrifice and its function. That is, this ritual requires decapitation, and through this rite the green of vegetative fecundity is ensured through the red of sacrificial blood. Such fertility sacrifices usually took place in the fields at midwinter, and the poet's words evoke the relationship between blood red and vegetable green. The significance of the color green and its associations with fertility help to draw together and explicate the acts of decapitation in the poem. After the departure of the Green Knight and the resumption of Arthur's Christmas feast, the poet compresses the following year into a few lines. Such compression of time is, of course, a common trait of the romance, but here references to the waxing and waning of the seasons—illustrated in part through the growth and decay of vegetable matter and the associated changes in color—serve to underscore the relationship between the Green Knight's decapitation and the fertility sacrifice of the Green Man.

That such vegetative fecundity may be associated with sexual potency may seem common sense, but in any case the poem is clear on this point in two ways. First, medieval appropriations of the Green Man motif often served as emblems of sexuality; although the figure of the Green Man in most fourteenth-century literature merely connoted youthful vitality, by this time the vegetative associations of the trappings of the Green Man also had come to be associated with sexuality. Second, during Sir Gawain's stay with his host Sir Bertilak (who is, of course, his verdant antagonist in disguise), Gawain undergoes a series of temptations by Sir Bertilak's wife; each of these he overcomes in turn, except for the last. The sexual nature of these temptations is clear enough, but what is really of importance is how and why Gawain fails at the last, and how this failure is marked concerning sexual fertility, castration anxiety, and the relationship between these and vegetative fertility and decapitation.

On his last day at Sir Bertilak's, while his host is out for his daily hunt, Bertilak's wife tries one last time to seduce Gawain. In this she fails, but she tries then to give him a gift, a keepsake of their time together. First she offers him a gold ring—which he refuses—but then she presses upon him her girdle, which is, of course, green. The association with fertility here is obvious: a beautiful young woman, who has been trying for days to seduce Gawain, offers to gird his loins with a sash from her own fertile hips; as if this were not enough, the girdle is green, representing her ability to reproduce, as well as (unknown to Gawain) her husband Bertilak's role as the Green Man, and therefore the fecundity of the natural world. At first Gawain resists, but he is soon overcome by the secret of the girdle: it will protect the life of whoever should wear it. Gawain's fear of decapitation is enough to overcome his sense of honor, and he accepts the gift and agrees to keep it secret, thereby violating the terms of his agreement with Bertilak. Gawain therefore attempts to protect his head by covering his loins. Clearly here Gawain's fear of death and decapitation may be equated with fear of castration, impotence, loss of virility—in short all of those trappings of sterility that the sacrifice of the Green Man promises to stave off in nature.

The next day Gawain goes off to meet his fate with the sash around his hips; he finds the Green Knight at the Green Chapel—which appears to be more of a grassy barrow, and which, with its doorways into the earth, clearly invokes the Celtic mythic conception of a portal to the otherworld, here cast by Gawain into the Christian hell—and fulfills his original compact with the knight by presenting his neck for the ax. After a series of feinted blows and remonstrations, the Green Knight nicks Gawain on the neck, absolves him from his debt, and reveals Bertilak and the Green Knight to be one and the same. It has been argued reasonably that this nick on the neck is representative of a male rite of passage, a circumcision of sorts; such sacramental acts at the threshold of manhood are ritual manifestations of the hero's journey and represent his victory over a symbolic death. Finally, the Green Knight claims ownership of the green girdle (and perhaps his wife's fecundity), and thus of the fertility attributed to the Green Man. In the words of the Green Knight, Gawain's only sin was fear of loss of life, a fear which could be associated with a fear of loss of virility, of sexual potency, of the power of the phallus represented by the head. Gawain himself then laments the weakness of his flesh and how it led him to sin, in terms that seem much more appropriate to sexual transgression than to the breaking of a vow to a host.

Sir Gawain and the Green Knight is a poem concerned with decapitation and fertility, and these concerns have important implications regarding comparative British mythology. The Celtic incarnation of the Green Man motif is reflected in this poem's treatment of the relationship between the beheading of the Green Knight and the changing of the seasons; further, a number of northern European mythic concepts concerning the power and potency residing in the head, the relationship between the head and the phallus, and that between agricultural fertility and sexual potency manifest themselves in the beheading game described in this tale. Finally, green is the color of fertility in *Sir Gawain,* and by trying to protect his head by girding his loins with the Green Knight's green sash, Gawain betrays a fear of the loss of his own life-giving potency, as well as a fear of the loss of his life; Gawain's act illustrates the link between decapitation and castration, and thus helps to explicate a conception of the totemic power of the human head that is much older than the Middle English poem.

The Love Quest to the Underworld:
Sir Orfeo Seeks the Land of Fairy

Once upon a time there lived a certain Sir Orfeo, who was a king of England and dwelt in Thrace, as Winchester was called at that time. Orfeo was the son of King

Pluto and Queen Juno, and was married to Lady Heurodis. Orfeo loved to play the harp, and honored and respected all fellow harpers; of all the harp players in the world, moreover, Orfeo was the best, and to hear him play might be compared to listening to the celestial strains of the angels themselves. It happened one lovely May day that Lady Heurodis went walking with two noble maidens in an orchard. At noontide they took their rest beneath a beautiful cultivated tree, and soon Heurodis was fast asleep. The maidens were loathe to rouse their queen from her slumber, and thus Lady Heurodis slept until afternoon.

Suddenly Lady Heurodis awoke screaming, thrashing about and tearing at her face and her clothes; unable to bear this horror, the maidens fled quickly to the palace, where they told all who would listen that their queen had gone mad. Knights, ladies, and more than sixty damsels sped to Lady Heurodis to restrain and calm her. But although they managed to bring her back to her bed, still she continually cried out and tried to flee. When Orfeo heard this news he rushed to her side with ten of his knights, attempting to calm and reassure her. Heurodis calmed enough then to tell him her story, but it was one that offered them little hope: they were to be together no more. When she had fallen asleep beneath the cultivated tree in the orchard at noontide, two knights had appeared to her as though in a dream; they had demanded that she accompany them to their king. When she refused, the knights spurred off, only to return moments later with their king and his vast retinue. All in the host were clothed in white and were mounted on snow white steeds; they were beautiful beyond comparison, and almost radiant in their brightness. The king had upon his head a crown—not of silver, nor of gold—wrought from one massive jewel, shining as bright as the full sun at midday, both beautiful and painful to gaze upon. As soon as the king came upon her he seized her and placed her upon a palfrey at his side; they then embarked on a tour of his vast domain, and he showed her his many castles, towers, rivers, forests, and flowers, and many rich estates. Then he returned her to her orchard, with the warning that she was to prepare to depart the next day at noontide, to live with him and his folk evermore. She was to meet him at the selfsame cultivated tree, and would be taken whole or in parts—torn limb from limb—at her option. Help would avail her not, he admonished her, and any resistance would only cause her pain.

Upon hearing her tale of woe, Orfeo declared that he would rather lose his life than his queen, and he sought counsel from all the wisest of his retainers. No one could offer advice on this matter. The next day, therefore, Orfeo surrounded Heurodis and the cultivated tree with a thousand armed knights, stern, grim, and watchful. All his preparations were for nought, however, as at the appointed hour Heurodis simply vanished from their midst. The consternation of Orfeo's people was doubled when he announced that he was soon to depart from them himself; he vowed to live the rest of his days in the wilderness with only the wild beasts for company. Orfeo appointed a steward to rule over the country in his absence, and instructed his people that they should, upon evidence of the death of Orfeo, convene a parliament to preside over the selection of a new king. Having made these arrangements, Orfeo exchanged his kingly garb for beggar's rags and made his way to the wilderness with only his harp for company. Over the next ten years he lived in the wilds, making do on what nature had to offer, growing thin and wasted, with long, lank black hair and beard to his waist. He kept his harp in a hollow tree trunk, and on clear days he beguiled all of nature with his playing, and birds and beasts drew near to hear; when he desisted, however, no living creature would draw near to him.

Often during this tenure in the wild, Orfeo noted that in the heat of the day—just at noontide—he might observe the Fairy King and all his rout out hunting, accompanied by baying hounds and huntsman's horns, but Orfeo could never make out their quarry or their destination. On other occasions he saw columns of fierce and beautiful fairy soldiers, fully armed and armored, marching to or from some field of combat. Still other times he witnessed a woodland dance, with beautiful lords and ladies dancing to lovely music, far from any court or palace. One particular day he spied a group of sixty such ladies—without a single man—riding down to the river side. Each lady bore a hawk, and once they had reached the shore the ladies sent up their birds of prey. Having been an avid falconer himself, Orfeo followed them, and approached one of the ladies, whom he quickly recognized as his wife; that she recognized him and the suffering he had undergone through his grief was evident by her reaction, for although she said not a word, her cheeks were soon bathed in tears. Noting her distress, the other ladies soon took her up, and they all rode off away from the river side and Orfeo.

Orfeo now resolved to follow his beloved wife, regardless of the consequences. The sixty ladies rode right into the side of a mountain, and passed through the stone for three miles; Orfeo followed them on foot. On the other side of that rocky passage—at the heart of the mountain—he found himself on a glorious green plain, as bright as a summer's day and level as could be, with no hill nor dale as far as the eye could see. In the midst of this great plain was a splendid castle, surrounded by a high wall of crystal and a hundred lovely and strong towers. Buttresses rose up from the moat fashioned from purest gold, and the vaulting was exquisitely enameled. All of the dwellings were wrought of precious stones, and the most humble pillar was of burnished gold. When the dark of night threatened to fall, great jewels brightened up the sky until it shone as bright as the sun at noon. It seemed to Orfeo as though he were gazing upon the court of heaven.

The ladies soon dismounted within the castle, and Orfeo attempted to follow them; at the gate he told the porter that he was a traveling minstrel come to entertain the lord, and he was soon granted admittance. Now within the walls, Orfeo looked about him and saw all manner of folk who had been brought thither and thought dead, but who in fact lived now here: Some stood without head; some had not arms; some had wounds through the body; some lay mad, and bound; some sat armed ahorse; some strangled as they ate; some were drowned in water; some were all shriveled from fire; some women lay in childbed, some dead, some mad; and very many more lay there besides, just as they had lain themselves down at noontide. Each was taken thus in this world, and carried off thither with the Fairy King. There he saw his own Lady Heurodis, asleep under the cultivated tree from his orchard; he recognized her by her clothes. Having thus had his fill of marvelous sights, Orfeo made his way into the king's hall, where lord and lady sat among their retinue, attired in garb and countenance so bright that Orfeo could scarcely bear to look upon them.

Orfeo bowed before the king and offered to play for him; the Fairy King was taken aback, as no mortal man had ever dared to come to his court without having been bidden. Orfeo played so sweetly, however, that the king offered to him whatever reward he cared to name, and Orfeo asked for the lovely lady asleep under the cultivated tree in the courtyard. At first the king refused, citing the disparity of their stations: one a high-born queen, the other a ragged beggar. Orfeo reminded the king, however, of his vow freely to give to Orfeo his choice of rewards, and the king thus bowed to honor and granted Heurodis to Orfeo. The happy pair then traveled the long road back to their kingdom, where Orfeo hid Heurodis in the cottage of a peasant until he had the chance to try the loyalty of his steward. Still dressed in rags, Orfeo presented himself to the steward in the street, who gladly accepted him and offered him a meal at court out of love for his lost lord, who was ever kind to fellow harpers. That evening Orfeo played for the court, and the Steward recognized the harp as that of his master; asked how he came by it, the still unrecognized Orfeo related a tale of a fellow wanderer rent to pieces by wild beasts. Seeing his steward's genuine distress at this news, Orfeo revealed himself to the gathered company, who were overjoyed to have their king and queen home again. Orfeo reigned again for many years, and after his passing the Steward was granted the throne as reward for his loyalty.

ORFEO'S QUEST FOR his lost love in the otherworld is a rendering of one of the most famous of the hero's journeys, and in the older mask of Orpheus of classical literature it is perhaps the best-known quest for love in the western tradition. *Sir Orfeo* survives in three manuscripts, the earliest of which dates from the first half of the fourteenth century; the story is composed in the dialect of southeast England, and probably predates the earliest manuscript version by no more than a hundred years. It is possible that this version of the story was based on or translated from a Breton Lay, which is to say a Celtic romance of French origin from the region of Brittany, where a thousand years before Celtic Britons fleeing the Germanic Anglo-Saxon invasion had found refuge. The fundamental source of *Sir Orfeo* is the Orpheus myth, a classical rendition of an ancient theme, treated most famously, perhaps, in Books X and XI of Ovid's first-century CE *Metamorphoses*, and also notably described in such works as Virgil's first-century BCE *Georgics* and the sixth-century CE *The Consolation of Philosophy* of Boethius. Indeed, the Orpheus myth has remained popular up to the present day, retold (and sometimes set to music) by such luminaries as Henryson (1508), Monteverdi (1607), Gluck (1762), and Offenbach (1858). But *Sir Orfeo* is far more than another retelling of the age-old Orpheus theme; in this work we see a number of traditions combined and refined, granting us, for example, a glimpse into the peculiarly British conception of the otherworld as fairy kingdom rather than simply the abode of the dead. Moreover, locating this otherworld beneath a hill or mountain clearly reminds us of the Irish mythic notion of the Tuatha De Danann and their migration beneath the surface of Ireland after the invasion of the Celts. Further, the combination in the fairies of *Sir Orfeo* of more or less ordinary human forms with magical properties also seems closely linked to Welsh tradition, notably the king and underworld of Annwn as these are represented in *The Mabinogion*.

Celtic mythic traditions note several pathways to such fairy kingdoms, some associated with place and others with time of day. In *Sir Orfeo*, the Modern English term "cultivated tree" (sometimes rendered "grafted tree") is a translation of the Middle English *ympe-tre*, which denotes an artificially created plant—that is, one that is neither wholly natural nor wholly man-made. Such a creation illustrates the arrogance of man in his attempt to emulate and perhaps improve upon the works of God, and thus provides an obvious portal to the land of the fairies, those supernatural beings who likewise span the gap between human and divine. These creatures were often associated with mounds, hills, groves, and trees, perhaps owing to the animistic and decentered nature of traditional Celtic spiritual life. Entrances to the fairy kingdom might be found in any of these places and could take various forms; sometimes these are straightforward, as in the case of a door which is set in the side of a hill or mound, as in *Sir Gawain and the Green Knight,* and sometimes these are more conceptual, as in the case of Lady Heurodis's *ympe-tre.* Time of day can also open the portals to the otherworld. What has been translated in this text consistently as "noontide" is actually the Middle English term *undertid,* denoting a time between mid-morning and mid-afternoon, say the period between 10:00 A.M. and 2:00 P.M. It is particularly noteworthy that *Sir Orfeo* is recounted as a romance, a medieval literary genre that is notoriously time-unspecific; that the author consistently reminds us of the notable hour of Lady Heurodis's abduction and Sir Orfeo's witnessing of the wild hunt seems therefore significant. The time itself is mysterious and suspect because it is neither morning nor afternoon, and is an ideal time for the Fairy King to engage in his wild hunt. Although some cultures have long embraced the custom of napping after a large noontime meal, here we see the conflation of Celtic traditions concerning the dangers of the fairy world with Christian canonical hours and a moral sensibility calling for regular prayer and useful activity between very early in the morning and quite late at night. This conflation also might indicate an attempt to warn workers about the dangers of napping on the job, and therefore might represent a rather crude folkloric attempt at social control. This preoccupation with the dangers of noontide is hardly limited to Celtic tradition, however; Psalm 91 mentions "the destruction that wasteth at noonday," and Milton takes up this biblical time theme in his description of Eve's temptation in Book IX of *Paradise Lost.*

The most notable consistencies in the descriptions of the fairy king and the fairy kingdom in *Sir Orfeo* concern the painful beauty and blinding brightness that clothe darker purposes and deeds. It may be significant that, in his first vision of the fairy kingdom, it seems to Orfeo *almost* the court of heaven. The Celtic tradition of the fairies has ancient pagan roots, and this vision of the otherworld conflates elements that Christian conceptions of the afterlife clearly divide into good and evil, heaven and hell. At the same time, a notion of a powerful ruler of the underworld whose courtly manner and superficial beauty belie his destructive and immoral intent lends itself to Christian interpretation. In the Celtic tradition, however, the fairies are both evil and good, or—more precisely—they are neither. They are removed from human affairs and moral sensibilities, and thus are more correctly termed amoral than immoral. With rare exceptions, the fairies, like the gods of the classical pantheons, do not necessarily care one way or the other about the fate of human beings; occasionally a foolish mortal may bring the wrath of the fairies upon himself, but most generally it is dumb luck or fate that places one in their path. We are to them—as Shakespeare once said of the gods—"as flies to wanton boys." The brilliant crown worn by the Fairy King, the shining countenance that is both painful and beautiful to look upon, the beautiful palace in the heart of the mountain—these are all indicative of one aspect of the paradoxical duality of the fairies, one half of their terrible beauty. The terror lurking beneath this beauty is represented, of course, by the countless maimed and mad abductees hidden within the crystal walls. To the fairies, human happiness and well-being simply do not count.

The fairy dance is an ancient and widespread Celtic tradition attested to in a number of sources, notably Walter Map's *De Nugis Curialum*. The basic premise is that a knight, having given over his wife's corpse to the grave and witnessed her burial, sees her alive again in a desert place, dancing among unknown beautiful and youthful companions. The story most usually continues that he steals up to the assembly and takes her back by force, enjoying thereby many more years of marriage with her and begetting many children upon her, the generations of which are thus known as "the sons of the dead mother." Sometimes such mysterious dances are come upon by those not mourning the loss of a spouse, in which cases the ring usually vanishes as the stranger approaches, sometimes leaving behind a single member who may subsequently marry the interloper. Chaucer's "Wife of Bath's Tale" deals with such a fairy dance, and the wisdom and magical properties of the old hag left to the errant young knight thus come as no surprise to a knowing audience. Further, Chaucer's tongue-in-cheek discussion, in the same tale, of the replacement of fairies and elves by mendicant Friars (ll. 857–881) notes some of the most usual traits and locations of fairy dances.

The wild hunt is an ancient tradition attested to in a number of Northern European traditions; here it has been clothed in the trappings of the medieval romance, focusing on the courtly elements of the pack of hounds, the gaily appareled rout, and so forth. Orfeo witnesses the hunt itself, but never realizes the nature of the quarry; although the author never makes this quarry explicit, it is obvious that the fairies are hunting mortals—prizes such as Heurodis that they may take back and display as trophies at court. In combination with the time-of-day theme, it seems that this tradition clearly has been conflated with a Christian sensibility concerning spiritual vigilance versus moral somnolence. Just as Odin and earlier proto-Germanic sky-gods led the wild hunt through the night sky in search of human prey—warriors to add to their menagerie—so too does Satan, the slayer of souls, hunt constantly for the spiritually unwary. In other words, literally the Fairy King leads the wild hunt in search of mortal quarry who have fallen asleep at an unwise hour; figuratively, however, the author has grafted this pagan tradition unto a Christian theme of spritual and moral wakefulness. The message is that it is dangerous to let down one's guard when the hunter is on the prowl.

The Penitential Quest: Transgression and Redemption in "The Wife of Bath's Tale"

Once upon a time, back in the days of King Arthur, all of Britain was filled with fairies; the Elf Queen and her maidens often danced in many a green and grassy meadow. But this was hundreds of years ago, and no one sees the elves anymore, and limiters and other holy friars saying prayers have chased these creatures from sight; indeed, friars seem to have taken their place in every nook and cranny in the land that once had been the territory of elves. Women now may walk through woods in dusky light, and no incubus will trouble them—save the friars—and these jolly men of God will do a maid nothing but dishonor.

It came to pass one fine day that a knight of King Arthur came riding from the banks of a river and saw before him a lovely young maiden, all alone. For what reason none can say, but this knight dishonored them both that day by taking from her by force her maidenhead, her sacred virginity; and for this ghastly crime Arthur deemed the knight as dead, and commanded that his head should pay his debt. But the Queen and her ladies begged the King that it should not be so, and that the sinful knight be placed in their judgment. After long and fervent supplication this request was granted. The Queen brought then this knight before her, and let him know that his was a stay of execution only, for a period of a year and a day; and at the end of that period, if he could reveal to her what it is that women most desire, then he should keep his head and his freedom. But if he returned after that space with no satisfactory answer to give, his head should be the forfeit.

Then this knight—who for a moment had been glad—was again sorrowful and despaired at solving such a riddle. But at length he realized that he had no choice but to seek the answer as well as he was able, and so he set off on his quest, hoping in God's mercy, and planning to return at the end of the year. He searched high and low in every house and dwelling place, but never did he hear the same answer twice: some said women loved wealth best, some said honor, some said pleasure; some claimed it was fine clothes that women most desired, some countered that it was good sport abed, and some implied that it was best to be oftened widowed and wedded. He heard that women best loved flattery, or to be free to make their own choices, or to be thought able to keep great secrets. So, search as the knight might, he found no definitive answer, and as his time was up, he turned toward home again sorrowful and afraid, for surely he must lose his life for his failure.

And it happened that upon his journey home he chanced into a clearing of a forest, where he saw before him four and twenty maidens and more, all joined together in a dance. But as he approached them they vanished—to where he knew not—and he was left alone on the meadow, save for one shriveled old crone. A fouler creature one can scarcely imagine, and the knight recoiled at her ugliness. Seeing him, however, the old biddy rose to her feet and greeted him, remarking that the clearing led to nowhere, and thus she surmised that he sought something; she bid him ask of her, as old folk often know that which eludes the young. So the knight told the old hag his plight, and she told him to put his mind at ease: she could give him the answer to his question, and her only condition was that he grant to her whatever she next desired of him. To her condition the knight quickly assented, and the crone whispered the secret of his salvation into the knight's ear. She told him to have no fear, and together they then made their way to Arthur's home.

When they arrived at court at last, the knight announced that he had returned as his covenant had required; further, he claimed to have found that which he sought, and was anxious to give his answer to the Queen and her ladies. Then many women gathered in the hall: young and old, rich and poor, maid, wife, and widow gathered around the Queen, who sat now in judgment. The knight strode forward confidently, and in a powerful voice declared that which women desire most: to have dominion over their husbands in marriage and in love, and thus to hold the reins of power. The knight stood by his answer, and asked them for death if it pleased them not. All agreed, however, that they could find no fault with his answer, and they therefore declared with one voice that he had won his life. Now the old hag sprang to her feet and demanded her due: the knight had promised her whatever she desired of him in return for the words that saved his life; now she called upon the Queen and her court to see justice done. The crone wished the knight to take her to wife. Shocked and appalled, the knight begged of her to make another request, and called upon his sovereign queen to save him and his family from such a degrading union; but it was all for nothing. Wed they would be, and soon it came to pass.

The tale of their wedding and the banquet is quickly told: he wedded her privately in the morning, and there was no feast; he hid himself in his rooms for shame, and lamented the foulness of his wife's features. Then came the moment of truth: their wedding night and nuptial bed seemed to the knight a greater tribulation than many a dangerous quest in arms. But there was no avoiding the inevitable, and soon they lay together between the sheets of their bed. The knight, however, was resolved to go no further in his marital duty and refused to consummate their union. For this his new bride gently reproved him, and asked what she could do to amend the situation he found so dire. The knight scoffed at this offer, however, and responded by lamenting her age and ugliness, her poverty and her base lineage. To each of these charges the wife reasonably responded, but then she offered him a choice to sooth his woe: he might have her as a beautiful and desirable wife, and yet always run the risk of being cuckolded by her; or ugly and old she would remain, but her loyalty to him would be guaranteed. The knight, however, made no choice and asked her to decide upon that which would provide them both with the most honor and pleasure. His wife then asked the knight if he indeed granted her dominion over him, to which he assented. As soon as his words were spoken, she revealed herself to him as a beautiful young maiden, and declared to him that—because he had granted her power over him—she would be for him both beautiful and loyal. Further, from that day forth she pleased him in every way and obeyed him in all things, and so they lived happily ever after.

THE KNIGHT IN "The Wife of Bath's Tale" is a sinner, and his search is that for penitence and forgiveness; this is one version of the age-old archetypal quest story, but this medieval rendering is also far more than that. "The Wife of Bath's Tale" is a part of Chaucer's *Canterbury Tales*, and so is rightfully examined in that context: that is, in the context of the *Canterbury Tales* as a whole; in that of the Wife of Bath as a character in that larger narrative; and in that of the Wife's Prologue, which precedes her tale. That said, in this tale—as in so many of the others—Chaucer has taken a series of narrative traditions and elements and used them for his larger purposes. As with the other romances retold in this conclusion, we are primarily interested in the mythic and folkloric elements recast in this particular medieval guise, and with the journey of the hero archetype as it is here retold. We are interested only tangentially with the narrative structure of the *Canterbury Tales*, or with the generic characteristics of the medieval romance. Still, a brief overview of the salient aspects of those narrative elements and generic characteristics may in fact bet-ter illuminate how "The Wife of Bath's Tale" engages mythic and folkloric material.

Chaucer began his *Canterbury Tales* in the mid 1380s, although some of the material contained in them is undoubtedly a bit earlier. Some eighty-four manuscripts and early printed versions still exist, and from these we may infer that Chaucer left some ten fragments of various sizes that were meant to be part of a larger whole. According to the General Prologue to the tales, some thirty pilgrims were each to tell two tales on the way to Canterbury, and two tales on the way back; nowhere near this many tales survive, however, and we have every reason to believe that Chaucer never completed this massive proj-ect. It has long been argued that the pilgrims who tell the tales are meant to be distinct and well-formed characters; thus Chaucer's descriptions of these characters, the tales that they tell, and the prologues to these tales are all meant to provide the evidence through which we can compile a "composite sketch" of each character. This theory works well for some characters, but not at all for others; it is our good luck that the Wife of Bath is one figure who is well fleshed out through her own words.

The Wife of Bath is a bold and assertive woman who has had five hus-bands and makes no secret of her amorous nature, nor of her use of her femi-nine wiles to control each of her husbands in turn. The prologue to the wife's tale, in fact, is a protracted account of the desire of women to have mastery over their husbands in marriage, as well as her own anecdotal confessions of her success in this endeavor. The prologue is in this case much longer than the tale, and it is clear that they are both linked to the wife's interest in what now is termed gender politics, and to her autobiographical account. In a way, then, the real hero of this tale is the hag, just as the knight is an antihero of sorts; the hag's role and her actions represent at one and the same time the wife's practical desire for sovereignty in marriage, her lustful need for a new young buck in her bed, and her wistful longing for the firm flesh and lovely features of her now lost youth. The representative audience of women—young and old and in between—at the trial of the knight, and indeed the tri-partite role of the major female figures in the tale—the young virgin upon whom the knight violently exerts his male dominance, the old hag who saves him and in return demands sovereignty from him, and the young wife who re-mans him—remind us of the tripartite goddess of the Celts: at once maiden, wife, and crone.

The immediate analogues of this tale are all in English, and some are clearly folkloric; two identify Sir Gawain as the knight in question, although in none of these other sources is the knight guilty of rape. The theme of the innocent maiden raped by the lone knight does appear in some French sources, although we cannot link them definitively to this tale. Rather, Chaucer seems to have chosen this heinous crime as perfectly suited to the wife's discussion of power, sexuality, and dominance. In this tale Chaucer has combined the mythic quest for penitence with elements of the fairy tale and of folklore as well as those of the romance. The Arthurian setting and the commonplace magic suggest the popular oral traditions of the times, and this may well be Chaucer's most populist tale. The best-known oral folkloric tradition used in this tale by Chaucer is that of the fairy dance, discussed at some length in our examination of *Sir Orfeo*.

Chaucer weaves these disparate elements together with the familiar romance motif of the perilous quest that ends with the hero's survival in the face of a threat of death. To those familiar with the mythic archetypes involved, it comes as no surprise that such heroes—such as Sir Gawain—often are reborn through a symbolic death. The knight's journey in this tale is one of penance, and through true penitence—which is hard to come by, it seems, and which this knight seems to lack in full measure—the sinner-hero may be reborn. In this tale—again, like that of Gawain—the threat of death comes from the suspended sentence of decapitation: For a year and a day this knight lives with the fear of a symbolic sword dangling over his head by the merest thread; this thread represents his hopes to find the answer to his quest, and thereby to serve his penance; but this searcher is driven by fear of death rather than by sorrow for his sin, and hence he is not able to discover the answer on his own. This seeker's quest for penance, therefore, only ends with the knight's submission to his ancient bride. Thus, according to the logic of the tale, he who imposed his will upon a powerless woman (and who felt no remorse for his act, but merely grief for his own fate) only may begin to expiate that horrible sin when he submits wholly and voluntarily to the power of a woman. Fear of beheading—as we discuss at length in our treatment of *Sir Gawain and the Green Knight*—usually resonates with castration anxiety; considering the issues of marital power and sovereignty at stake in this tale, it is clear that the knight's sense of his manhood is indeed at risk. This association seems particularly fitting considering the nature of the knight's crime; in other words, the threat of a symbolic castration seems an apt punishment for one who forcibly has taken "maiden head."

The Hero's Trial by Fire: Myths of Justice in *Athelston*

Once upon a time there lived four royal messengers who bore letters throughout the kingdom of England. Each of them was from a different precinct, and one day they met in a forest at a standing cross by the highway; this was under a linden tree. They soon became fast friends and swore blood-brotherhood, although they were not from the same family. The eldest of them was named Athelston, and he was close kin to the king, the son of the king's uncle. Soon thereafter the king died without heir, and as the nearest relation, Athelston ascended the throne. Athelston forgot not the oath he had sworn to his blood-brothers in the forest, and he called them all to him. The eldest of the three was named Wymound, and Athelston made him Earl of Dover. The next was named Egelan, and Athelston made him Earl of Stone, and married him to his own sister Edif; Edif and Egelond had two sons, who were fifteen and thirteen at the time of this tale. The youngest of the blood-brothers was named Alryke, and he was a priest; Athelston appointed him to be Archbishop of Canterbury.

Athelston loved Edif, Egelond, and his two dear nephews more than his own life, and he showed them great favor; he consulted them in all matters, both private and public, and weighed their advice most heavily. Wymound, the earl of Dover, began to resent this favoritism, and envied Egelond's position. He decided to advance himself at the earl of Stone's cost by secretly accusing him of treason. Dover therefore made his way to the king, and asked to speak with him in private. Once they were alone, Dover told Athelston that there was a traitor in the land who wished to replace him upon the throne. Athelston demanded the scoundrel's name, but this Dover refused to provide until Athelston had given his word that he would never reveal the source of his information. To this condition Athelston quickly assented, and then Dover laid before him the false plot he had devised: that Edif and Egelond were not satisfied with their favored position, but wished to rise to be queen and king in his stead by poisoning him. Athelston was outraged and promised to put them to death immediately. Dover, his dastardly purpose fulfilled, returned to his home well satisfied.

Athelston quickly dispatched a messenger to Stone, telling him to bring his wife and family immediately, for he wished to dub the boys knights. Stone thought to delay the journey, as his wife was heavy with child and soon to be delivered, but Edif would not think of waiting; she was anxious to see her boys knighted. Upon their arrival at court, Athelston had the boys and their father promptly placed in irons and thrust into the dungeon; he was deaf to Edif's pleas, and had his own sister—pregnant and soon to give birth—cast into prison. Word of this calamity soon reached the queen, who was herself with child, and she went quickly to Athelston to learn his purpose and to beg for clemency. Athelston was so outraged at his wife's interference that he kicked her in the stomach, slaying his own unborn son in her womb. Taken to her bed and delivered of her slaughtered child, the queen managed to arrange for the messenger who had summoned Stone to wend his way to Alryke, the Archbishop of Canterbury, to see what influence he could bring to bear upon the king. The queen offered the messenger gold and lands for his efforts, but these he nobly declined; he did, however, demand a meal before he reentered the saddle.

His sustenance provided, the messenger sought out the archbishop, who was horrified to learn of Stone's plight. He sprang into the saddle and returned with the messenger, whose weary horse collapsed and died of exhaustion as they crossed back over London Bridge. Promising the messenger a new steed for his troubles, Canterbury made his way to the royal residence. The king was at church, praying that justice be done to those in his prisons. Finishing his prayer, Athelston looked up and saw Canterbury coming toward him; he rose and greeted his friend warmly. The archbishop pleaded to be allowed fully and fairly to examine Stone's case, to determine if he was in fact guilty of a crime; once again, however, Stone's advocate found himself the brunt of the wrath of Athelston. Blinded by fury, the king revoked Alryke's office as archbishop. Canterbury calmly answered that, if Athelston should choose to deprive him of his seat, he would have no choice but to deprive the king and kingdom of Christianity. This he did, pronouncing an Interdict that forbade priests to say Mass or to provide any of the sacraments. Athelston was soon brought to his knees by this act, and was forced to allow the archbishop to examine Stone's treason through a trial by ordeal.

The archbishop prepared a path of nine plowshares, laid out upon a bed of glowing coals. He explained that, if the accused were indeed innocent, they need not fear the doom of passing through the flames upon the red-hot metal shares.

They brought forth first Egelond, who removed his scarlet hose and shoes. Canterbury hallowed the way nine times, and then Egelond passed through; he was unblemished, foot and hand. Seeing this, the crowd thanked God for his justice, and rejoiced at Egelond's innocence. Next the children underwent the ordeal. They removed their scarlet hose and shoes, but when they saw the hideous red fire, they swooned as if they were dead. The archbishop took them by the hand and told them not to dread; then the children stood and laughed, saying that the flames were cold. They passed through; they were unblemished foot and hand. The crowd thanked God for his grace. Then Edif was brought forth, great with child. As she neared the fire, she prayed to the Saviour that no enemy of the king might quickly leave that blaze. Then she entered the fair fire, quickly advancing through the first third; there she paused, calling the flames merry and bright. Then bitter, strong labor pains overtook her, both in her back and in her womb. As these passed, so she passed through the rest of the fire, blood bursting from her nose; she was unblemished, foot and hand. She kneeled there upon the ground and gave birth to St. Edmund. Seeing her innocence, Athelston bequeathed upon the child half his lands and revenue while he lived, and all upon his death.

The archbishop then called upon the king to renounce the foul traitor who had slandered Egelond, but the king replied that he had sworn never to reveal the name of the informant. Canterbury offered to absolve Athelston of the sin of breaking this vow, and further, threatened to force Athelston to undergo the same trial that Egelond and his family had passed. The king then acquiesced, and named Wymound as the villain. Shocked, the archbishop pronounced that Wymound, if guilty of this deed, would be hanged from three trees and drawn by five horses. Athelston then summoned Dover, claiming that Egelond had been executed, and offering his estates to Wymound; the villain soon made his way to court, where Athelston confronted him with his accusation. Wymound denied the charge, and all present thought to resolve the issue with the ordeal. Again Canterbury prepared a path of nine plowshares, laid out upon a bed of glowing coals; again he hallowed the path nine times. Wymound quickly made his way through the first third, but then collapsed onto the coals; he was blinded by the heat, and might no longer find his way. Then Stone's sons ran into the fire for Wymound and pulled him out. Wymound confessed his sin: That he had conspired against Stone out of envy because Athelston loved Stone too much and Dover too little. Then Dover was put to death, drawn and hanged as Canterbury had proclaimed.

ATHELSTON'S ORDEAL BY fire represents the archetype of the trials and tribulations of the hero; in this case the trial is not transformative, but rather clarifying, in that it brings to life the true nature and identity of the hero. Composed in the mid-fourteenth century, the Middle English verse romance *Athelston* is on the surface a highly entertaining tale of the political rise of a group of sworn blood-brothers. The relationships between these men are marred, however, by treachery and deceit, and finally the tensions between motives of loyalty, self-interest, and jealousy are relieved through the (quite literally) purging fires of judgment and vindication. What is superficially a good story of human strengths and frailties is, upon further reflection, also a fascinating social document wherein we might discover the struggle between several traditions of legal and mythic authority as elements of this struggle were captured in the popular imagination of fourteenth-century England.

Trial by ordeal had been extremely widespread under Anglo-Saxon law, but it had been entirely supplanted in English legal practice by the time that *Athelston* was composed. As late as the mid-fourteenth century, however, the concept of a legal system such as the ordeal in which God, and not man, was the judge and final arbiter was still deeply imbedded in the popular imagination. *Athelston* therefore illustrates a tension between officially sanctioned and popularly conceived models of authority. The mythic core of the Germanic concept of the ordeal was passed down from pagan times, and had as its basis the belief that the state of the soul of an accused person might be manifested physically upon the body of that person. Such ordeals normally consisted of a religious ceremony culminating with some painful ritual act, such as the grasping of a red-hot iron bar or the plunging of an arm into a cauldron of boiling water. The wounded member then would be sealed up, and it would be examined after a statutory period of time (quite often three days). The results of the trial would then be read in the flesh of the accused: a festering wound meant guilt, while a clean and healing wound composed a testament to innocence.

For the four centuries prior to the Fourth Lateran Council of 1215, trial by ordeal was one basis for the legal system for much of Europe, and there is ample evidence extant to prove how common and widespread it was. Types of ordeals and the situations for which they were invoked varied widely, but the ordeal of the boiling water (or "the cauldron") seems to have been the most common. Cold water and hot iron ordeals were also employed, among several others. The ordeal of the red-hot plowshares, which is similar to that ordeal which forms the climax of *Athelston,* is recorded in a number of sources. In fact, the wife of Charles the Fat cleared herself of charges of adultery through such an ordeal. Two other recorded episodes are of particular interest: the first is included in an account of the life of Cunigunda, the wife of the emperor Henry II. She is represented in an illuminated manuscript walking without concern over hot plowshares, led by bishops holding each of her hands; the scene of ordeal described in *Athelston* seems clearly along the same lines. The second account is English in origin: it is recorded that the English Queen Emma underwent this ordeal in 1043. According to this account, Emma felt no pain whatsoever and was unaware until after the fact that she had walked over the plowshares. These episodes, and notably the reactions of the accused, are remarkably similar in tone and content to the ordeal scenes in *Athelston.*

Such ordeals are notable for two major characteristics: first, the spiritual state of the accused determines the effect of the ordeal upon his or her flesh; second, this spiritual state likewise determines how painful the experience is for that person. This twofold barometer of guilt links the philosophy of the ordeal with the concept of the fire of judgment, especially as this barometer is manifested in ordeals of fire. While such a concept may be related to any ordeal, the parallels between some versions of the fire of judgment and the ordeal of the red-hot plowshares described in *Athelston* are truly striking.

The concept of purgatory was not acknowledged as doctrinally sound until the Council of Florence in 1439, almost a century after the composition of *Athelston*. Prior to the development of the concept of purgatory, the fire of judgment was a widespread model of the judgment to be expected by mankind on doomsday, and it was certainly a popular notion in early medieval England. According to this conception of judgment, on doomsday all souls would walk through the fire of judgment, and the condition of each soul would determine the effect of the flames upon that soul. The righteous would be unscathed or refined, those whose sins were not mortal would be purified through the heat of the furnace, and the wicked would be entirely consumed. This concept was derived from a number of models of judgment postulated by early Church fathers, most notably that described by Ambrose, which utilized a metallurgical metaphor. According to Ambrose, the wicked are like lead in the holy flames, and bubble and burn and are consumed, while the righteous are like pure silver, and are refreshed by the heat. Those who are neither too wicked nor completely holy are like a mixture of lead and silver, and burn in the fire however long it takes to rid them of their impurities. By constructing his vision of the judgment in the terms of metal-working, Ambrose was drawing upon the beliefs of a philosophical school far older than he might have imagined. Similar metaphors for spiritual purification were common in ancient Egypt, to cite just one example, and have been widespread throughout the globe; most metal-working cultures have developed analogous ideas. Indeed, the medieval and renaissance conception of Alchemy—through which the practitioner hopes to render base metal into gold—is based upon the same philosophical foundation.

After 1215 the employment of the ordeal was drastically curtailed. The Fourth Lateran council forbade such employment, and this moratorium left a vacuum in the structure of many legal systems, and notably in that of England. This same council made confession an annual obligation of all Christians, and thus confession became central to everyday life, and eventually to the legal system. Jury trial had been in use for some time, although only in unusual circumstances. Jury trial was soon utilized to fill the void in English jurisprudence left by trial by ordeal, and the oaths and compurgation of Germanic law were replaced by confession. A system requiring verbal admission of guilt thus supplanted one in which God was expected to arbitrate.

The judgment of men is largely irrelevant to the trial by ordeal, while the concept of God's judgment is central. In the world in which *Athelston* was composed, evidence of guilt or innocence was compiled and evaluated by men, who also were called upon to pronounce judgment. In the earlier system that is reflected in the narrative of the poem, however, men are portrayed as unreliable judges, and the ordeal is presented as a means through which one might call as witness a temporal manifestation of the judgment of God. In *Athelston* the justice of man is clearly called into question through the injustice and abuse of power manifested in the person of King Athelston. The underhanded way in which Egelan is accused by Wymound, for example, serves to underscore the inherent injustice of temporal judgment. Further, Athelston's lack of reason, and his injudicious and despotic actions—tempered only through Canterbury's threat of interdict—recall the ravings of the tyrant Herod, the medieval type of the power-mad dictator. Indeed, Athelston's slaying of his own son in the queen's womb typifies the rage associated with the archetypical tyrant, and would be associated by a medieval audience with the biblical slaughter of the innocents under Herod. Moreover, this injustice is born of sibling rivalry, that basest of family tensions: Wymound is jealous of the favor shown to Egelan by Athelston, and such jealousy exemplifies the kind of petty, temporal concern that renders the institutions of man flawed and suspect. In such a world, the divine judgment of the trial by ordeal seems reasonable and desirable: while the innocence of Egelan and his family is made manifest through their unblemished limbs and through the painless effect of the flames upon them, so is Wymound's guilt revealed through the pain and bodily destruction that he suffers during his ordeal. This result certainly resonates with the doomsday model of the fire of judgment, but further, it underscores the truth and justice of a system of judgment that is dependent upon divine intervention. Wymound the traitor is guilty, God's judgment is against him, and these facts are made manifest through his experience of the ordeal. *Athelston* offers a literary echo of popular mythic tradition regarding the ordeal; this tradition privileges the judgment of God over that of man, a privileging which is founded upon a fear of the corrupt nature of man-made institutions.

Athelston is a particularly interesting medieval literary example of the mythic tradition of the ordeal in that it illuminates both the social and Christian doctrinal influences associated with that tradition. In *Athelston* we see a model of a legal system unsullied by the corruption of man-made institutions. The invocation of such a system in this romance reflects a popular fear of the miscarriage of justice at the hands of one's fellow man. Although the concept of being judged by one's peers may seem to a modern audience far superior to an expectation of divine intervention, there is ample evidence to suggest that the ordeal was preferred in the popular imagination of medieval England. There are a number of reasons for such a view: First, the substitution of human for divine judgment was suspect on the grounds of human fallibility. Second, God seems to have been in the habit of acquitting the accused. Third, the abolition of the ordeal left a vacuum in the legal system, destroying as it did the most widely recognized system of producing proofs. The legal system of England never assimilated judicial torture as a means of procuring confession, and thus had a particularly difficult time finding procedures to fill this vacuum; this it did only slowly and piecemeal, over time and by consulting a growing body of precedents. The immediate result of this void in the English system of jurisprudence was a series of stop-gap measures, including most notably a moratorium on capital punishment; this moratorium directly and unequivocally reflected a concern with condemning the accused without recourse to divine ratification.

The Hero's Trial by Tribulation:
The Transformation of Sir Isumbras

Once upon a time there was a man by the name of Sir Isumbras, who was so mighty of hand and so doughty in battle that none would dare to stand against him. He was also rich, and was noble and gracious, and was loved by all. Sir Isumbras was generous and refined, and was generally considered to be a very fine man. He kept minstrels in his hall, and supplied them with rich clothes and with payment in gold and silver. Sir Isumbras was married to as lovely a lady as ever walked upon the earth, and together they had three handsome sons. Sir Isumbras was so well blessed with the things of this world, however, that his pride grew all out of bounds, and he forgot to be thankful for the grace and blessings of his Lord in heaven. Finally Jesus would abide the arrogance of Sir Isumbras no longer, and sent a messenger to the prideful man.

It so happened that Isumbras was used to going abroad into the forest by certain paths unknown to most, and on a certain day as he wandered along this way a bird spoke to him, telling him of the wrath of the Lord brought down upon him as a result of his pride, and offering him a choice: Isumbras might have health and wealth in youth, and suffer in old age, or he might suffer in youth and find comfort in his dotage. Suddenly the scales fell from the eyes of Isumbras, and he was aware of his faults; falling humbly to his knees before the bird, Isumbras yielded himself before the will of the Lord in true and heartfelt repentance. He then reasoned that it would be easier for him to bear suffering in youth than among the gathered infirmities of age, and thus he made his choice: to be poor in his youth and to be recompensed in old age.

As soon as the bird had flown away, the horse under Sir Isumbras fell dead to the ground, and his hounds and hawks seemed to go wild; all alone in the wilderness, Isumbras made his way home afoot. On his way he was met by a servant who told him that his hall and buildings were now no more than smoldering ruins, and that most of his men had been slain; on the heels of these grim tidings Isumbras learned that his cattle and livestock all had been stolen. Still the man was content in his heart to suffer his just penance, and wanted nothing more in the world than to see his wife and children safe. These he found before the ruin of the house, naked as they had come from bed, and lamenting their loss. Isumbras bade them all to suffer in silence, and acknowledged that all that befell them came as a result of his own pride. Then he covered his wife with his mantle and clad his children with the clothes off his back, and cut the sign of a cross onto his bare shoulder, as a sign of his contrition. Then Isumbras and his family left their own country, and his greatest sorrow was that he could not offer any aid to those of his servants who were left behind.

Through the lands of two kings the wretched family passed in the next six days, and in all that time neither food nor drink passed their lips. They were happy, therefore, when they came upon the rushing flood of a mighty river; soon their joy was to turn to sorrow. Isumbras carried his eldest son across the flood upon his shoulders, and sat him upon a stump to amuse himself while his father fetched the others. Isumbras then crossed back over and got the middle son. Halfway across the river with the second boy upon his back, Isumbras could do nothing but stare and weep as he saw a lion streak out of the woods and seize his oldest child. Shaking with grief, Sir Isumbras had to leave his second son upon the same stump as he returned back across the river a last time to get his wife and youngest child. These two the man carried together, and great was their horror when they saw a leopard snatch the middle son off the stump and rush back into the forest. The little family was wracked in grief, and it was all Isumbras could do to convince his wife that she must accept the will of the Lord; indeed, that poor lady nearly killed herself in her sorrow.

The family went on, and finally they reached the shore of the Greek Sea, where they saw a great gathering of ships; unknown to them, a heathen king from afar meant to conquer Christendom. As his family had not eaten for a week, and were all the fainter from their grief, Isumbras approached the greatest of the ships—that of the king—in order to beg for some food in the name of Christian charity. At first the king thought Isumbras some Christian spy come to ferret out the secrets of his invasion; thus he ordered the poor man to be thrown off his ship. Then one of the king's men noted Isumbras's noble bearing and fine physique, and the ivory complexion and fine features of his wife; surely, thought the heathens, here was a man of quality, a warrior they might employ in their service. The king then had Isumbras fetched back, and offered to him gold and power and dignity if he would but forswear Christ and enter into the service of the king. This offer Isumbras rejected out of hand, as he never again wished to strive against Christ. Then the king offered him gold and costly garments in exchange for his wife, whom he thought to make the empress of his realms. Isumbras—joined to his wife through the bonds of Christian matrimony—was horrified by this offer, but his wife was taken through force of arms. The king paid no heed to Isumbras's refusal and paid out gold into a red mantle, which was then folded together. Poor Isumbras then was beaten black and blue and cast upon the sand next to his youngest son.

Before her ship sailed, however, Lady Isumbras convinced her new king that she be allowed to say some parting words to her husband. When they met upon the beach she gave to him a ring as a token of their love, and she bade him to seek her in whatever land she might be held. There, she foretold, he would slay the heathen king and rise to power in his stead, thereby ending his woe. She gave to Isumbras enough food for a week for him and for their son. Then the lady was taken back to the ship, swooning thrice as she bade farewell to her husband and son. Isumbras, for his part, wept so long as the sails of her ship were visible on the horizon. Isumbras then took his young son by the hand, and together they walked off the beach and through that land until they reached a tree within a great gray forest. Then they wept until they couldn't see each other, and as their weeping slackened they ate, and then they put the rest of their food with the gold in their mantle. Then they climbed a high hill, and here they set themselves down to sleep, for they could go no farther. In the morning Isumbras was awakened by the sound of a griffin flying away with their gold and their food; it had been attracted by the red color of the wrapping. Isumbras chased the creature until it flew out over the Greek Sea, and he returned downcast, only to find that his son had been borne away in the meantime.

Now, for the first time since he had met the bird in the wood, Isumbras was utterly overcome by despair. He lamented the loss of his family, and he cried aloud to God for some guidance, as he had no idea where he was or to whence he should travel. The prayers of Isumbras were answered when he heard the clamor of smiths at work nearby. He asked them for charity and they traded him bread for work; seven years he labored in the smithy, and he taxed his body mightily. But at the end of that time he knew all of smithing and of armoring, and could make all manner of things, and best of all those necessary to a knight. All this while the heathen king had harried the Christian kingdom thereabout, and a great battle was soon to commence that might end this struggle for once and for all. Isumbras mounted a horse that had been used for hauling coal to the smithy, and he joined the forces of the Christian king. Isumbras fought bravely and strongly, and his enemies fled before him, until his poor horse was slain; then an earl lifted him from the battle and rearmed and remounted him, and Isumbras reentered the battle like a whirlwind. He slew all who stood before him, and in the end he brought death to the heathen king and his chosen bodyguards.

Then the Christian king marveled at the prowess of this unknown man, and ordered that he be brought before him. A group of knights and squires carried Isumbras thither, although he was sorely wounded. The king was amazed to hear that this was a smith, and he left the wounded Isumbras at a convent to heal, swearing that, if he recovered, Isumbras should be dubbed a knight. Isumbras, however, had other plans, and once he had healed he set out again for the Greek Sea, now attired as a pilgrim; he found at the shore a ship bound for the Holy Land, and so he there embarked and remained a palmer for seven years, and never shirked his penance, although greatly did he suffer. He had no food nor drink, but one night an angel appeared unto him, bearing both bread and wine; this messenger brought the glad tidings that God had forgiven the sins of Isumbras because of his faithful penance. The Lord now commanded Isumbras to return, but the man knew not how, and so he set off again to find his fate.

As he traveled through that land he came upon a mighty castle that was home to a rich queen of whom much good was said. It seems that she was generous without measure to the poor, and each day she dispensed money to those who clamored at her gate, and took in many of the sickest and poorest. Isumbras was among these, and the queen honored him greatly, listening to his tales of lands abroad and deeds of old. She gave to him a place to live, and food and drink for life, all for the soul of her lost lord, and for his love if he yet lived. Isumbras thus lived in her household for seven years, and was so honored and exalted by the queen that many envied him; but never could he forget his sorrow or his loss. The Saracens he gave no quarter, and so they arranged a tournament for the land thereabouts; they horsed him on a lame steed, but Isumbras amazed them all with his prowess, and many a Saracen regretted meeting Isumbras upon the field. The queen, meanwhile, was pleased to see his might, and thought him well worth her expense in keeping him.

One day Isumbras was wandering through the forest, as was his wont, when the fluttering of scarlet cloth high above him caught his eye. He struggled up to it, and there he found a griffin nest; within it he discovered the gold that bought his wife, wrapped in the tattered shreds of the red mantle. His old sorrow welled up anew, and weeping he hid what he had found under his bed. Now Isumbras was sick with grief and couldn't leave his room by day or by night for some time; those who were jealous of his favor with the queen told her that this was a sure sign of his guilt for some treachery against her. So it was that—some days later, when Isumbras finally made his way from his room—some squires broke into his room and found the treasure secreted under his bed. This they showed to the queen, and she swooned as she saw it, for she knew it belonged to her lost lord, Sir Isumbras. She ordered that the pilgrim be brought before her, that she might learn what he knew of her rightful husband.

When Isumbras was brought before her, the queen questioned him closely concerning the treasure and the scarlet mantle; Isumbras opened his heart to her then, and out spilled his whole story. When he mentioned the ring that Isumbras had received as a token of love and fidelity from his wife, she asked to see it; he replied that she had broken it in two, and had given him half. His half of the ring he produced; all present gasped when the queen drew the matching half from a finely wrought purse she kept at her bosom. The lady announced with joy that she had been reunited at long last with her own Sir Isumbras, her true husband; she swooned three times from the intensity of her emotion at this reunion. Now Isumbras was crowned king of that land, and was granted even greater power and fortune than he had held before his penance. The first act of King Isumbras was to declare Christianity the religion of the state; messengers poured into every nook and cranny of that land, spreading the gospel of Christ. All the Saracens of that kingdom, however, were dissatisfied with this conversion, and sought to displace Isumbras. For that reason a trial at arms was declared, and a great battle was planned: Isumbras would fight for Christ, while the heathens, under two heathen kings, would fight to retain their ancient ways.

On the day of the battle, each and every one of Isumbras's followers deserted him for the other side. He was woeful indeed as he bade farewell to the lady he had long sought, for he knew that he would never look upon her again in this life. She, however, would part from him no more, and so she armed and armored herself as a knight, so that they might meet their end together. The two rode side by side to battle, the lone Christian combatants facing a host of thirty thousand or more Saracens. Just as they joined battle against their foes they heard the sound of great confusion; turning, they saw that they were being joined by three other kings, each riding in the most amazing fashion: one was mounted on a leopard, one on a unicorn, and one on a lion; this last was their eldest child. The beasts were both wild and ferocious, and they set upon the heathen hosts like wildfire, driving their enemies before them. The three sons of Isumbras slew two heathen kings, and many others besides, some thirty thousand and three Saracens in all. After the slaughter the three kings came before Isumbras and revealed themselves to be his sons, and his joy was complete; he gave unto each a share of his new kingdom, and crowned them kings with his own hand, and they converted and christened all who lived under their power. And thus was the penance of Isumbras at an end, and he and his lady lived together happily for the rest of their days.

THE TRIALS AND tribulations of Isumbras are a classic example of a reformulation of the archetype of the hero's coming-of-age transformation. The hubris of Isumbras is the cause for his fall, and through the adversity he faces he is able at last to expiate the sin of pride; further, through his true penitence he is reborn into a mature and properly humble hero. It is interesting that the wife of Isumbras does not recognize him for such a long time, but the severe change in appearance wrought by his deprivations is a common romance theme; here such change also serves as an outward manifestation of the inner change wrought through his tribulations. Sir Isumbras's search for his stolen wife is likewise a familiar theme, and his journey to heathen lands to seek her smacks of Orfeo's quest to the land of Fairy; indeed, the non-Christians in this tale are represented as little short of demonic. *Sir Isumbras* was composed in the early fourteenth century in the East Midlands dialect. The theme of the man tried by fate is common to the genre of the romance, and has its origins in European literature in the tales of St. Eustace, tales which are Eastern in origin. The Eustace legend is the basis of many romances from throughout Britain and is, for example, an important aspect of the Third Branch of *The Mabinogion*, in which Manawydan and Pryderi lose their realms through enchantment, and must betake themselves to crafts for their bread. We might well compare the Eustace legend to the Constance theme, which is the tale of the loyal wife put to outrageous tests by her suspicious husband. The Constance legend is best exemplified in Medieval English literature by Emare of the romance of the same name, and by Griselda from Chaucer's "Clerk's Tale." The theme of the falsely accused or unfairly punished wife also reappears several times in *The Mabinogion*, in which both Rhiannon and Branwen suffer such persecution.

Final Word

The battle for mythic Britain was not, after all, a monumental clash of titanic deities in the sky, but rather a slow, laborious ground war of sorts, and its foot soldiers were mythic archetypes of gods, legendary sagas of mighty heroes and of lesser men, and folkloric customs and beliefs. Christianity and literacy came together to Britain to stay at the dawn of the Middle Ages, and so medieval literature might be said to be a prime battleground of this mythic conflict. Further, it is often thought that the battle between the gods of Britain was a war between Christian and Pagan, between civilization and savagery, and between the tall tales of ancient oral epics and the hard facts of the Western literary tradition. Moreover, the very metaphor of warfare—although apt in some ways—misleads us to think of the waves of myth that flooded Britain as universally antagonistic; after all, Roman fought Celt, Celt fought Saxon, and Saxon fought Viking, and earlier peoples were brutally pushed to the margins of the islands far more often than they were gently assimilated. But assimilation, in the end, occurred on many levels, and indeed, the conflict between any mythic traditions often is the struggle between competing masks of the same ancient beings.

In other words, it is only on the surface that Wodan replaced Lugh, or that Christ replaced Baldr and Thunor; in archetypal terms, Wodan and Lugh represent different manifestations of the same human thirst for divine expression, and Christ has attributes that bring to mind facets of Wodan, Baldr, and Thunor. In a similar way Beowulf and Bodvar Bjarki and Peredur and Gawain all represent different masks of the same hero, a creature of both myth and legend who lives to give voice to the cares, desires, and anxieties of all human beings. Finally, it is in the everyday details of folklore and folk custom that the assimilation of ancient ways into medieval and even modern practices is most clear; governments and even individual gods may rise and fall, but certain universal concerns remain constant: proper planting, fertile soil, a timely and sufficient harvest; these factors are of concern to any who would eat, just as passion—lust, greed, jealousy, selfless love—inflames all hearts equally. Gawain's sacrificial quest speaks to a universal need for a bountiful harvest, just as Orfeo plumbs the depths of hell for the true love we all desire, and the trial of Athelston represents the longing in most of us for justice and fair play. The battle for Britain represents the ongoing attempt by humans everywhere to make sense of their present reality by drawing on those aspects of past traditions that fit the most appropriate mask.

FURTHER READING

General Mythology

Leeming, David A. *The World of Myth*. New York: Oxford University Press, 1990.
Puhvel, Jaan. *Comparative Mythology*. Baltimore: The Johns Hopkins University Press, 1987.

Anglo-Saxon Mythology and *Beowulf*

Allen, Michael J. B., and Daniel G. Calder. *Sources and Analogues of Old English Poetry: The Major Latin Texts in Translation*. Totowa, NJ: Rowman and Littlefield, 1976.
Bradley, S. A. J., ed. *Anglo-Saxon Poetry*. Rutland, VT: Charles E. Tuttle Co., 1994.
Branston, Brian. *The Lost Gods of England*. New York: Thames & Hudson, 1957.
Calder, Daniel G., et al. *Sources and Analogues of Old English Poetry II: The Major Germanic and Celtic Texts in Translation*. Totowa, NJ: Barnes and Noble, 1983.
Webb, J. F., trans. *The Age of Bede*. Rev. ed. New York: Viking Penguin, 1998.

Anglo-Saxon History

Campbell, James, ed. *The Anglo-Saxons*. New York: Penguin Books, 1991.
Fletcher, Richard. *Who's Who in Roman Britain and Anglo-Saxon England*. London: Shepheard-Walwyn, 1989.
Stenton, Frank. *Anglo-Saxon England*. 3rd ed. New York: Oxford University Press, 1989.
Welch, Martin. *The English Heritage Book of Anglo-Saxon England*. London: B.T. Batsford, 1992.

Celtic Mythology

Green, Miranda. *Celtic Myths*. The Legendary Past Series. London: The British Museum Press, 1993.
———. *The Gods of the Celts*. Godalming, Surrey: Bramley Books, 1986.

Celtic History

Armit, Ian. *Historic Scotland: Celtic Scotland*. London: B.T. Batsford, 1997.

Chadwick, Nora K. *Celtic Britain*. Ancient Peoples and Places Series Number 34. New York: Frederick A. Praeger, 1963.

———. *The Celts*. New ed. New York: Penguin Books, 1997.

Millett, Martin. *The English Heritage Book of Roman Britain*. London: B.T. Batsford, 1995.

Norse Mythology

Crossley-Holland, Kevin. *The Norse Myths*. New York: Pantheon, 1980.

Davidson, H. R. Ellis. *Gods and Myths of Northern Europe*. Middlesex: Penguin, 1964.

Page, R. I. *Norse Myths*. The Legendary Past Series. London: The British Museum Press, 1990.

Norse History and The History of Viking Britain

Graham-Campbell, James, ed. *Cultural Atlas of the Viking World*. Oxfordshire, England: Andromeda Oxford, 1994.

Hall, Richard. *The English Heritage Book of Viking Age York*. London: B.T. Batsford, 1994.

Jones, Gwyn. *A History of the Vikings*. Rev. ed. Oxford: Oxford University Press, 1984.

Loyn, Henry. *The Vikings in Britain*. Malden, MA: Blackwell Publishers, 1994.

Magnusson, Magnus, and Hermann Palsson, trans. *King Harald's Saga*. Penguin Classics. New York: Viking Penguin, 1987.

Palsson, Hermann, and Paul Edwards, trans. *Egil's Saga*. Penguin Classics. New York: Viking Penguin, 1987.

———, trans. *Orkneyinga Saga: The History of the Earls of Orkney*. Penguin Classics. New York: Viking Penguin, 1987.

Ritchie, Anna. *Historic Scotland: Viking Scotland*. London: B.T. Batsford, 1993.

Ritchie, Anna, and David Breeze. *Historic Scotland: Invaders of Scotland*. Edinburgh: HMSO, 1991.

Medieval British and Irish Literature

Beidler, Peter G., ed. *Geoffrey Chaucer: The Wife of Bath*. Case Studies in Contemporary Criticism. Ross C. Murfin, Series ed. New York: Bedford Books, 1996.

Jones, Gwyn, and Thomas Jones, trans. *The Mabinogion*. New rev. ed. Everyman Library. Rutland, VT: Charles E. Tuttle Co., 1993.

Kinsella, Thomas, trans. *The Tain*. Oxford: Oxford University Press, 1970.

Lewis, Thorpe, trans. *The History of the Kings of Britain*. Reprint ed. New York: Viking Penguin, 1981.

Mills, Maldwyn, ed. *Six Middle English Romances*. Totowa, NJ: Rowman and Littlefield, 1973.

Stone, Brian, trans. *Sir Gawain and the Green Knight*. 2nd ed. New York: Viking Penguin, 1959.

BIBLIOGRAPHY

Allen, Michael J. B., and Daniel G. Calder. *Sources and Analogues of Old English Poetry: The Major Latin Texts in Translation*. Totowa, NJ: Rowman and Little-field, 1976.

Armit, Ian. *Historic Scotland: Celtic Scotland*. London: B.T. Batsford, 1997.

Beidler, Peter G., ed. *Geoffrey Chaucer: The Wife of Bath*. Case Studies in Contemporary Criticism. Ross C. Murfin, Series ed. New York: Bedford Books, 1996.

Bjork, Robert E., and John D. Niles, eds. *A Beowulf Handbook*. Lincoln, NE: University of Nebraska Press, 1997.

Bowker, John, ed. *The Oxford Dictionary of World Religions*. New York and Oxford: Oxford University Press, 1997.

Bradley, S. A. J., ed. *Anglo-Saxon Poetry*. Rutland, VT: Charles E. Tuttle Co., 1994.

Branston, Brian. *Gods of the North*. New York: Thames & Hudson, 1955 & 1980.

———. *The Lost Gods of England*. New York: Thames & Hudson, 1957.

Breeze, David. *Historic Scotland: Roman Scotland*. London: B.T. Batsford, 1996.

Burrow, J. A., ed. *Sir Gawain and the Green Knight*. New Haven: Yale University Press, 1982.

Byock, Jesse L., trans. *The Saga of King Hrolf Kraki*. Penguin Classics. New York: Penguin Putnam, 1998.

———, trans. *The Saga of the Volsungs: The Norse Epic of Sigurd the Dragon Slayer*. Berkeley, CA: University of California Press, 1990.

Calder, Daniel G., et al. *Sources and Analogues of Old English Poetry II: The Major Germanic and Celtic Texts in Translation*. Totowa, NJ: Barnes and Noble, 1983.

Campbell, James, ed. *The Anglo-Saxons*. New York: Penguin Books, 1991.

Campbell, Joseph. *The Masks of God: Occidental Mythology*. New York: Viking, 1964.

Cassidy, Brendan, ed. *The Ruthwell Cross: Papers from the Colloquium*. Index of Christian Art Occasional Papers I. Princeton, NJ: Department of Art and Archaeology, Princeton University, 1992.

Chadwick, Nora K. *Celtic Britain*. Ancient Peoples and Places Series Number 34. New York: Frederick A. Praeger, 1963.

———. *The Celts*. New ed. New York: Penguin Books, 1997.

Chance, Jane. *Woman as Hero in Old English Literature*. Syracuse, NY: Syracuse University Press, 1986.

Clarke, Lindsay. *Essential Celtic Mythology*. San Francisco: HarperCollins, 1997.

Cooper, Helen. *Oxford Guides to Chaucer: The Canterbury Tales*. 2nd ed. New York: Oxford University Press, 1989.

Crossley-Holland, Kevin. *The Norse Myths*. New York: Pantheon, 1980.

Cunliffe, Barry. *The Ancient Celts*. New York: Oxford University Press, 1997.

———. *The Celtic World*. New York: McGraw-Hill, 1979.

Damico, Helen. *Beowulf's Wealhtheow and the Valkyrie Tradition*. Madison, WI: University of Wisconsin Press, 1984.

Damico, Helen, and Alexandra Hennessey Olsen, eds. *New Readings on Women in Old English Literature*. Bloomington, IN: Indiana University Press, 1990.

Davidson, H. R. Ellis. *Gods and Myths of Northern Europe*. Middlesex: Penguin, 1964.

———. *Myths and Symbols in Pagan Europe: Early Scandinavian and Celtic Religions*. Syracuse, NY: Syracuse University Press, 1988.

———. *Roles of the Northern Goddess*. New York: Routledge, 1998.

DuBois, Thomas A. *Nordic Religions in the Viking Age*. Philadelphia: University of Pennsylvania Press, 1999.

Eliade, Mircea, ed. *The Encyclopedia of Religion*. 16 vols. New York: Macmillan, 1987.

Ellis, Peter Berresford. *Caesar's Invasion of Britain*. London: Orbis, 1978.

———. *The Celtic Empire: The First Millennium of Celtic History, c. 1000 BC-51 AD*. Durham, NC: Carolina Academic Press, 1990.

———. *Dictionary of Celtic Mythology*. Santa Barbara, CA: ABC-CLIO, 1992.

Fletcher, Richard. *Who's Who in Roman Britain and Anglo-Saxon England*. London: Shepheard-Walwyn, 1989.

Fox, Denton, and Hermann Palsson, trans. *Grettir's Saga*. Penguin Classics ed. Toronto: University of Toronto Press, 1974.

Fulk, R. D., ed. *Interpretations of Beowulf*. Bloomington, IN: Indiana University Press, 1991.

Gordon, E. V. *An Introduction to Old Norse*. 2nd ed. Rev. by A. R. Taylor. Oxford: Oxford University Press, 1956.

Graham-Campbell, James, ed. *Cultural Atlas of the Viking World*. Oxfordshire, England: Andromeda Oxford, 1994.

Green, Miranda. *Celtic Myths*. The Legendary Past Series. London: The British Museum Press, 1993.

———. *The Gods of the Celts*. Godalming, Surrey: Bramley Books, 1986.

———. *The Gods of Roman Britain*. Shire Archaeology. James Dyer, Series ed. Aylesbury, Bucks: Shire Publications, 1983.

———, ed. *The Celtic World*. New York: Routledge, 1995.

———. *The World of the Druids*. New York: Thames & Hudson, 1997.

Hall, Richard. *The English Heritage Book of Viking Age York*. London: B.T. Batsford, 1994.

Henig, Martin. *Religion in Roman Britain*. New York: St. Martin's Press, 1984.

Hollander, Lee M., trans. *Heimskringla: History of the Kings of Norway, by Snorri Sturluson*. Austin, TX: University of Texas Press, 1992.

———, trans. *The Poetic Edda*. 2nd ed., rev. Austin, TX: University of Texas Press, 1962.

Irving, Edward B., Jr. *A Reading of Beowulf*. New Haven, CT: Yale University Press, 1968.

Jackson, Guida M. *Encyclopedia of Traditional Epics*. Santa Barbara, CA: ABC-CLIO, 1994.

Jones, Gwyn. A *History of the Vikings*. Rev. ed. Oxford: Oxford University Press, 1984.

Jones, Gwyn, and Thomas Jones, trans. *The Mabinogion*. New rev. ed. Everyman Library. Rutland, VT: Charles E. Tuttle Co., 1993.

Joyce, Timothy. *Celtic Christianity: A Sacred Tradition, a Vision of Hope*. Maryknoll, NY: Orbis, 1998.

Kinsella, Thomas, trans. *The Tain*. Oxford: Oxford University Press, 1970.

Larrington, Carolyne, ed. *The Woman's Companion to Mythology*. London: Pandora, an imprint of HarperCollins, 1992.

Leach, Maria, ed. *Funk and Wagnalls Standard Dictionary of Folklore, Mythology, and Religion*. San Francisco: Harper and Row, 1984.

Leeming, David A. *Mythology: The Voyage of the Hero*, 3rd ed. New York: Oxford University Press, 1998.

———. *The World of Myth*. New York: Oxford University Press, 1990.

Leeming, David A., and Margaret A. Leeming. *A Dictionary of Creation Myths*. New York: Oxford University Press, 1995.

Le Goff, Jacques. *The Birth of Purgatory*. Arthur Goldhammer, trans. Chicago: University of Chicago Press, 1984.

Lewis, Thrope, trans. *The History of the Kings of Britain*. Reprint ed. New York: Viking Penguin, 1981.

Lonigan, Paul R. *The Druids: Priests of the Ancient Celts*. Contributions to the Study of Religion, Number 45. Westport, CT: Greenwood Press, 1996.

Loyn, Henry. *The Vikings in Britain*. Malden, MA: Blackwell Publishers, 1994.

Mac Cana, Proinsias. "Celtic Religion." *The Encyclopedia of Religion*, edited by Mircea Eliade, vol. pp.3, 148–166. New York: Macmillan, 1987.

MacKillop, James. *Fionn mac Cumhaill: Celtic Myth in English Literature*. Irish Studies Series. Syracuse, NY: Syracuse University Press, 1986.

Magnusson, Magnus, and Hermann Palsson, trans. *King Harald's Saga*. Penguin Classics. New York: Viking Penguin, 1987.

———, trans. *Laxdaela Saga*. Penguin Classics. New York: Viking Penguin, 1987.

———, trans. *Njal's Saga*. Penguin Classics. New York: Viking Penguin, 1987.

———, trans. *The Vinland Sagas*. Penguin Classics. New York: Viking Penguin, 1987.

Miller, Miriam Youngerman, and Jane Chance, eds. *Approaches to Teaching Sir Gawain and the Green Knight*. MLA Approaches to Teaching World Literature, Number 9. New York: MLA, 1986.

Millett, Martin. *The English Heritage Book of Roman Britain*. London: B.T. Batsford, 1995.

Mills, Maldwyn, ed. *Six Middle English Romances*. Totowa, NJ: Rowman and Littlefield, 1973.

Munch, Peter Andreas. *Norse Mythology: Legends of Gods and Heroes*. Rev. by Magnus Olsen; Sigurd Bernhard Hustvedt, trans. New York: The American-Scandinavian Foundation, 1926.

Nagy, Joseph Falaky. *Conversing with Angels and Ancients: Literary Myths of Medieval Ireland*. Ithaca, NY: Cornell University Press, 1997.

Page, R. I. *Norse Myths*. The Legendary Past Series. London: The British Museum Press, 1990.

———. *Runes*. Reading the Past Series. London: The British Museum Press, 1987.

Palsson, Hermann, trans. *Hrafnkel's Saga and other Icelandic Stories*. Penguin Classics. New York: Viking Penguin, 1987.

Palsson, Hermann and Paul Edwards, trans. *Egil's Saga*. Penguin Classics. New York: Viking Penguin, 1987.

———, trans. *Eyrbyggja Saga*. Penguin Classics. New York: Viking Penguin, 1989.

———, trans. *Orkneyinga Saga: The History of the Earls of Orkney*. Penguin Classics. New York: Viking Penguin, 1987.

Piggott, Stuart. *The Druids*. New ed. New York: Thames & Hudson, 1975.

Polome, Edgar C. "Germanic Religion." *The Encyclopedia of Religion* edited by Mircea Eliade, vol. 5, 520–536. New York: Macmillan, 1987.

Powell, T. G. E. *The Celts*. New ed. New York: Thames & Hudson, 1980.

Puhvel, Jaan. *Comparative Mythology*. Baltimore: The Johns Hopkins University Press, 1987.

Rees, Alwyn, and Brinley Rees. *Celtic Heritage: Ancient Tradition in Ireland and Wales*. London: Thames and Hudson, 1961.

Ritchie, Anna. *Historic Scotland: Viking Scotland*. London: B.T. Batsford, 1993.

Ritchie, Anna, and David Breeze. *Historic Scotland: Invaders of Scotland*. Edinburgh: HMSO, 1991.

Short, Douglas D. *Beowulf Scholarship: An Annotated Bibliography*. New York: Garland Publishing, 1980.

Simek, Rudolf. *Dictionary of Northern Mythology*. Angela Hall, trans. Rochester: Boydell & Brewer, 1993.

Stenton, Frank. *Anglo-Saxon England*. 3rd ed. New York: Oxford University Press, 1989.

Stone, Brian, trans. *Sir Gawain and the Green Knight*. 2nd ed. New York: Viking Penguin, 1959.

Swanton, Michael, ed. *The Dream of the Rood*. New York: Barnes and Noble, 1970.

Webb, J. F., trans. *The Age of Bede*. Rev. ed. New York: Viking Penguin, 1998.

Webster, Graham. *Celtic Religion in Roman Britain*. Totowa, NJ: Barnes and Noble, 1986.

Welch, Martin. *The English Heritage Book of Anglo-Saxon England*. London: B.T. Batsford, 1992.

Young, Jean I., trans. *The Prose Edda of Snorri Sturluson: Tales from Norse Mythology*. Berkeley, CA: University of California Press, 1954.

INDEX